RESILIENT GODS

To Robert Putnam -
With Much Appreciation
for Your Work.

REGINALD W. BIBBY

RESILIENT GODS

BEING PRO-RELIGIOUS, LOW RELIGIOUS, OR NO RELIGIOUS IN CANADA

UBCPress · Vancouver · Toronto

26 25 24 23 22 21 20 19 18 17   5 4 3 2 1

Printed in Canada on FSC-certified ancient-forest-free paper
(100% post-consumer recycled) that is processed chlorine- and acid-free.

Library and Archives Canada Cataloguing in Publication

Bibby, Reginald W. (Reginald Wayne), author
Resilient gods: being pro-religious, low religious, or no religious in Canada /
Reginald W. Bibby.

Includes bibliographical references and index.
Issued in print and electronic formats.
ISBN 978-0-7748-9005-2 (hardcover). – ISBN 978-0-7748-9006-9 (pbk.)
ISBN 978-0-7748-9007-6 (PDF).

1. Canada – Religion – 21st century. 2. Irreligion – Canada. I. Title.

BL2530.C3B536 2017   306.6'0971   2017-900290-2
                                                 C2017-900291-0

Canadä

UBC Press gratefully acknowledges the financial support for our publishing
program of the Government of Canada (through the Canada Book Fund),
the Canada Council for the Arts, and the British Columbia Arts Council.

UBC Press
The University of British Columbia
2029 West Mall
Vancouver, BC V6T 1Z2
www.ubcpress.ca

To

LITA AND SAHARA,

*whose patience
with my failing to draw a line
between work and play
is nothing short of remarkable*

Contents

Preface

The exponential growth of information available in the world today means that books and articles run the risk of being obsolete shortly after they appear. It's not a new reality, just a reality that has become all the more accentuated, largely because of the arrival of the Internet in the early 1990s.

I thought that my "gods series" of books did a reasonably good job of keeping up with trends and literature when they appeared in 1987 (*Fragmented Gods*), 1993 (*Unknown Gods*), and 2001 (*Restless Gods*). But the birth of *Beyond the Gods and Back* in 2011 took place at a time when information was exploding at a remarkable rate. In the six years since its release, I have clarified and refined my thinking on religious polarization. I have also generated and been exposed to much new data. As a result, while *Beyond the Gods and Back* is the informing backbone to this book – as reflected in the first two chapters – not much else remains the same.

This book benefits from the availability of considerable new data, both global and Canadian in scope. The two key players for me in recent years have been the Pew Research Center based in Washington, DC, and the Angus Reid Institute in Canada. I am immensely indebted to both, along with Andrew Grenville, my colleague and friend with the Vision Critical research division of the Maru Group, who has played a central role in helping me to generate considerable new survey data.

This book has also benefited from feedback from colleagues and students who used its predecessor as a text. I want to single out Joel

Thiessen, whose early review of *Beyond the Gods and Back* was extremely insightful and valuable.[1] This book further clarifies key ideas such as polarization and secularization, deletes anything extraneous, and adds fresh and helpful material. The result is not only a new book but a substantially improved one. As I always remind readers, I have no illusions that this book says it all. But I think that it says a lot.

The primary sources of support for my work – and my life, for that matter – remain much the same. At the top of the list are my wife, Lita, and my daughter, Sahara, now 14, who has taken over my office since *Beyond the Gods and Back* but lets me use it once in a while (primarily when she is sleeping). My grown-up sons, Reggie, Dave, and Russ, continue to be major sources of both encouragement and enjoyment, in the midst of doing acrobatics with their own burgeoning families.

I also remain extremely grateful to the University of Lethbridge for having provided me with tranquility and resources for more than four decades now. Many thanks as well to the people at UBC Press – beginning with its director, Melissa Pitts; Emily Andrew, who offered early enthusiastic support; and Holly Keller, who has overseen production of the manuscript – for their positive response to this project as well as their hands-on editorial contributions.

And thanks to you – yes, you – for taking the time to read the book. As always, my hope is that it will stimulate some thought and even elevate life.

Reginald Bibby
Lethbridge, Alberta
April 2017

RESILIENT GODS

Introduction

One of the most basic features of sociology that I have always emphasized to my students is the importance of social environments. If we want to understand people in a comprehensive way, then we have to understand the social settings from which they come.

The old cliché that no one is an island carries much wisdom. What we think and how we act are determined in large part by social factors, beginning with the influence of our parents and our friends, what we see and hear, and what we experience. Social environments determine just about everything.

So it is that Canada is not an island unto itself. We all know that our multifaceted culture has been largely the product of people coming here from other places, dating back to the first individuals who – most scholars believe – probably found their way here via the Bering Strait. Our collective life ever since has been shaped by the arrival of new waves of people from around the world.

As seemingly obvious as such a reality is, we sometimes lose our balance and think in insular terms. We get caught up in national, regional, and local developments and lose our global perspective. That is especially true of how we interpret religion, especially organized religion.

Although the Canadian religious landscape has a clear historical imprint in which explicit lines can be drawn from the dominant Catholic and Protestant groups to their predominantly European roots, observers of religious developments have been reading the times with remarkably limited demographic perspectives. Ironically, in seeking the input of wise academics, our best scholars have had the naive notion that they can be enlightened by widening the conversation to long-deceased Europeans, like Comte, Durkheim, Marx, and Freud, none of whom ever set foot in Canada (as far as I know), let alone had any way of comprehending our global contemporary times.

Many observers, consequently, have spent considerable time, money, and energy writing about religious ideas that have been of limited accuracy. To our shame, those views and interpretations have also been of limited help to students and others with vested interests in clearly understanding what has been happening. It's time for us to do much better.

Canadian academics and religious leaders spend endless hours, much ink, and many computer bytes talking and writing about whether or not the religious sky is falling in this country. In the process, we have been like kids huddled in a tent, wondering whether or not there is a leak in the canvas. In the meantime, a major tornado is about to land. Or the beautiful weather outside makes it – yes – "an academic argument" whether or not the pinprick in the tent actually matters. These days a global religious tsunami is taking place. Christianity, Islam, and many other major and minor religions are experiencing explosive growth.

For reasons readily identified by Statistics Canada, in the next several decades immigrants will form a higher proportion of the national population than at almost any other time in Canada's history – approaching levels seen during the early European settlement of Canada. The decline in our national population growth by natural increase and the need to offset this decline with accelerated immigration are starting to transform the Canadian religious scene.

What we do in the tent matters. But what is happening in the world around the tent matters much more. That is what this book is all about.

I have written *Resilient Gods* for two primary reasons. The first is the opportunity and need to draw on invaluable new national and global data. The second is my strong belief that the polarization framework that I unveiled in *Beyond the Gods and Back* is enormously helpful in making sense of religious developments in Canada and around the world. The framework therefore needs to be more extensively delineated, documented, and disseminated.

In the past few years, many important developments have taken place in Canada and elsewhere. They have been accompanied by a large number of rich national and global readings provided by research organizations led by the Pew Research Center, along with Gallup, the World Values Survey, and the International Social Survey Programme. Colleague and friend Rodney Stark has published a fair amount of global data drawn from these sources and carried out the legwork in offering a number of valuable summaries.[1] It has also been a gift to be able to analyze the General Social Survey (GSS) data sets available online for both the United States and Canada.

This book has benefited enormously from numerous data sources, including my own Project Canada national surveys spanning 1975 through 2005. In 2015, I completed a simulation of a new Project Canada national survey by generating data from eight Angus Reid and Vision Critical omnibus surveys. The largest by far was a major survey of religion in March 2015, carried out in partnership with the Angus Reid Institute. This online survey of more than 3,000 Canadians allowed me to monitor an array of religious trends dating back to 1975 and provided important updates on new religious developments in Canada. These surveys are ongoing. Together the data are sheer gold, particularly when placed in the Project Canada survey series.

But beyond the data, another major potential contribution of this book lies in the clarification and use of the polarization framework. Canada is characterized by a religious situation in which a significant number of people continue to embrace religion, a growing number of people reject it, and a large number lie somewhere in the middle. This situation is hardly limited to Canada. On the contrary, it characterizes virtually every country, region, city, community, and group around the world. Everywhere the inclination to adopt religion coexists with the inclination to reject it, with many people typically falling between the two poles. What is fascinating for social scientists to examine is the extent to which the three inclinations are found in any specific setting.

But that's just the starting point. The second intriguing question is "so what?" What are the implications for personal and collective life of people variously embracing religion, rejecting it, or opting for that middle position? On an individual level, do such choices make any difference when it comes to personal well-being? Are the devout happier than others? Are those who reject religion more compassionate than others? Are those in the middle more likely to be accepting of believers than those who reject faith and more accepting of atheists than those who value faith? And, on balance, do the three inclinations lead countries and communities and groups to have higher or lower levels of physical and interpersonal well-being – enhanced standards of living, less crime and conflict, more civility and compassion? And how do people with these different outlooks toward religion deal with death?

These central questions concerning the inclinations of and consequences for people today opting for religion, passing on religion, or choosing a middle position are at the heart of this book.

1

The Early Days of God's Dominion

He shall have dominion also from sea to sea.

– Psalm 72.8, KJV

Viewing religion across Canada these days is like viewing devastation after some tragedy has hit. It's as if a fire of secularization has devastated much of what, through the early 1960s, was a flourishing religious forest.

Around 1950, national religious service attendance, led by Quebec and the Atlantic region, was actually higher than that of the United States. Churchgoing was relatively high pretty much everywhere. To varying degrees, Protestant and Catholic groups had significant places in Canadian life, as exemplified by the large number of people heading to services on almost any Sunday morning; the "Blue Laws," which restricted business transactions on Sundays; the Christian radio stations and broadcasts; the recitation of the Lord's Prayer in schools; and the prominence of religion in the lives of community leaders such as Tommy Douglas in Saskatchewan, E.C. Manning in Alberta, and Cardinal Paul-Émile Léger in Quebec.

Now, some 70 years later, that blaze of secularization has destroyed much of religion's presence and influence, as determined by weekly church attendance (Figure 1.1). The collective devotion of the Atlantic

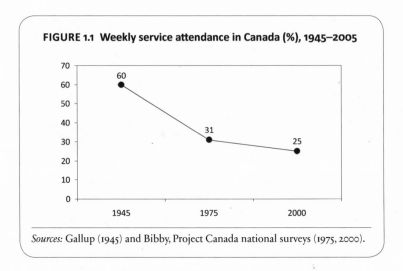

FIGURE 1.1 **Weekly service attendance in Canada (%), 1945–2005**

Sources: Gallup (1945) and Bibby, Project Canada national surveys (1975, 2000).

region has been significantly reduced both by scandal and by modernization. In Quebec, the Quiet Revolution of the early 1960s was accompanied
by a "quieter religious revolution" that decimated religious participation
and authority. In Ontario, western Canada, and the North, the blaze
torched Mainline Protestantism in particular.

However, as is often the case with devastating fires, secularization has
not consumed everything. In some instances, there has been scorching
rather than torching. Amid the rubble, there are pockets of life – even
vitality. Evangelical Protestant churches have been left largely untouched
in many parts of the country, as have a large number of Roman Catholic
dioceses and congregations and some Mainline Protestant groups.

And just when it seemed that much of the Canadian religious forest
was reduced to ruins, new seeds and new plants from other countries
began to replenish it. Growing numbers of Muslims, Hindus, Sikhs, and
Buddhists, for example, have added new diversity and life to the fire-
ravaged forest (Table 1.1).

So it is that the Canadian religious situation is characterized today
by death and life, disintegration and reorganization, abandonment and
participation, aging congregations and youthful congregations, disbelief
and belief, and discarding and embracing of religious rituals surrounding

Resilient Gods

TABLE 1.1 Canadian identification with select major world faiths, 1991 and 2011

	1991	2011
Islam	253,265	1,053,945
Hinduism	157,015	497,960
Sikhism	147,440	454,965
Buddhism	163,415	366,830
Percentage of Canadian population	2.6	7.0

Sources: Statistics Canada 1991 census and 2011 National Household Survey.

marriage, birth, and death. This book aims to offer a coherent picture of the seemingly disparate patterns of religion in Canada today.

Religious Identification in Early Canada

Historians tell us that the new country of Canada that came into being on July 1, 1867, was collectively a highly religious country. It was a time, wrote historian John Webster Grant, when membership in a particular group "ranked high as a badge of personal identity." To know a person's religious affiliation, he said, was to have an important clue about his or her moral and political leanings, school system preferences, and even favourite newspaper.[1]

The First Nations across the country placed considerable importance on spirituality. To varying degrees, they believed in a Creator as the source of everything that lived. Extensive beliefs and forms of worship and celebration existed. By 1867, missionary work had seen large numbers become at least nominally Christian.[2] In some instances, Christianity left room for elements of Indigenous spirituality, resulting in syncretistic expressions of faith.

In Quebec – previously Canada East and earlier Lower Canada – settlement from France dating back to the early 17th century had been accompanied by the arrival of Roman Catholicism. The Quebec Act of

TABLE 1.2 Religious identification in Canada (%), early 1840s

	Upper Canada, 1842	Lower Canada, 1844
Roman Catholic	13	82
Church of England	22	6
Presbyterian	20	5
Methodist	17	2
Baptist	3	1
Jewish	<1	<1
Other denominations	8	1
No response	17	3

Source: Census of Canada, 1870–71, cited in Kalbach and McVey (1976, 223).

1774 gave French-speaking citizens the right to practise the Catholic faith and French civil law. At the time of Confederation, the province was heavily Catholic – with observers claiming that much of the public and private lives of Quebeckers was controlled by the church.

In Ontario – previously Canada West and earlier Upper Canada – the arrival of large numbers of settlers from England resulted in Anglicanism being the numerically dominant religion in 1867. Presbyterians, Methodists, and Congregationalists were also prominent, in large part because of the magnitude of immigration from England and Scotland. Immigration also produced a significant Catholic presence: the Irish Famine of the 1840s, for example, resulted in the arrival of some 40,000 Irish Catholics (Table 1.2).

The other two British colonies part of the new country – Nova Scotia and New Brunswick – also had a pronounced religious presence. Immigration from France brought Acadians to Nova Scotia, where they coexisted with Protestant immigrants from Britain. The creation of New Brunswick in 1784 occurred in large part because of the arrival of significant numbers of United Empire Loyalists on the heels of the American Revolution.

The influx of large numbers of slaves from the United States via the Underground Railroad added to the early religious mosaic as black

Resilient Gods

TABLE 1.3 Religious identification of Canadians (%), 1871–1961

	1871	1901	1931	1961
Roman Catholic	42	42	41	47
Protestant	56	56	54	49
Eastern Orthodox	<1	<1	1	1
Other faiths	2	2	3	2
No religion	<1	<1	<1	<1

Source: Canadian census data.

Baptists took up residence, particularly in Nova Scotia and southern Ontario.

As the young nation expanded to include Manitoba and the Northwest Territories (1870), British Columbia (1871), Prince Edward Island (1873), the Yukon (1898), Saskatchewan and Alberta (1905), and Newfoundland (1949), the number of people with religious ties also grew.

There is nothing surprising about the early Christian monopoly. It was the direct result of heavy immigration from France, Britain, and other western European countries where Christianity was pervasive – patterns documented thoroughly in two recent valuable works compiled by Paul Bramadat and David Seljak.[3] Religious group numbers, as with the population as a whole, are primarily a function of net gains via immigration and birth, along with intergroup "switching." The early years favoured Christians.

Immigration consequently played a major role in Protestants and Catholics making up more than 95% of the national population from the time of the first census in 1871 through 1961 (Table 1.3). Over the 90-year period, the percentage of people claiming to have "no religion" never reached 1%.

Religious Participation in Early Canada

Hard data on actual *involvement* in religious groups, rather than mere identification with them, are difficult to locate for the early years of Canada.

Yet, in describing the religious situation just after Confederation, Grant wrote that "the morale of the churches was higher than ever. They were building larger edifices, devising more effective programs, and successfully shaping the moral values of the nation."[4]

More specifically, sociologist Peter Beyer notes that things were looking good numerically for organized religion as Canada entered the 20th century. Allowing for more than one service per Sunday, churches had enough seating capacity in 1901 to accommodate more than the total Canadian population – "3,842,332 seats for a total population of 5,371,315." A survey carried out by Toronto newspapers in 1896 showed that 57% of the available seats in the Toronto area were occupied during any given service.[5]

But church attendance seems to have become even better. The years following the Second World War, the 1940s and 1950s, appear to have been a golden age for church attendance and influence in Canada. According to the first known national attendance poll, conducted by the Gallup organization in 1945, 65% of Canadians over the age of 20 said that they had attended a religious service in a three-week period following Easter Sunday. Gallup noted in its press release that a similar survey it had conducted in the United States around the same time had found that 58% of Americans had attended a service over a four-week period following Easter.

The Canadian poll found that levels here were slightly higher for those 21 to 29 (69%) than for older adults (64%) and for women (73%) than for men (61%). In Quebec, where Catholics made up 95% of the population, 9 of 10 people said that they had been to Mass during the three-week period. The pollster noted that the levels were lower in "some western provinces" than elsewhere and suggested that the levels might have been related to "greater distances to travel."

The Gallup release concluded with this additional informative statement: "The present survey complements the one conducted by the Poll some months ago, in which ninety-five per cent of Canadians expressed their belief in God; and eighty-four per cent, their belief in a life after death."[6]

Such high levels of religious participation continued in Canada through the 1950s and 1960s (Table 1.4).

TABLE 1.4 Membership in selected religious groups in Canada (1,000s), 1871–1966

	United	Anglican	Baptist	Pentecostal	Lutheran	Presbyterian	Roman Catholic
1871	–	–	–	–	–	–	1,586
1881	170*	–	–	–	–	117	1,773
1901	289*	368	–	–	–	214	2,256
1921	401	690	–	–	–	351	3,427
1931	671	794	132	–	–	181	4,047
1941	717	836	134	–	–	174	4,806
1951	834	1,096	135	45	121	177	6,069
1961	1,037	1,358	138	60	172	201	8,343
1966	1,062	1,293	137	65	189	200	9,160

* United figures for 1881 and 1901 = Methodist.

Notes: Anglican figures = inclusive membership; in 1967, for example, full Anglican membership = 657,000 versus 1,060,000 for United. Roman Catholic = approximate full membership based on percentages of Canadian population. Baptist = Canadian Baptist Federation. Pentecostal = Pentecostal Assemblies of Canada. Lutheran = Evangelical Church of Canada, Lutheran Church in America, and Lutheran Church-Canada (Missouri Synod).

Sources: Anglican, Baptist, Lutheran, Pentecostal, Presbyterian, and United yearbooks; Beyer (1997); Bibby (2002, 11); McLeod (1982); Statistics Canada, the *Daily*, June 1, 1993; *Yearbook of American and Canadian Churches, 1916–1966*.

- Attendance at Catholic churches appears to have held steady at about 85% both in Quebec and in the rest of the country, while weekly attendance at Protestant churches remained strong at around 45%.[7] This was a time when Cardinal Léger could say this of Montreal: "When I bow to say the evening rosary, all of Montreal bows with me."[8]
- Membership in the United and Anglican churches peaked at over 1 million in 1965. During these heady days of the mid-1940s to mid-1960s, the United Church alone built 1,500 new churches and halls.[9]
- Other faith groups were growing as well. Between 1941 and the end of the 1960s, the number of Jews jumped from 169,000 to 275,000. During the same period, Jehovah's Witnesses experienced explosive growth, increasing from 7,000 to 170,000.[10]

The religion business seemed to be booming.

Religious Influence in Early Canada

There is widespread consensus that religion once had an impact on Canadian life. Writers tell us that religion was a central feature in the lives of early First Nations peoples, that they were "deeply committed to religious attitudes, beliefs, and practices" grounded in "communion with nature and a connectedness with all of life."[11] Religion is also seen as having been an integral part of the earliest Roman Catholic and Protestant settlements.

Religion appears to have had a major place during Canada's first century, from the 1860s to the 1960s. As one thinks of the past, it is difficult to envision Quebec without Roman Catholics, Ontario without Anglicans or Presbyterians, the Prairies with no evangelical Protestant presence, British Columbia and the Atlantic region without the Church of England.

Religion was blatant in many of our early institutions:

- A large number of hospitals and social service programs across the country were initiated by religious groups.
- Individual schools and entire school systems were created by religious groups, notably Roman Catholics.

- Universities – including McMaster, Queen's, Ryerson, Wilfrid Laurier, Ottawa, Montreal, Laval, Acadia, Mount Allison, St. Mary's, Winnipeg, Brandon, and Regina – were founded by religious organizations.
- Initiatives to establish fairness in the workplace, including supporting labour unions, were undertaken by many groups, including Roman Catholics in Quebec and social gospel–oriented Protestant denominations elsewhere, notably the United and Anglican churches of Canada.
- The influence of religious groups was also evident in the public sphere generally and the political sphere specifically. CBC footage of a religious event in Montreal in the 1960s reveals three prominent platform guests: Mayor Jean Drapeau, René Lévesque, and Cardinal Léger.[12]

One obvious reason why religion had significant input into Canadian institutions was because it also had an important place in many individual lives. At its best, religion is supposed to play itself out in everyday life. It is therefore not surprising that, to varying degrees, the faith practices of individual Canadians involved in religious groups had an impact on them, beginning with their families. For example, large numbers of their children were attending Sunday schools or receiving other forms of religious instruction (Table 1.5).

TABLE 1.5 **Frequency of religious instruction of children in Canada (%), 1975–2005**

"How frequently – if at all – do your children attend Sunday School or classes of religious instruction that are not part of their regular school days?"	1975	1990	2005
Regularly	36	28	19
Often	10	7	6
Sometimes	31	26	24
Never	23	39	51

Sources: Bibby, Project Canada national surveys (1975, 1990, 2005).

Moreover, through individuals and the efforts of the groups them-selves, religion's reach extended to the institutional sphere in Canada – schools, the economy, the government, the media, social services, sports and leisure, and so on. To the extent that religion was important to indi-viduals, it coloured life in Canada. American historian Mark Noll goes so far as to say that, as of around 1950, Canada had a much stronger claim as a Christian nation than the United States.[13]

Today, in the early years of the 21st century, things have changed. Religion no longer occupies centre stage. Protestantism is not a pivotal feature of Anglo culture, while Catholicism is no longer at the heart of Québécois culture. Religion's importance for many other cultural groups has similarly declined as those groups have been increasingly integrated into mainstream Canadian life.

Religion obviously continues to have a presence. Old and new places of worship serve as reminders that it remains important for some people.

TABLE 1.6 Religious identification of immigrants (%) in the 20th century

	Pre-1946	1956–60	1976–80	1996–2000
Roman Catholic	14	41	27	21
Anglican	26	7	6	1
United	4	3	<1	<1
Presbyterian	4	1	<1	<1
Lutheran	3	6	<1	<1
Baptist	5	<1	1	<1
Jewish	<1	4	1	1
Muslim	<1	<1	7	16
Hindu	<1	<1	3	8
Sikh	<1	<1	4	3
Buddhist	<1	<1	5	3
No Religion	10	15	21	20
Other	29	18	22	23
Total	100	100	100	100

Source: Statistics Canada General Social Survey (2012).

Resilient Gods

We welcome visits by the pope or Dalai Lama, just as we welcome visits of the queen or a president.

Yet religion is expected to be both non-partisan and respectful of pluralism. Graduation invocations are no longer prayers, and religious symbols have been decreed to have no place in public buildings. Even the declaration in the Canadian Charter of Rights and Freedoms that "Canada is founded upon principles that recognize the supremacy of God and the rule of law" sounds somewhat anachronistic.

For many Baby Boomers, the poetry of Kris Kristofferson still applies: the things that remind them of religion, such as a church bell or a Sunday School chorus, have been lost "somehow, somewhere along the way."[14] For most post-Boomers and Millennial youth, however, the bell is just a bell, the chorus just another kind of music.

The obvious question is "what happened?" Two factors appear to have been central. The first key factor was a shift in immigration patterns. During the last few decades of the 20th century, Mainline Protestants in particular saw their immigration pipelines largely dry up. Conversely, the Catholic Church continued to benefit from large numbers of arrivals from other countries, as did other world faiths, particularly Islam (Table 1.6). The Mainline Protestant immigration void was not filled up via births. Something had to give, and it did. The second key factor was the changing mindsets of Canadians, led by the Baby Boomers. Many began to see old things in new ways – placing unprecedented importance on themes including diversity, gratification, and input. The impact on Canadian life and institutions would be pervasive and powerful.

2

Declining Religious Participation
among Boomers

The age where religious leaders could appeal to
obligation and duty to get people into the pews is over.
– Reginald W. Bibby, *The Boomer Factor*, 2006

Demographically, what led to the decline of religious participation in Canada was fairly straightforward. The Great Religious Recession took place largely because Mainline Protestant groups no longer had the luxury of gushing immigration pipelines. To make matters worse, their birthrates were down, and their policies and strategies for retaining their children's religious participation were not always well developed and well executed. Their third and last numerical lifeline – recruiting outsiders – was not really a viable solution given the low priority that many assigned to evangelism.

Consequently, by the 1970s, the number of active members dying was greater than the number of people taking their places. Some social analysts at the time spoke of the inevitability of cultural forces eroding organized religion (see Chapter 3). Some theologians spoke of the death of Christendom.[1] In retrospect, the demographer probably deserved the A.

But immigration changes, declining birth rates, and limited "switching" tell only part of the national story and little of the Quebec story.

Historian Mark Noll recently offered a provocative analysis of the marginalization of Christian groups as organizations in the post-1960s. He sketched the impact of rising nationalism on the Catholic Church in Quebec, governments' co-opting of personal welfare on the United Church, disestablishment on the Anglican Church, and isolation on evangelical groups.[2]

At the individual level, decline in the importance of organized religion coincided with a number of significant social and cultural shifts in Quebec and the rest of Canada, the United States, and much of the Western world. Occupying centre stage, because of both historical timing and their sheer size, were the Baby Boomers.

Boomers and Religious Involvement

The post–Second World War Baby Boom saw an annual average of 400,000 children born in Canada between the mid-1940s and the mid-1960s. As observers such as David Foote of the University of Toronto remind us, Boomers were bound to have a dramatic impact on Canadian life, if for no other reason than "there were so many of them."[3]

By 1966, the oldest members of the cohort were entering their 20s, while the youngest reached that age by 1986. From about 1980 to 2000, Boomers comprised more than 50% of all adults in the critical and influential cohort of those aged 20 to 64, and they were thus positioned to have significant impacts on all spheres of Canadian life. As of 2015, they made up only 30% of that strategic cohort, and by 2020 they will have slipped to 20%. But since the 1960s, Baby Boomers have had an impact on everything that they have touched – including, of course, religion.

Gallup polls found that, in 1956, 61% of Canadians claimed that they had attended a religious service "in the last seven days," a figure very similar to that for 1946. But by 1965 that level had dropped to 55% and by 1975 to 41%. The somewhat stricter measure used in our Project Canada national surveys – "how often do you attend religious services?" – produced a lower figure for 1975, with 31% of Canadians reporting that they attended a religious service weekly (Table 2.1; also see Figure 2.1).

TABLE 2.1 Weekly attendance at religious services by age cohort (%), 1975 and 2005

	Canada	Quebec	Canada outside Quebec
1975			
Pre-Boomers	37	48	33
Boomers	15	11	16
Total percentage of Canadian population attending weekly services	31	35	29
2005			
Pre-Boomers	37	33	37
Boomers	18	7	22
Post-Boomers	24	13	28
Total percentage of Canadian population attending weekly services	25	15	28

Note: Pre-Boomers are those born before 1946, Boomers are those born between 1946 and 1965, and post-Boomers are those born after 1965.
Sources: Bibby, Project Canada national surveys (1975, 2005).

The drop in attendance that began to show up in the mid-1960s was largely a Boomer phenomenon. The Project Canada national surveys show that weekly attendance at services among pre-Boomers – people born before 1945 – remained a consistent 37% between 1975 and 2005. However, as early as 1975, Boomer attendance was much lower (15%), and it remained near that level right through 2005 (18%).

In Quebec, pre-Boomer and Boomer differences were dramatic as early as 1975 (48% versus 11%). Pre-Boomer attendance slipped somewhat (to 33%), while Boomer attendance, rather than showing signs of recovery, fell further (to 7%). In the apt line of journalist Konrad Yakabuski, "church attendance in Quebec didn't so much collapse as vaporize – at least among those born after 1945."[4]

Elsewhere in Canada, there was a mild increase by 2005, but the Boomer level (22%) remained well below the pre-Boomer level (37%).

In short, contrary to some highly publicized rumours, Boomers never "returned to church" in sufficient numbers to offset earlier losses. The

Resilient Gods

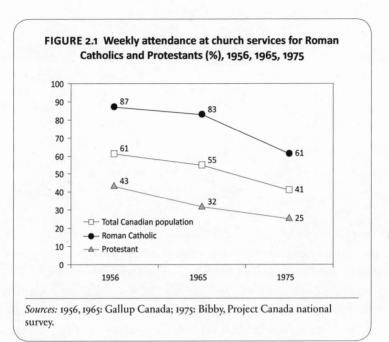

FIGURE 2.1 Weekly attendance at church services for Roman Catholics and Protestants (%), 1956, 1965, 1975

Sources: 1956, 1965: Gallup Canada; 1975: Bibby, Project Canada national survey.

generation that has followed them – the post-Boomers – has exhibited higher levels of attendance, but their level of participation is still well below that of their pre-Boomer grandparents.

These findings clearly show that the religious recession of the post-1960s was tied not only to changes in immigration patterns but also to the inclination of large numbers of Boomers to stay away from churches. This leads us again to ask "why?"

Four Critical Shifts

The 1960s brought with them a number of key cultural and social trends. I discussed 10 of them in detail in *The Boomer Factor*.[5] Four shifts appear to have been particularly significant in reshaping religion.

From Dominance to Diversity

Boomers were strongly influenced in the 1960s by "rights revolutions" relating to civil rights, sexuality, women, and countercultural lifestyles. In Canada, many Boomers grew up with bilingualism, multiculturalism,

**TABLE 2.2 Social attitudes of pre-Boomers and Boomers
(% in agreement), 1975**

	Pre-Boomers	Boomers
Whites and blacks marrying	46	81
Homosexual relations	21	43
Women employed when their husbands can support them	58	84

Source: Bibby, Project Canada national survey (1975).

and the Charter. The result was what some writers have referred to as "the death of the monoculture"[6] – the movement from sameness to diversity, accompanied by the explosion of choices in every sphere of life.

As I suggested more than 25 years ago in *Mosaic Madness,* Canada is a country with multiple mosaics that go well beyond intergroup relations. Pluralism at group and individual levels has become part of the Canadian psyche. For some time now, we have had not only a cultural mosaic but also a moral mosaic, a meaning system mosaic, a family structure mosaic, a sexual mosaic. And that's just the shortlist. Pluralism has come to pervade Canadian minds and Canadian institutions.[7]

The legitimation of choice can be seen as far back as the mid-1970s. Our Project Canada national surveys show that young Boomers – in a remarkably short time – broke dramatically from their parents and grandparents in their views on things like racial intermarriage, women being employed outside the home, sexual orientation, family life, and valid religions (Table 2.2). In retrospect, the portrayals of intergenerational conflict between Archie and "Meathead" in those *All in the Family* episodes in the 1970s – remembered by at least a few of us – were not exaggerations. They summed up pervasive differences in outlook between pre-Boomers and Boomers in both the United States and Canada.

The emergence of options and the increasing view of truth in relativistic terms were hardly conducive to any religion that proclaimed absolutes and exhibited intolerance of difference. In fact, any religion that didn't champion flexibility and freedom could expect to see its market share shrink.

　　　　　　　　　　　　　　　　　　　　　　　　　Resilient Gods

Yet, ironically, religions that aligned themselves with social changes ran the risk of becoming indistinguishable from culture and – in the memorable words of Canadian Lutheran theologian William Hordern – failing "to tell the world something that the world [was] not already telling itself."[8]

From Obligation to Gratification

Many of us who lived back in the 1950s and 1960s now find those days very different from today with respect to what motivates people. To a fair extent, people back then seemed to be moved by loyalty, obligation, and duty – even, on some occasions, altruism. There was a sense that one should be loyal to one's country, old school, and maybe even local grocery store or gas station. Some people thought that it was their duty to get out of bed on a Sunday morning and attend church (Table 2.3). It wasn't unusual to find someone who would spontaneously help out when needed. They'd change a stranger's flat tire, offer a couple of dollars if a person came up short at a checkout till, or lend a hand shovelling a neighbour's driveway – all with no expectation of return.

What's more, themes of obligation were drawn on by organizations and companies, including sports teams. There was a sense that a parent

TABLE 2.3 Churchgoing in Canada perceived as a duty (%), 2005

	"My parents believed that they were supposed to go to church."
Roman Catholics: Quebec	79
Pre-Boomers	88
Boomers	81
Post-Boomers	64
Roman Catholics: outside Quebec	71
Christian: unspecified	66
Conservative Protestant	61
Mainline Protestant	56
No religion	48
Other faith	48

Source: Bibby, Project Canada national survey (2005).

should help out at school, that a Catholic should attend Mass, that a Canadian cultural icon like Eaton's should receive our support. People were called on in Regina to save the Riders and in Calgary to save the Stamps, while in Winnipeg and Quebec City people were asked to get behind efforts to save the Jets and Nordiques. Why? Because, depending on the situation, it was our civic duty, or national duty, or religious duty.

And then, of course, there was marriage. Ceremonies involved declarations that marriage was not to be entered into lightly – with couples solemnly swearing that they would remain faithful to each other, "for richer, for poorer, in sickness and in health, so long as [they] both shall live."

The Boomer era saw a major shift in motivational emphasis from obligation to gratification. Themes like duty and loyalty were replaced by a market model. That model stressed the importance of following the axiom of marketing gurus: successful organizations determine needs and then meet them. In the process, they emphasize what's in it for us. And they offer "value-added" features such as travel points or seasonal discounts or gift vouchers. We don't get just something we pay for; we get "more." By the new century, such an outlook had become pervasive,

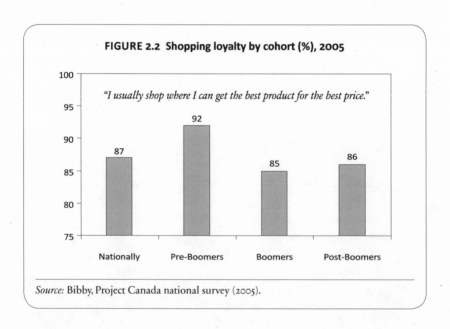

FIGURE 2.2 Shopping loyalty by cohort (%), 2005

Source: Bibby, Project Canada national survey (2005).

shared by Canadians of all ages. So it is that, for some time now, most of us have been highly selective consumers in every area of life (Figure 2.2).

Religion has not received an exemption. To the extent that people consider joining religious groups, they do so in highly pragmatic, consumer-like fashion. Many of their parents might have considered that churchgoing was a duty – for example, something becoming of "a good Catholic" – with no questions asked. But as the new century began, the dominant sense of Canadians of all ages, close to 90% of them, was that people should attend services not out of a sense of obligation but because they find doing so worthwhile.[9]

Lest religious leaders take such selective consumption personally, they need only look at how Canadians, younger and older, approach relationships: "We want relationships to last forever. But if they don't add very much to our lives we follow the advice of the relationship guru and discard them, 'turn the page,' and move on. After all, if people don't enrich our lives why should we bother with them?"[10] Of course, some people continue to be motivated by duty and loyalty. There are still some who act out of concern for others. But they are in the minority. So, if religious leaders still expect people to show up for services because that's what a good person does, then my message is simple: "Good luck!"

From Deference to Discernment

For Canadians who lived in the 1950s and 1960s, a buzzword was *respect*. People were expected to respect their elders and parents, teachers and ministers, doctors and police, journalists and politicians – pretty much everyone who was an adult and definitely anyone who had credentials. There was also a high level of deference shown to institutions, including schools, universities, governments, and churches. Acquiescence to the church was allegedly widespread among Roman Catholics in Quebec.

For Boomers, higher levels of individual freedom have included freedom of expression. Better educated, exposed to television and travel, and equipped in recent years with the Internet, Boomers have led the way insisting that they have a voice in every realm of life. They want input. They are also extremely demanding.

The result is that individuals and institutions are now carefully scrutinized. They have to earn the right to be seen as authoritative and to

TABLE 2.4 Attitudes toward authority by cohort (%), 2005

	Nationally	Pre-Boomers	Boomers	Post-Boomers
"My parents taught me to respect people in authority."	95	96	95	94
"I think that today people in authority have to earn our respect."	86	94	85	82
"Critical thinking – whereby we evaluate our leaders and experts – is generally a good thing."	95	96	95	94

Source: Bibby, Project Canada national survey (2005).

be respected. We take it for granted that the critical evaluation of our leaders and experts is a positive thing (Table 2.4). Consider the following examples.

▶ A doctor's diagnosis is checked and supplemented with information gleaned from the Internet – giving new meaning to the old cliché about "getting a second opinion."
▶ A teacher's or counsellor's assessment of our children is evaluated in terms of what we ourselves know and further information gained from "googling" on ADD, a learning disability, or a speech delay.

Individuals who serve as coaches and referees for our children find themselves having to contend with parents not lost for thoughts on abilities, playing time, and good and bad calls.

So it is that almost every business and organization today offers us "contact" information. Every media outlet offers us a "feedback" opportunity. Every big talent show offers us "viewer" input. The emphasis on facilitating interaction is captured by the fact that businesses and organizations, large or small, are on Facebook and Twitter, inviting us to enter

TABLE 2.5 Canadians' confidence in leaders (%), 1975–2005

Have "a great deal" or "quite a bit" of confidence in	1975	2005
Police	75	69
Schools	49	47
Newspapers	40	43
Court system	49	42
Radio	–	40
Religious groups	51	34
Television	44	33
Major businesses	–	33
Provincial government	31	27
Labour unions	21	27
Federal government	30	21

Sources: Bibby, Project Canada national surveys (1975, 2005).

into conversations with them. It's not as if they have a choice. If they want to be successful, then they have to be willing to hear us out.

But try as they might, virtually all of our primary institutions have had difficulty garnering high levels of confidence – with the trend suggesting that things will get worse before they get better. As shown in Table 2.5, only the police enjoy the confidence of a clear majority of Canadians; schools, the media, the court system, religious leaders, politicians, and labour unions fare much worse. In general, levels of confidence have declined since the 1970s.

The highly critical outlook of Canadians can also be seen in survey results reported by Leger Marketing. In recent years, the polling company has found a decline in our trust of people in virtually every occupation. Firefighters and nurses rank at the top; teachers, doctors, and police officers also fare quite well. But there is trust slippage when it comes to bankers, church representatives, and – gasp – pollsters, along with lawyers and journalists. Trust in publicists has dropped significantly. Trust in politicians – well, let's just say that it remains very low.[11]

Indicative of "the death of deference," a national poll in the United States found that, by the turn of the new century, younger Roman Catholics were far less inclined than their older counterparts to blindly

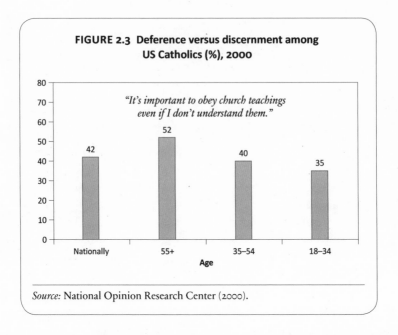

FIGURE 2.3 Deference versus discernment among US Catholics (%), 2000

"It's important to obey church teachings even if I don't understand them."

Source: National Opinion Research Center (2000).

accept the teachings of the church (Figure 2.3). Deferential obedience was giving way to critical discernment.

Another American research finding that might be equally applicable to Canada is that Catholic teenagers are now no more likely than other teens to express feelings of guilt. Christian Smith's research suggests that Catholic young people often do not know enough about church teachings to feel guilt; others are aware of teachings but disregard them rather than internalize them.[12]

The shift from deference to discernment has put considerable pressure on religious groups to respond. People want opportunities for input, yet groups have been put in the position of determining what is negotiable and what isn't negotiable. They have also had to cope with heightened expectations and have not always been successful.

Canadians not actively involved in religious groups in 2000 were asked if they would be receptive to greater involvement if they "found it to be worthwhile" for themselves or their families. Some 65% said either "yes" or "perhaps." Asked "what kinds of things would make it worthwhile?" 37% cited ministry factors – better meeting of spiritual, personal, and relational needs. But another 30% said that organizational factors

Resilient Gods

TABLE 2.6 Factors that would make religious involvement more worthwhile for those attending less than monthly (%), 2005

	% in agreement
Ministry factors	37
Organizational factors	30
Changes in style and outlook	23
Better leadership	3
Other	4
Respondent factors	30
Other factors	3

Source: Bibby (2002, 221).

were an issue – wanting changes in style, outlook, and leadership. Most of the remaining 33% indicated that the problem was with factors related to themselves, like work schedule, family indifference, and getting older (Table 2.6).[13] These findings indicate that large numbers of people have strong feelings about what they expect from religious groups. The days of passive acquiescence are over.

Consistent with such thinking, McGill University philosopher Charles Taylor has written that, during the 1950s and 1960s, the secular mindset that dated back to the Enlightenment made a leap from the intellectual sphere to the public sphere. One key component was a "coming of age narrative" in which people thought that they did not need to look beyond themselves for norms and values.[14] "Self-authorization," says Taylor, is "an axiomatic feature of modernity."[15] He maintains that such a sense of self-authorization has done more to advance secularism than scientific thinking.

From Homes to Careers

Between 1960 and 2000, the proportion of women employed outside the home doubled from 29% to 58% (Figure 2.4). In 1930, the figure had been around 20%. A similar shift took place during the same period in the United States.

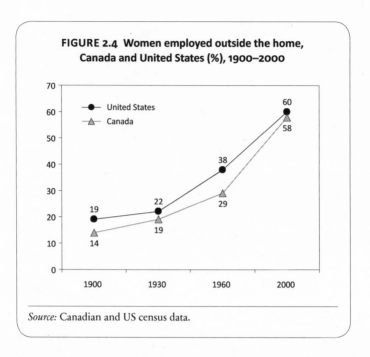

FIGURE 2.4 Women employed outside the home, Canada and United States (%), 1900–2000

Source: Canadian and US census data.

The social impact of this dramatic escalation in female employment during the Boomer era is difficult to overestimate. It affected family life, altering both the age at which couples married and the inclination to marry or the need to remain married. It affected the number of children that a couple could have. It altered the amount of time that women and men could give to their children and each other. It created new pressures on time, adding a significant level of pragmatism to time-use choices. In the process, it significantly affected social and organizational involvement – including churchgoing.

Sociologist Robert Putnam of Harvard University, in his best-selling book *Bowling Alone*, released in 2000, maintains that the increase in the number of women in the labour force in the United States was "the most portentous social change of the last half century." Controlling for other factors, Putnam says, "full-time employment appears to cut home entertaining by roughly 10 percent and church attendance by roughly 15 percent, informal visiting with friends by 25 percent, and volunteering by more than 50 percent. Moreover," he adds, "husbands of women who work

TABLE 2.7 Lack of time among employed parents in Canada
with school-age children (%), 2003

	"I never seem to have enough time."
Total	47
Married mothers	77
Cohabiting mothers	65
Married fathers	59
Divorced/separated mothers	58
Non-employed mothers	49

Source: Bibby (2006, 82).

full-time are, like their wives, less likely to attend church, volunteer, and entertain at home."[16]

In short, something like a revolution was taking place in how personal life, family life, and work life were being experienced. One of the most prominent correlates was the widespread feeling of being short of time. Of course, couples had felt busy in the past. But employment outside the home brought with it loss of control over schedule and location. It translated into large numbers of people feeling that they were being pulled in an array of directions and simply lacking time (Table 2.7).

The available data suggest that employed husbands and wives in post-1950s Canada frequently felt pressed for time and thus became increasingly pragmatic about how they spent their time and their resources more generally. They were open to things that added to family life.

If parents could arrive at a church service and find that the religious group was ready for them and their children, providing a relaxing, uplifting, and gratifying atmosphere, then great! However, there is little evidence that religious groups – even those like the United Church who saw themselves as progressive and in touch with the times – were ready, that they understood the magnitude of the family and workplace transformations taking place.[17]

On the contrary, when groups should have been adding resources that would result in improved ministry to children, teenagers, and tired moms and dads, often the opposite was taking place.

- Between the 1960s and 1990s, Mainline Protestant groups cut back on their number of Sunday Schools.
- Catholics, despite their official commitment to a "family, parish, and school" model of ministry, did not provide environments particularly conducive to stressed-out parents and children.
- Evangelical groups might have been an exception, not so much because they read the times better, but more so because "they lucked out": many already had good children and youth ministries in place, almost accidentally possessing the infrastructure to minister to the dual employed.

As a result, rather than abandoning their faith and traditions, many pragmatically minded Boomers gave churches the time that they thought they warranted, in keeping with what they added to their lives and those of their families. For many, that meant not dropping out altogether but showing up on special occasions, notably Easter and Christmas, along with baptisms and christenings, weddings and funerals. The Project Canada national surveys since 1995 have shown that large numbers didn't rule out greater involvement. But such participation had to enrich their lives and those of their family members.

In light of such findings, one is hard pressed to escape the conclusion that the problems of organized religion in the post-1960s were tied, in large part, to the fact that Canada's groups too often did a poor job of responding to the changing family roles and needs of Boomers. As a result, most people continued to place a measure of importance on faith and retain their psychological and emotional ties with religious traditions. But, on weekends, sizable numbers found better things to do with their time.

The Aftermath

The reluctance of Boomers to embrace organized religion is reflected in the finding that weekly attendance in Canada slipped from more than 50% in 1960 to about 30% in 1980 and to 25% by 2005 (Table 2.8). However, except for Quebec Catholics, the core people actively involved in

TABLE 2.8 Weekly church attendance in Canada (%), 1957, 1980, and 2005

	1957	1980	2005
Canada	53	28	25
Protestant	38	24	29
Conservative	51	53	64
Mainline	35	19	20
Roman Catholic	83	41	29
Outside Quebec	75	44	42
Quebec	88	38	14
Other faiths	35	11	22

Sources: 1957: March Gallup poll; 1980, 2005: Bibby, Project Canada national surveys.

groups stabilized by 1980 and has in fact increased since then for Conservative Protestants and members of other faiths.

It is important to remember, however, that to base a percentage on which people identify with which group can be misleading if the sizes of the pools are shrinking. Such is the case with Mainline Protestants – the United, Anglican, Presbyterian, and Lutheran Churches. On the surface, their combined core of weekly attenders has remained steady at about 20% since about 1980. However, the percentage of Canadians identifying with the four groups dropped from 32% in 1981 to 20% in 2001 (Table 2.9). In light of their age structures as of the 2001 census, there is good reason to believe that the combined total of the Mainline Protestant pool might now be no higher than around 15%.

This brings us back to the importance of immigration in determining group sizes. In analyzing the findings for the 2001 census, Statistics Canada noted that one reason for Roman Catholic growth has been immigration. Catholics accounted for nearly one-quarter of the 1.8 million people who came to Canada between 1991 and 2001. The pattern is not new: Catholics "have remained the largest [single] religious denomination within each new wave of immigrants since the 1960s."[18]

TABLE 2.9 Canadians identifying with Catholic and Protestant faiths (%), 1931–2001

	1931	1961	1981	2001
Roman Catholic	40	46	46	43
Mainline Protestant	48	41	32	20
United	20	20	16	10
Anglican	16	13	10	7
Presbyterian	8	4	3	1
Lutheran	4	4	3	2
Conservative Protestant	8	8	8	8
Baptist	4	3	3	3
Pentecostal	<1	<1	1	1
Other	3	5	4	4

Source: Statistics Canada census data.

As a result of what amounts to "a global circulation of the saints," Catholics in Canada have continued to benefit from the arrival of Catholics from other parts of the world. In the Greater Toronto Area (GTA), for example, the church has some 2 million Catholics in close to 225 parishes and celebrates Mass each week in about 40 different ethnic and linguistic communities.[19]

Since the early 1960s, Protestants have not been nearly as fortunate. Their share of "the immigrant market" has decreased steadily, being surpassed first by Catholics and then by new arrivals who either identified with other world faiths or said that they had no religion. With few exceptions, the primary countries of origin have been changing in favour of Catholics, other world faiths, and people with no religion (Figure 2.5).

The Legacy

Young people obviously do not emerge out of a cultural vacuum. The key to understanding Canadian youth today is to look at their Boomer and post-Boomer parents. Our most recent Project Teen Canada national

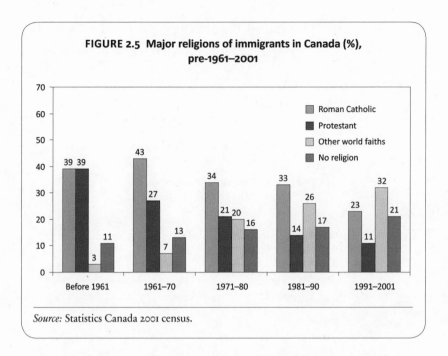

FIGURE 2.5 Major religions of immigrants in Canada (%), pre-1961–2001

Legend:
- Roman Catholic
- Protestant
- Other world faiths
- No religion

Before 1961: 39, 39, 3, 11
1961–70: 43, 27, 7, 13
1971–80: 34, 21, 20, 16
1981–90: 33, 14, 26, 17
1991–2001: 23, 11, 32, 21

Source: Statistics Canada 2001 census.

survey of teenagers between the ages of 15 and 19 allows us to do just that. The survey, the latest in a series conducted every eight years since 1984, had a sample of more than 5,500 young people, including a special over-sampling of Aboriginals.[20] It provides an intriguing snapshot of the children and grandchildren of Boomers in light of many of the explicit goals, efforts, and emphases of Boomers.

We know – thanks to the census – that the percentage of Canadians who said that they had no religion jumped from 4% in 1971 to 16% in 2001. Their children and grandchildren would be expected to follow suit – and they have. Today's teens are reporting the highest level of non-affiliation in Canadian history: 32% say that they have "no religion" – up dramatically from 12% in 1984 (Table 2.10).

The declines and diminished pools among Quebec Catholics and the United and Anglican Churches are almost breathtaking.

▶ Between 1984 and 2008, Quebec teens who said that they were Roman Catholic dropped from 21% to 9%.

- During the same period, the percentage of teenagers across the country who identified with the United Church fell from 10% to 1%.
- The drop-off in Anglican Church identification has also been sizable – from 8% to 2%.

TABLE 2.10 Religious identification of teens (%), 1984 and 2008

	1984	2008
Roman Catholic	50	32
Outside Quebec	29	23
Inside Quebec	21	9
Protestant	35	13
United	10	1
Anglican	8	2
Baptist	3	1
Lutheran	2	1
Pentecostal	2	1
Presbyterian	2	1
Other/unspecified	8	6
Orthodox	–	2
Christian (unspecified)	–	3
Other faiths	3	16
Islam	<1	5
Buddhism	<1	3
Judaism	1	2
Hinduism	<1	2
Sikhism	<1	2
Aboriginal spirituality	<1	2
Other/unspecified	2	2
None	12	32

Source: Bibby, Project Teen Canada national surveys (1984, 2008).

And, if the findings on identification and attendance are not bad enough for religious groups, a further headline finding should be more than a shade unnerving: *God is slipping in the polls.* The 2008 youth survey found that the proportion of teens who said that they were atheist was higher than any pollster had previously found.

Such findings undoubtedly lead observers to conclude that we are seeing further evidence of rampant secularization. One prominent media commentator recently proclaimed that, "if the future for institutional religion lies in the hearts and minds of the young, a dark night is sweeping down on the country's churches, synagogues, and temples."[21]

Actually, such a conclusion is a misreading of the times.

A synopsis of the new reality was provided by a highly publicized debate in Toronto between prominent atheist Christopher Hitchens and prominent believer former British prime minister Tony Blair in December 2010. In noting that it was the fastest-selling show in the history of Roy Thomson Hall, journalist Lorna Dueck suggested that the level of interest was "a sign that religion is far from dead in the public imagination."[22] The fact that the two combatants had two different fan bases provided an important clue as to what is happening with religion in Canada.

3

Pro-Religion, Low Religion, and No Religion

> Sure, lots of people are leaving, but lots of people are also staying.
>
> – A beleaguered church leader

Secularization seemed to sum up the Canadian religious situation well as the 20th century came to a close. Proponents of the thesis, dating back to luminaries like Comte, Durkheim, Marx, and Freud, all saw religion as giving way to science as civilization evolved. More recently, the argument had been echoed and updated by prominent sociologists, including Bryan Wilson, Karel Dobbelaere, Collum Brown, and Steve Bruce. Significantly, all of these individuals have been Europeans.

This "old story" about religion is still the story that the media typically tell. In December 2010, Michael Valpy and Joe Friesen expressed things this way in the introduction to a five-part *Globe and Mail* series on the future of faith in Canada: "What we've seen is a sea of change in 40 years, a march toward secularization that mirrors what's happened in Europe."[1]

The Secularization Argument

Simply put, secularization refers to the decline of the influence of organized religion. While the line is not perfectly straight, it is nonetheless linear: secularization proceeds in a fairly relentless and irreversible fashion.[2]

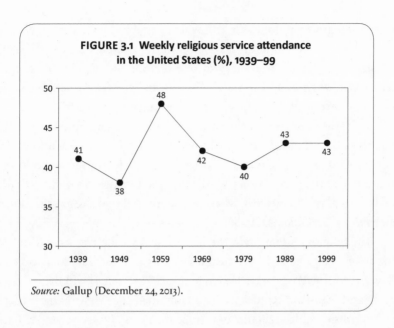

FIGURE 3.1 Weekly religious service attendance in the United States (%), 1939–99

Source: Gallup (December 24, 2013).

Dobbelaere, the Belgian sociologist, offered an important clarification of the concept in pointing out that it has at least three major dimensions: institutional, personal, and organizational.[3] The spheres of life over which religion has authority decrease, and its role becomes more and more specialized. Religion has less and less of an impact on the daily lives of individuals – what Peter Berger has referred to as "a secularization of consciousness."[4] Religious organizations themselves are increasingly influenced by society and culture in terms of how they operate – their goals, their means, their content, how they measure success, for example.

By the 1980s and 1990s, all three dimensions of secularization were generally recognized as characterizing much of Protestant Europe as well as Canada. The United States, as one of the world's most advanced societies, appeared to be an important exception to the secularization rule. Such an apparent anomaly, however, was readily explained away by many prominent observers, including Berger and Thomas Luckmann.[5]

They argued back in the early 1960s that, despite high levels of religious participation in America (Figure 3.1), secularization was already rampant. Their explanation was that it was taking the form of "secularization from within" rather than "secularization from without." On the surface, religion was flourishing, they said, but if one looked more closely the structures and contents of religion in the United States were being ravished by secularism. By way of one memorable illustration, Berger wrote that, when it came to values, "American Christians [held] the same values as anyone else – only with more emphatic solemnity."[6]

So it was that, even in the case of the United States, prominent observers of the religious scene, including Harvard University's influential Harvey Cox, assumed that secularization was sweeping the country.[7] Indicative of the pervasiveness of the explanation, in 1968 Rodney Stark, no less, used the framework when he coauthored the classic work *American Piety* with Charles Glock.[8]

The religious situation in the United States aside, the secularization thesis was assumed to be applicable to Canada. Observers such as Peter Beyer, Kurt Bowen, Lorne Dawson and Joel Thiessen, David Eagle, Mark Noll, and Jean-Paul Rouleau have maintained that Canada has experienced considerable secularization since the 1950s.[9] Over the years, I have certainly concurred, providing considerable documentation in support of the argument in *Fragmented Gods* (1987) and *Unknown Gods* (1993). There didn't seem to be much more to say. Things appeared to be bad and getting worse for organized religion "up here."

The Revitalization Argument

What makes life interesting, of course, is when the unexpected occurs.

In 2000, a surprising finding emerged from the Project Canada national teen survey. In 1984, we had found that 23% of teenagers claimed to be attending services on approximately a weekly basis. In 1992, that figure had dropped to 18%. When we did the survey in 2000, I expected the teen attendance level to have dropped another five percentage points or so – to around 13%.

It didn't happen. Instead, we found that the percentage of weekly attending teenagers had risen to 21% – reaching essentially the same level as that in 1984. Increases took place across all major religious groups – Catholicism, Protestantism, and other world faiths, with the exception of Catholicism in Quebec, where attendance continued to drop off.

TABLE 3.1 Weekly religious service attendance in Canada by denomination (%), 1957–2000

	1957	1975	1990	2000
National	53	31	24	21
Protestant	38	27	22	25
Conservative	51	41	49	58
Mainline	35	23	14	15
Roman Catholic	83	45	33	26
Outside Quebec	75	48	37	32
Quebec	88	42	28	20
Other faiths	35	17	12	7

Sources: 1957: March Gallup poll; 1975, 1990, 2000: Bibby, Project Canada national surveys.

That surprising national finding led me to reflect on a fairly radical possibility – that a modest resurgence in religious participation was taking place in Canada. After all, people like Berger and Cox were acknowledging that they had made an error in buying into secularization thinking and underestimating the resiliency of religion.[10] Maybe I had too.

Later in 2000, we completed the Project Canada national adult survey, providing an opportunity to obtain a new reading of adult attendance. The new survey revealed that attendance had slipped modestly from 1990 – the weekly level from 24% to 21%, the monthly level from 34% to 30% (Table 3.1). However, on closer examination, I discovered that the apparent decline camouflaged some signs of life corroborated using Statistics Canada data.[11]

- ▶ Among Conservative Protestant groups, an increase in attendance had taken place since 1990.
- ▶ In the case of Mainline Protestants – the United, Anglican, Lutheran, and Presbyterian denominations – the collective hemorrhaging had stopped in the 1990s.

- As for Roman Catholics, attendance declines during the decade had slowed significantly both inside and outside Quebec – though levels in Quebec remained very low.
- Other major faith groups, despite facing problems of sustaining growth, had experienced heightened profiles and, to varying degrees, added quantitative and qualitative vitality to the Canadian religious scene.

In presenting these data in *Restless Gods*,[12] I concluded that "these overall findings about the churches suggest that some important new developments are taking place – that there is something of a renaissance of organized religion in Canada."[13] Whether or not it continued seemed to be highly dependent on how the dominant religious groups responded to readily apparent consumer demand. Here my thinking was influenced considerably by Rodney Stark.

Stark's Challenging of Secularization
I had met Stark in 1972 when I was a graduate student at Washington State University (WSU) and he was a newly arrived professor at Seattle's University of Washington on the other side of the state. A decade or so earlier, he had been a graduate school student at Berkeley with my primary WSU mentor, Armand Mauss. Originally from North Dakota, Stark started out as a journalist; he also played football briefly for the Winnipeg Blue Bombers.

Stark took chances with flair. In the early 1980s, he took on the secularization school of thought by posing a simple but creative and compelling argument – the kind of argument that, after the fact, left many of us wondering "why didn't we think of that?" His provocative argument, now well known, has been variously described as a market model and rational choice theory.

Put succinctly, Stark – in collaboration with key associates William Bainbridge, Roger Finke, and Laurence Iannaccone[14] – maintained that there are some needs "that only the gods can provide."[15] They pertain particularly to death, along with purpose and meaning, including the meaning of life and the meaning of events in life.

Using a market analogy, Stark argued that the persistence of such questions means that, in any setting, there is a fairly constant market demand for religious responses. What varies is the supply side. In societies where the religious economy has been "deregulated," groups or "firms" that have difficulties will lose "market share" to groups that are more vigorous and less worldly.

Consequently, for Stark, secularization does not lead to the end of religion; on the contrary, it stimulates innovation. He gave particular attention to the emergence of sects (breakaway groups from existing religious bodies) and cults (new religious traditions).[16] So it is, said Stark, that, "in an endless cycle, faith is revived and new faiths [are] born to take the places of those withered denominations that lost their sense of the supernatural."[17]

As for which groups tend to win and which ones tend to lose, the key is costs versus benefits. The higher the costs of membership, the greater the material, social, and religious benefits. "People tend to value religion according to how much it costs," wrote Finke and Stark, and, "because 'reasonable' and 'sociable' religion costs little, it is not valued greatly."[18] Individuals consequently make "a rational choice" to belong and participate.[19] Conversely, as religious bodies ask less of their members, their ability to reward them declines. In short, the more mainline a denomination becomes, the lower the value of belonging to it, eventually resulting in widespread defection.

Stark and his associates have claimed considerable support for their general thesis as a result of their research in the United States, Canada, and Europe. They have found a consistent positive correlation between the existence of cult centres and people who have no religion.[20]

A Canadian Adaptation of Stark

The problem with trying to apply Stark's stimulating thinking to religious developments in Canada is that things don't fit all that well. As I pointed out in detail in Restless Gods, census data on religious identification over time reveal two distinct patterns: the stable dominance that established Christian groups enjoy and the difficulty that new groups confront in cracking their monopoly.[21]

TABLE 3.2 Religious composition of Canada (%), 1891–1991

	1891	1941	1991
Catholic	42	44	47
Protestant	56	52	36
Other	2	3	5
No religion	<1	<1	12

Source: Canadian census data.

TABLE 3.3 Percentages of select religious groups in Canada, 1951 and 2001

	1951	2001
Baha'i	–	0.1
Jehovah's Witnesses	0.2	0.5
Latter Day Saints	0.2	0.3
Unitarians	0.1	0.1

Source: Canadian census data.

TABLE 3.4 Populations of select religious groups in Canada, 2001

Religious group	Population
Pagan	21,080
Baha'i	18,020
New Thought*	4,000
Humanist†	2,105
New Age	1,530
Scientology	1,525
Gnostic	1,160
Rastafarian	1,135
Satanist	850

* Includes Unity, New Thought, and Pantheist.
† Technically not a religious group.
Source: Statistics Canada 2001 census.

Between 1891 and 1991, the Catholic share of the population grew, while the Protestant share declined (Table 3.2). The drop for Protestants, however, was not because of the expansion of new groups. The decrease in the size of their market share coincided instead with a rise in the proportion of Canadians who said that they had "no religion" – an increase stemming in large part from the methodological fact that "no religion" became an acceptable census option only in 1971.[22]

During the period 1951–2001, when "the market" was seemingly ripe for newer entries to make inroads, groups such as Jehovah's Witnesses and Latter Day Saints made tiny gains (Table 3.3).

Further, at the beginning of the 21st century – by which time the country's well-established groups had been in numerical decline for three decades – the actual numbers for would-be competitors were extremely small. For all the media hype about disenchanted and disaffiliated Canadians turning to new options, relatively few actually seized the opportunity to do so. In a nation of some 30 million people, fewer than 25,000 identified with highly publicized alternatives like Pagan (including Wicca), with the figures for New Age and Scientology under 2,000 (Table 3.4). The New Age total in allegedly receptive British Columbia was 690, with the numbers for Ontario and Quebec only 380 and 25 respectively. These data point to the fact that we have an extremely tight "religious market" in Canada, dominated by Catholic and Protestant "companies." New groups find the going very tough.

A more plausible argument compatible with Stark's thesis is that secularization may stimulate not only the birth of new groups but also the rejuvenation of older ones.[23] Throughout his work, Stark stresses that religious economies will be stimulated by religious pluralism resulting from "deregulation." Presumably, some of the older companies will go back to the drawing boards in light of changing times and a more competitive marketplace. In fact, in the last chapter of his third major work on the topic, he and Roger Finke acknowledged such a possibility, whereby "the sect to church cycle" reverses itself. They commented that the literature provided few hints of such a possibility, despite the historical example of something as blatant as the Counter-Reformation of the 17th century. They saw a key component of such possible resurgence to be new, highly committed clergy who in turn call their congregations to commitment and emphasize traditional religious content. Only people like this, they maintained, will be motivated to be involved in declining groups in which secular rewards are low. Growth, they theorized, will take place initially at the congregational level, and they provided preliminary data on a number of American groups that are consistent with their argument.[24]

Long-standing major corporations and other organizations realize that, in order to survive and thrive, they have to be in an ongoing mode of change. The primary players who occupy the Canadian religious scene are no exception.

As I reminded readers over a decade ago, Anglican, United Church, Presbyterian, and Lutheran denominations, along with the Roman Catholic Church in Quebec and elsewhere, are no fly-by-night operations.[25] They have long histories and recuperative powers. They don't just roll over and die. Many are parts of durable multinational corporations with headquarters in places like Rome and Canterbury. Such well-established religious groups don't readily perish. They retreat, retrench, revamp, and resurface.[26]

To sum up, declines in participation are neither inevitable nor irreversible. On the contrary, (1) if people continue to identify, (2) if they are reluctant to turn elsewhere, (3) if they have interests and needs, and (4) if the groups with which they identify respond, then it will be only a matter of time before the established groups experience numerical revitalization.

Theoretically, it all seemed to make perfect sense.

Widening the Discussion

So which is it? Secularization or revitalization? Is religion in Canada in a downward spiral that dates back to the 1960s? Or are there signs of new life as the country's dominant religious groups respond to ongoing interests and needs?

Before we attempt to resolve the debate, it might be helpful to hear from some other respected people who have not been lost for thoughts on the matter. In the past few decades, a number of individuals have updated and debated the explanatory value of the secularization and market models. Here are a few examples:

▶ Mark Chaves of Duke University has maintained that we need to emphasize the decline of religious authority as a key component of secularization.[27]

▶ The University of Ottawa's Peter Beyer has argued that the two frameworks – secularization and the market model – are complementary and that religious developments in Canada specifically can best be understood when seen from both viewpoints.[28]

▶ José Casanova of Georgetown University in Washington, DC, has echoed Dobbelaere's thinking in similarly calling for recognition of the personal, institutional, and organizational facets of secularization, and he sees much of the disagreement between the secularization and market model perspectives as resulting from proponents of the former emphasizing institutional changes and proponents of the latter focusing on personal religiousness.[29]

▶ Peter Berger, while at Boston University, wrote that the assumption that we are living in a secular world is false. Modernization has had secularizing effects, but it has also provoked powerful movements of counter-secularization.[30]

▶ Charles Taylor of McGill University, in his highly acclaimed work *A Secular Age*, acknowledges that many observers are thinking of these two features of secularization when they talk about what is secular. But he maintains that the key feature of secularity is a new context characterized by what he calls "exclusive humanism," which puts an end to acknowledging things transcendent and "claims which go beyond human flourishing."[31]

▶ In a comprehensive review of secularization theories, Jay Demerath of the University of Massachusetts offers the stimulating point that secularization "is not a process that sweeps everything sacred before it" but can also involve *sacralization* – "the process by which the secular becomes sacred or other new forms of the sacred emerge."[32]

In light of such debates, one can again raise the important question. In the case of Canada, which is it? Secularization or revitalization? Actually, the answer is that both are facets of the dominant pattern that helps to clarify everything: *polarization*.

The New Religious Reality in Canada

In charting trends of religious participation in Canada, we did what most pollsters and observers of poll data do: we looked at who was attending religious services. The data were highly convincing: around 1950, 60% of Canadians were attending services weekly; by 1975, that figure had fallen to 30% and by 2000 to 20%.

The seemingly obvious conclusion was that religion's importance had decreased significantly. And, further to observers like Dobbelaere, what was happening at the individual level was also taking place at the institutional level, where religion was increasingly being experienced on the margins of everyday life. In addition, religious organizations themselves were looking increasingly a lot like other social institutions. Following Dobbelaere, Luckmann, and Berger, there was ample evidence that secularization had not stopped at the church steps but had invaded many congregations and denominations. Secularization was widely visible "within."

The fact that the decline in religious participation did not continue unabated – as seen in the increase in regular teenage attendance and the levelling off of adult attendance in the 1990s – led a few of us to speculate about a comeback of religion. Even a respected public opinion pulse reader like Allan Gregg mused about the possibility.[33]

The speculation was hardly limited to survey findings. Stark's theorizing provided a reputable and credible academic explanation of the unexpected resurgence that seemed to be showing up in national surveys.

Blame It on the Pollsters

Somewhat remarkably, in probing participation trends, what I and so many people have failed to do is keep a close eye on everyone – not only the religiously active but also those who are not particularly active or not active at all. As a result, the photos we have been using to splice together the religion story have been incomplete. A lot of key people have been left out – like having dad or a couple of the kids missing from the family photo, leading to a misreading of the overall situation.

For example, typical Gallup polls over the years focused on the percentage of Canadians who had attended a religious service "in the past seven days." I myself have zeroed in on people who say that they attend services at least weekly or monthly. In the United States, Gallup's regular reports on attendance were interpreted in the same way. As the proportions went down, we saw evidence of secularization. As the proportions levelled off, or even went up, we saw evidence of revitalization.

Here's a quick, two-question test.

❶ *Approximately what percentage of Canadians attend services every week?*
❷ *Approximately what percentage of Canadians never attend services?*

If you follow polls reasonably closely, then chances are you would say, in response to the first question, "between 20% and 25%" (Figure 3.2). For the second question, you – like just about everyone else – would draw a big blank.

Sometimes it takes a simple empirical observation to stimulate an epiphany. In my case, it took place when I was analyzing the Project

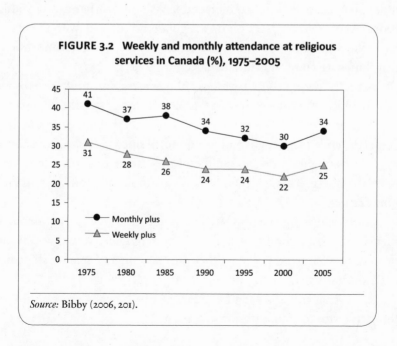

FIGURE 3.2 Weekly and monthly attendance at religious services in Canada (%), 1975–2005

Source: Bibby (2006, 201).

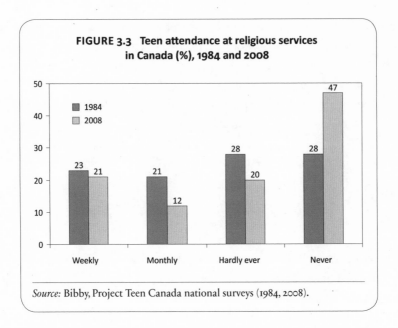

FIGURE 3.3 Teen attendance at religious services in Canada (%), 1984 and 2008

Source: Bibby, Project Teen Canada national surveys (1984, 2008).

Canada findings on teen attendance from 1984 to 2008. If one only looks at what amounts to weekly or monthly-plus attendance, then the religious situation appears to be remarkably stable. As noted earlier, 23% of young people were attending services on a regular basis in 1984, with the figure for 2008 a similar 21%. A typical and seemingly obvious interpretation is that things haven't changed much. Right?

Actually, wrong. When we reset the camera and took a snapshot that included everyone by looking at other responses to the attendance item, we found that the percentage of teenagers who said that they "never" attended services had almost doubled since the 1980s, from about 25% to 50% (Figure 3.3). The middle of the attendance continuum had been shrinking. This, everybody, is an example of growing religious polarization.

Now everything starts to become much clearer. In recent decades, there has been an important shift away from religion. We are well aware from census data and poll data that the "no religion" market share has been increasing. Growing numbers of people are living life "beyond the gods." That trend is what led many of us – actually most of us – to think in terms of secularization.

Resilient Gods

Pro-religious	Religious middle	No religious

However, what tended to be minimized was the fact that, during the same period, a significant number of Canadians continued to value religion. The proportion of pro-religious people has been decreasing, particularly in recent years, but remains sizable. To the extent that it has shown signs of increasing, a few of us have raised the possibility that *revitalization* could be taking place. But when we look at the trend data for everyone – the involved and non-involved alike – what we see is a pattern of growing *polarization*.

I need to emphasize something that I minimized in 2011 in *Beyond the Gods and Back*. The Canadian reality is not just that we have large numbers of people who continue to value faith and growing numbers who do not. We also have a large and important segment of the population who constitute "the religious middle" – a point emphasized by Thiessen.[34] They are neither embracing nor rejecting religion. They show inclinations that are both "pro-religious" and "no religious." Just as sociologist Glenn Vernon recognized six decades ago that it was important to study "Religious Nones" along with the devout, so too in our time it is essential that we give adequate attention to the religious middle.[35] We need to recognize not only the pro-religious and no religious but also what we might dub the "low religious."

A Closer Look at the Religious Middle

A stimulating exposition of some of the people who comprise the religious middle has recently been offered by Phil Zuckerman, a professor at Pitzer College in Claremont, California. He specializes in the sociology of secularity. He describes "Sally," a woman in her mid-40s who was raised Catholic but rejected the tradition long ago and, with her husband, has raised kids who have no religious involvement. But Zuckerman writes that there is "a hint of worry or self-doubt in Sally's laugh as she describes her kids as 'nothings.'" Her secularity is not absolute, says Zuckerman.

> In her heart of hearts, Sally does believe. In God? Well, that depends on what you mean by "God." She believes in something. And although religion is not at all a part of her daily life, she does have a small stash of assorted angels that she adores, which she displays with pride as part of her household decorations every Christmas.

Zuckerman concludes that "the point here is that Sally is like millions of Americans: not religious, but not totally secular either."[36] The idea, he reminds us, is also shared by people like Putnam, who talks about "liminals" – people who are "betwixt and between" a religious and secular identity, standing halfway in and halfway out of a given religious/irreligious identity.[37] Such people can believe and not belong, to use British sociologist Grace Davie's well-known phrase,[38] or belong but not believe. The line of Zuckerman's Jewish father is playful but poignant: "Shlomo goes to synagogue to talk to God. I go to synagogue to talk to Shlomo."[39]

The bottom line for Zuckerman is this: "The simple binary of religious/secular won't do – at least not in the real world." And now some three years after I first said it (or think that I first said it!), Zuckerman echoes my thinking, which he in turn attributes to anthropologist Frank Pasquale: one useful way to conceive of the complexity of religiosity and secularity is to consider them "as existing on an imagined continuum, such as a ten-point scale." But he cautions that "precious few people are complete 1s or 10s. Most are somewhere in between ... even veering in different directions at different times throughout the course of their lives."[40]

Here Zuckerman converges with previous work of Canadians Bruce Hunsberger of Wilfrid Laurier University and Bob Altemeyer of the University of Manitoba,[41] along with current survey findings and analyses of prominent American pollsters, in acknowledging that "more and more people are now veering more closely toward the secular end of the continuum than ever before."[42]

Yet those in the middle – who might resemble the "marginals" examined recently by Thiessen in *The Meaning of Sunday*[43] – should not be overlooked.

A Simple if Confusing Concept

In using the term "religious polarization," I am simply talking about the inclination of people to embrace religion, reject religion, or occupy a middle position between the two tendencies. No more, no less. But my use of it since 2011 has been associated with a fair amount of confusion.

One reason is because of its prior use, particularly in the United States. There the term has been frequently associated with cultural wars as well as political orientations. As many readers know, the term "culture wars" was popularized by James Davison Hunter in his book of that title published in 1991. Hunter emphasized the conflict between conservative and liberal values evident in debates about issues like abortion, homosexuality, immigration, global warming, recreational drug use, state gun laws, and censorship. He spoke of polarization in describing the emerging intensification of positions on such issues. More recently, Chaves has used the term the same way in *American Religion*.[44]

That's not what I'm talking about.

When I first used the term in *Beyond the Gods and Back* in 2011, I thought that I was being somewhat original in applying the idea to religious inclinations. But as the wise writer of Ecclesiastes reminded us many centuries ago, "there is nothing new under the sun" (Ecclesiastes 1.9).

I was subsequently surprised to learn that in the first chapter of *Amazing Grace*, a book that literally passed mine in production, Robert Putnam and David Campbell wrote about "religious polarization in America." In reflecting on changes over the past half century, they noted a trend similar to what I was emphasizing: "Perhaps the most noticeable shift is how Americans have become polarized along religious lines. Americans are increasingly concentrated at opposite ends of the religious spectrum – the highly religious at one pole, and the avowedly secular at the other. The moderate religious middle is shrinking."[45]

As a further reminder that I had not invented the religious polarization wheel, in August 2012 my colleague and friend Bob Brym at the

University of Toronto contacted me with this surprising claim: "I first wrote about religious polarization in my co-authored US intro textbook that appeared in 2005."[46] Brym and his colleague John Lie have maintained that polarization in American society is visible in a number of institutions, including religion. In a 2013 update to their text, they wrote that

> It is an exaggeration to claim ... that the whole world is gradually becoming "disenchanted." But certainly part of it is. It seems to us, however, that the two contradictory social processes of secularization and revival are likely to persist for some time to come, resulting in a world that is neither more religious nor more secular, but one that is certainly more polarized.[47]

Along with Putnam and Campbell, Brym and I – independent of each other as well – have been thinking along similar lines. In his email to me, he colourfully put things this way about our convergence of thought: "If a Christian believer and a Jewish atheist can come to the same conclusion about religion, sociology must be a science."[48] He just might be right!

In the past few years, the concept has been used fairly extensively by Sarah Wilkins-Laflamme of the University of Waterloo.[49] In correspondence with me, she noted that "lots of us define religious polarization in slightly different ways, which makes things difficult. Nevertheless," she said, "I found it has real potential to reflect at least some of the empirical trends I'm observing."[50]

Clarifying the Concept

For my part, I'm "merely" reminding everyone that, in every society and every conceivable group setting – national, regional, local, and immediate – some people are religious, some are not, and some are in between.

So expressed, polarization is a self-evident, axiomatic, and fairly prosaic observation. There's not much to debate, apart from ongoing variations and their sources, along with the correlates of being pro-, no, and low religion. But it is an extremely important reality that frequently seems to be missed – with vital implications for understanding past, present, and future religious trends.

I would encourage people not to read more into the framework than I am intending. For example, in a recent essay, another colleague and friend, Sam Reimer, has gone to great lengths to explain what polarization has meant to some people and drawn on data from Canada and Europe to conclude that evidence for polarization is weak.[51] In fairness to him, my previous delineation of religious polarization was not very clear and not very developed. I can now lay things out with much more clarity.

Evidence of polarization – people variously embracing, rejecting, or taking a middle position toward religion – is everywhere. The debate is not between polarization and secularization. On the contrary, when we recognize the three primary inclinations toward religion, the place of secularization and its countertrend – desecularization – come into focus. Rather than being in conflict and warranting academic arm-wrestling, the two patterns are part of the broader reality of polarization (Figure 3.5).

▶ *Secularization* describes the movement away from religion.
▶ *Desecularization* describes the movement toward religion.

In the context of polarization, it is hardly surprising that academics and others have been observing both secularization and desecularization patterns. One is not accurate and the other inaccurate. Both trends describe movement along an ever-changing, dynamic polarization continuum.

FIGURE 3.5 Secularization, desecularization, and polarization

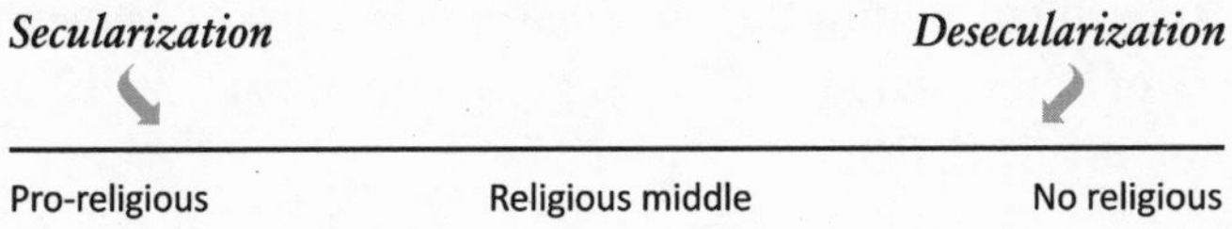

Secularization   *Desecularization*

Pro-religious   Religious middle   No religious

At any point in time, a society's tendency to opt for religion, no religion, or the religious middle will vary, depending on organizational and cultural factors. But the proclivity to opt for religion will always coexist with the proclivity to reject it, with noteworthy numbers of people comprising an ambivalent middle.

The three primary academic questions? One, to what extent do given populations tend to gravitate toward one end of the continuum versus the other? Two, why do such variations occur? Three, what are their correlates or consequences for personal and collective life?

In sum, polarization is the backdrop for understanding the dynamic, ongoing inclinations for people anywhere to embrace or reject religion. Secularization describes movement in the no religion direction, while desecularization (sometimes referred to as "sacralization") describes movement in the pro-religion direction. In some situations, growing secularization might be apparent; in other cases, desecularization might be evident; in many situations, neither pattern will be pronounced. But these various developments will take place in the context of polarization.

The Religious Reality Worldwide

Within the polarization framework, religious trends in pretty much any setting become much clearer. Take the United States, for example. Recent growth in the no religion category documented by surveys carried out by Gallup and the Pew Research Center has startled many observers.[52] However, seen through the polarization framework, things are not startling at all. The reason is that so-called American religious exceptionalism is proving to be not so exceptional after all.[53]

Historically, the polarization continuum in the United States has been weighted heavily on the pro-religion side. Currently, there is some modest movement toward the no religion side. Such movement in the directions of both religion and no religion is universal. The balances are always potentially in flux.

However, as with other geographical settings, the story is hardly final. We need to keep the camera running. The religious markets in the United

States, Canada, and everywhere else are always "up for grabs." Things are never over. Depending on religious group activity and social and cultural developments, proportional placement on the polarization continuum will always be changing.

Following Stark, the increase in the percentage of those with no religion in the United States, for example, means that the opportunity exists for religious groups to increase their market shares. There is little doubt that we will see accelerated activity in the religious marketplace.[54] Frank Newport, editor-in-chief of the Gallup poll, has gone so far as to say that, despite the rise of those with no religion, religion is poised for a renaissance – led by the influx of Hispanics and the aging of Boomers.[55]

But arguments about whether secularization is or is not prevailing have to be carried out in the context of polarization. The extent of secularization or religiousness will vary from setting to setting across the planet. But everywhere those patterns are illuminated when they are viewed in the context of the polarization continuum.

In locating the Canadian polarization in a global perspective, we now have a number of invaluable poll resources.

> ▶ The World Values Survey (WVS), produced by a cooperative network of social scientists, dates back to 1984 and has been repeated about every 10 years. It now includes some 100 societies and 90% of the world's population.[56]
> ▶ Since 2005, Gallup has conducted worldwide polls that have included more than 140 countries.[57]
> ▶ Global data have been generated through the International Social Survey Programme, whereby researchers from 50 countries have included topical sections in their national surveys dating back to the mid-1980s.
> ▶ The Pew Research Center in the United States has carried out international surveys since 2001.[58]

Recently, an invaluable synthesis of the global survey work to date was produced by Tom Smith, the highly regarded survey director and prolific author at the National Opinion Research Center in Chicago.[59]

His comprehensive report for the Templeton Foundation was released in late 2009. It is entitled *Religious Change around the World* and claims to be "the most comprehensive analysis to date of global religious trends."[60]

Looking at data for the United States, Europe, Asia, Latin America, and Muslim countries, Smith concludes that "no simple generalization adequately captures the complexity and nuance of the religious change that has been occurring."[61] He offers a number of key points in his summary.[62]

❶ On balance, the evidence indicates that the world, including the United States, has been moving in a secular direction. Modernization and education are associated with a tendency for religious beliefs and behaviour to decline. However, these correlations are neither overly strong nor uniform. They do not add up to simple confirmation of the secularization theory.

❷ The patterns of religious decline are characterized by variation and diversity. In Europe, for example, secularization has continued. But overall changes are modest and less striking than differences between nations. In Eastern Europe, the collapse of communist rule has seen religion rebound in some places but not in others. There is no uniform post-communist pattern.

❸ In many settings, there are clear elements of transformation in addition to decline. Still, on average, there has been "a secular tilt to religious change."

❹ All that said, secularization is not inevitable. Religion exhibits resilience.

It is easy to drown in all the numbers that can be presented. Consequently, I want to remind readers of something that I invariably emphasize in presentations: I myself am not particularly interested in numbers; I am interested in ideas. As a result, I want to present just enough numbers to allow us to get a good reading of religiousness around the world. Every country will not be included. However, I will provide information on my sources so that the statistics for many other countries of interest can be pursued.

Three measures of religion – attendance, identification, and belief – provide an initial reading of religiosity and non-religiosity around the planet. Salience – religion being a part of one's daily life – is also a valuable measure in making comparisons across groups (Table 3.5). Worship service attendance, for example, might not be equally valued. While cutting points are far from absolute, some general patterns are fairly clear.

▶ Extremely high levels of religiosity are found in settings such as Thailand, Nigeria, the Philippines, and India.
▶ A second tier of high religiousness is found in countries like Brazil, Iraq, Iran, and El Salvador.
▶ A third tier includes Mexico, Italy, Poland, and the United States.
▶ With the fourth tier – Israel, Spain, Canada, Germany, Russia, and Australia – polarization is more pronounced.
▶ In the fifth tier, religiosity is low. Countries include France, Britain, Hong Kong, the Czech Republic, Sweden, and China.

Some countries – like the Philippines, Pakistan, Greece, and Ukraine – are enigmatic, knowing high levels of salience, identification, and belief yet relatively low levels of attendance. Japan is characterized by levels of salience and identification that fall below those of belief and attendance. Overall, global variations in religiousness are readily evident. I leave it to readers to draw their own cut-off points depending on the importance that one gives to each of the four measures of religiosity.

Generally speaking, religion is viewed as personally important by higher percentages of women than men in many countries, including Canada (Table 3.6). Gender differences are predictably smaller in settings where levels of religiousness are very high, like Nigeria, Pakistan, and Indonesia. That said, it is not so readily evident why pronounced gender differences in the importance accorded to religion are found in a fairly large and diverse number of settings. Among them are places where religious identification is high – Honduras, Peru, Brazil, and Poland – but also settings where it is much lower, including Ukraine and Russia. And we still haven't really answered the question of gender difference in either Canada or the United States.

TABLE 3.5 Four measures of religion in select countries (%)

	Salience	Identification	Belief	Attendance
Nigeria	98	99	99	74
Thailand	97	99	99	69
Saudi Arabia	97	99	99	70
Pakistan	96	99	99	56
Philippines	95	99	99	65
Ethiopia	90*	99	99*	78*
Brazil	89	92	99	49
Dominican Republic	88	99	97*	51
El Salvador	88	83	98*	65
Iraq	86	99	99	51
India	85	99	98	67
South Africa	85	85	99	58
Iran	83	99	99	47
Greece	72	99	95	33
Italy	70	80	97	48
Mexico	66	95	98	58
Poland	64	92*	95	73
United States	66	77[†]	96	46
Ireland	54	94	98	56
Israel	48	98*	95*	35
Ukraine	47	92*	95	24
Spain	44	98*	93	31
Republic of Korea	43	57	71	35
Canada	43	76[†]	85[†]	27
Germany	40	80*	93	30
Cuba	35	90*	75*	20
Russia	34*	50*	93	15*
New Zealand	33	60	93	26
Netherlands	32	58	90	23
Australia	32	78	84	21
Finland	29	75	97	13
United Kingdom	29	74	91	20
France	27	75	93	19
Japan	26	95*	89	29
Hong Kong	25	95*	95	19
Czech Republic	25	65	92	14
Sweden	13	75*	83	16
China	–	48	73	9*

Note: The item for attendance was "have you attended a place of worship or religious service in the past seven days?"
Sources: For *salience* and *attendance*, China World Values Survey; * Gallup Worldview (2010); Stark (2015). For *identification*, CIA (2016); * estimates from varied sources (e.g., for Canada, 2011 NHS; for the United States, Pew Research Center 2015b). For *belief,* Stark (2015); * computed from the World Religion Database in Smith (2009, 284–87); † ARI Religion Survey (2015).

TABLE 3.6 Differences in attendance, prayer, and salience between women and men in select countries (% differences)

	Weekly attendance	Daily prayer	Salience
Italy	20	20	17
Philippines	15	8	0
Peru	14	16	11
Brazil	12	15	11
Mexico	10	11	0
United States	8	17	13
Canada	6	0	0
United Kingdom	5	9	6
Poland	0	17	19
Japan	0	11	5
Germany	0	9	0
Russia	0	7	6
Australia	0	6	7
France	0	6	0
China	0	0	0
India	–	0	0
Iran	–10	0	0
Nigeria	–10	3	0
Indonesia	–36	0	0
Turkey	–47	0	0
Pakistan	72	0	0

Note: Positive difference figures indicate more participation by women than men; negative difference figures indicate more participation by men than women.
Source: Pew Research Center (2016a).

Assessment

Canada is experiencing increasing religious polarization. As such, it stands in contrast to settings characterized by both religious and secular monopolies. Canada most closely resembles countries like Ukraine, Germany, and Australia.

However, religious polarization is not uniform across the country. There are considerable variations, for example by region, age, and religious group. What has been largely overlooked and offers many surprises is what I am calling the religious middle.

I want to turn next to an examination of the religious self-definitions of Canadians and what is associated with how they see themselves.

4

The Polarized Mosaic

Everyone knows that Canada's Bible Belt is Alberta.
– prevalent folk wisdom

When I set out to measure the prevalence of religious polarization in Canada in *Beyond the Gods and Back*, I thought that I could make use of three measures: service attendance, religious identification, and belief in God. I then proceeded to dichotomize between weeklies and nevers, affiliates and non-affiliates, and theists and atheists. In the rest of the book, I used these dichotomies to explore four centrally important correlates: personal well-being, social well-being, spirituality, and death.[1]

Looking back, it wasn't a bad strategy. But there were two serious limitations. First, I pretty much omitted the large number of Canadians in between the two extremes: the religious middle. Second, I created these polar opposites by imposing objective criteria on people without letting them have a say in things.

For better or worse – and I obviously believe for better – I have followed two basic rules when I do research. The first rule – a debt that I have to the pioneering work in the sociology of religion of Glock in tandem with Stark[2] – is that I don't tell people what their religious inclinations are; I ask them to tell me, and then I measure them. The second rule I learned from sociologist Howard Becker, who, in the course of studying "deviants" many years ago, wrote that "there is something wrong with our research if people don't recognize themselves in the descriptions we are providing of them."[3] Good methodological advice on both counts.

Measuring Religious Polarization

As mentioned in the Introduction, in the spring of 2015, I carried out a major new national online survey of 3,041 Canadians in partnership with Angus Reid and the Angus Reid Institute. The sample and its size produced data that reflect the characteristics of the national population with a high level of accuracy. We continued to probe things like attendance, identification, and belief. But in order to get a better understanding of polarization, we went further. We asked respondents if they recognized themselves in the categories of the polarization continuum. They were given the following statement and question:

> *Some people say Canadians variously (1) embrace religion, (2) reject religion, or (3) are somewhere in between the two extremes. Where would you tend to locate yourself?*

The three response options were (1) I am inclined to embrace religion, (2) I am inclined to reject religion, and (3) I am somewhere in between.

We found that 30% of Canadians maintain they are inclined to embrace religion (Figure 4.1).[4] They provide evidence that the days of religiously committed people are hardly over. But their numbers have been shrinking. Another 26% report that they are inclined to reject religion. Located primarily in the "no religion" category, their numbers have been growing in recent decades. The remaining 44% acknowledge that they are somewhere in between the two positions. As we will see shortly, they do not see themselves as particularly devout, but they have not completely abandoned religion. We don't have explicit trend data on the religious middle, but it is easily the largest of the three categories. As we saw, Putnam and Campbell maintain that this segment is shrinking in the

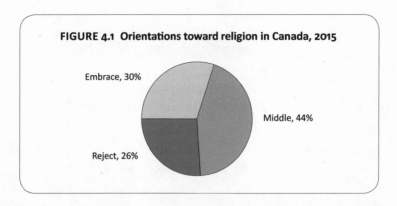

FIGURE 4.1 Orientations toward religion in Canada, 2015

Embrace, 30%

Middle, 44%

Reject, 26%

United States.[5] It is still sizable in Canada, perhaps pointing to a different distribution here.

Some Corroborative Religious Characteristics

What's the relationship between the three orientations and the three common indicators of attendance, identification, and belief in God? Our data readily allow us to address this question (Table 4.1).

- As we would expect, the correlations are fairly high, especially in the case of attendance. Among weekly attenders, 83% say that they embrace faith versus just 6% of those who never attend services. However, it is important to note that the relationships are far from perfect. One in two monthly attendees and one of four yearly attendees maintain that they embrace faith.
- Many people who identify with a religion see themselves in the religious middle.
- Although a large number of individuals who express unequivocal belief in God embrace faith (57%), significant numbers locate themselves in the religious middle (35%). That inclination is especially pronounced among equivocal atheists (46%).

Now let's change the vantage point and look at the characteristics of religiosity among people who embrace, reject, or take a middle position on religion (Table 4.2).

TABLE 4.1 Religious inclinations by attendance, identification, and belief in God (%)

	All	Embrace (n = 906)	Middle (n = 1,336)	Reject (n = 799)	Totals (n = 3,041)
Canada		30	44	26	100
Attendance					
Weekly	16	83	14	3	100
Monthly	7	54	37	9	100
Yearly	47	24	59	17	100
Never	30	6	38	56	100
Identification					
Yes	79	37	48	15	100
No	21	2	27	71	100
Belief in God/higher power					
Yes, I definitely do	41	57	35	8	100
Yes, I think so	32	17	66	17	100
No, I don't think so	14	5	46	49	100
No, I definitely do not	13	1	16	83	100

▶ People who embrace faith include large numbers who attend services only a few times a year or even less. Almost all identify with a religion, and almost all are theists.

▶ The religious middle tends to be made up of infrequent attendees, but they identify with a religion and are somewhat ambivalent theists versus atheists.

▶ Those who reject religion either never or seldom attend services, yet almost one in two identifies with a religious tradition, and, while not inclined to be theists, just 40% are explicit atheists.

Some Corroborative Attitudinal Characteristics
More than a few critics will likely wonder if the three inclinations toward religion reflect empirical reality versus some kind of statistical construct of yours truly.

TABLE 4.2 Attendance, identification, and belief in God by religious inclinations (%)

	Embrace	Middle	Reject
Canada	30	44	26
Attendance			
Weekly	43	5	2
Monthly	13	6	2
Yearly	37	63	32
Never	7	26	64
Identification			
Yes	99	87	44
No	1	13	56
Belief in God/higher power			
Yes, I definitely do	79	32	13
Yes, I think so	18	49	21
No, I don't think so	2	15	26
No, I definitely do not	<1	4	40
Totals	100	100	100

One way to check is to look at a number of attitudes of people in these three categories and see if they match what most of us find makes sense – in methodological jargon, providing us with some "face validity" (Table 4.3).

▶ The idea that "morality and good values" are tied to theism and churchgoing is solidly endorsed by Canadians who embrace religion, but it is almost equally panned by those who reject religion or occupy the middle ground.

▶ Yet the cultural pervasiveness of the Ten Commandments can be seen in the fact that a majority of people in all three groups – even 53% among those who reject religion – maintain that the Ten Commandments still apply today. That said, the pervasiveness of the idea of moral relativity can also be seen in widespread agreement with the seemingly contradictory claim that "what's right or wrong is a matter of personal opinion" – endorsed by even 40% of those who embrace religion.

▶ Differences among the three religious inclinations are sizable and predictable when it comes to beliefs about the positive impact of religion on the world and the impact of declining involvement and increasing atheism in Canada. Here those in the religious middle are nowhere as negative as those who reject religion. As

TABLE 4.3 Attitudes toward religion by religious inclinations (%)

	Embrace	Middle	Reject	All
It is not necessary to go to church to be moral and have good values.	80	91	95	89
It is not necessary to believe in God to be moral and have good values.	68	86	91	82
The Ten Commandments still apply today.	91	73	53	73
What's right or wrong is a matter of personal opinion.	40	57	55	51
The overall impact of religion on the world is positive.	80	52	15	51
The decline in religious involvement has been a bad thing for Canada.	86	44	11	48
I think that the growth in atheism is a good thing for life in Canada.	10	27	69	33
I have a high level of confidence in religious leaders.	61	21	6	29
I'd be open to more involvement with religious groups if I found it worthwhile.	49	42	22	39
I prefer to live life without God or congregation.	9	31	79	37
I sometimes feel guilty for not being more involved in religion.	54	33	8	33

would be expected, confidence in religious leadership decreases as one moves from the pro-religious to the no religious.

▶ Openness to more involvement is fairly high but predictably different – 49% for those who embrace faith, 42% for those in the religious middle, and 22% for those who reject faith.

▶ Perhaps one of the better indicators of the distinctiveness among the three religious inclinations is seen in how people respond to the statement "I prefer to live life without God or congregation." Those agreeing include 79% of those with no religion, 31% of those in the religious middle, and just 9% of those who embrace faith.

▶ Similarly in keeping with what one would expect are responses to the statement "I sometimes feel guilty for not being more involved in religion." Here just 8% of those who reject religion agree, compared with 33% of those in the religious middle and 54% of those who embrace religion.

What already stands out in the analysis is the fact that people in the religious middle – those with low faith – are very different from either those who embrace faith or those who reject faith. This finding underlines the fact that to focus exclusively on high levels of involvement (e.g., weekly church attendance) and to ignore both the non-involved ("the nevers") and those in between ("the occasionals") is to clumsily crop the Canadian religious photo and cut out two of the three family members.

Some Key Correlates of Religious Inclinations

An obvious question that arises is what kinds of people are drawn to religion, and what kinds tend to bypass it or opt for a middle position?

Social and Demographic Features
Our 2015 national survey has found that the pro-religious, no religious, or low religious differ little by gender and only slightly by either age or education. Older adults with somewhat lower educational levels are a bit more inclined than others to embrace religion.

This lack of variation is intriguing. It suggests that whether one is attracted to religion or chooses to take a pass is pretty random. The literature

TABLE 4.4 Religious inclinations by gender, age, and education (%)

	Embrace	Middle	Reject	Totals
Canada	30	44	26	100
Gender				
Female	30	48	22	100
Male	29	40	31	100
Age				
18–34	28	44	28	100
35–54	25	47	28	100
55 plus	35	41	24	100
Education				
Degree plus	27	41	32	100
Some postsecondary	28	45	27	100
High school or less	33	45	22	100

on religious involvement is replete with old ideas about women being more inclined to be religious than men, older people more devout than younger people, and the less educated more religious than the better educated (Table 4.4). When we throw in the religious middle, we find that only about one in four Canadians are actually rejecting religion. Well-worn generalizations about differences by gender, age, and education apply only modestly to the minority who see themselves as by-passing faith.

What is more pronounced are differences by birthplace and region (Table 4.5).

▶ People born outside Canada are more likely than those born here to embrace religion, though there is little difference by birthplace in the inclination to reject faith. This finding is very important, given the dramatic increase now and into the foreseeable future of Canadians who will arrive from other countries.

▶ Regionally, the pro-religious inclination is highest in the Atlantic region and the two prairie provinces of Saskatchewan and

TABLE 4.5 Religious inclinations by birthplace and region (%)

	Embrace	Middle	Reject	Totals
Canada	30	44	26	100
Birthplace				
Born in Canada	29	45	26	100
Born outside Canada	38	38	24	100
Region				
Atlantic	38	44	18	100
Saskatchewan	38	42	20	100
Manitoba	38	38	24	100
Alberta	32	43	25	100
Ontario	31	44	25	100
Quebec	24	48	28	100
British Columbia	24	39	37	100

Manitoba; the rejection of religion is highest in British Columbia. Somewhere in the course of recent Canadian history, the infamous "Bible Belt" shifted away from Alberta.

▶ Yet, as with gender, age, and education, the largest percentage of people in every part of the country identify with a middle position.

▶ Significantly, Quebec – often stereotyped as rejecting religion in the post-1960s – actually has the largest proportion of people in the religious middle. To repeat an old but accurate adage, "They may not be coming. But they're not leaving."

Religion and Spirituality
The tendency to embrace faith is considerably higher among Conservative Protestants (evangelicals) than others. They are followed by other non-Mainline Protestant Christian groups, along with Roman Catholics outside Quebec.

Yet, as I have been emphasizing, fairly small numbers of people who identify with religious groups actually reject faith. That is most common

TABLE 4.6 Religious inclinations by religious identification (%)

	Embrace	Middle	Reject	Totals
Canada	30	44	26	100
Conservative Protestant	70	22	8	100
Protestant, neither Conservative nor Mainline	47	43	10	100
Roman Catholic outside Quebec	42	48	10	100
Other world faith	31	58	11	100
Mainline Protestant	31	56	13	100
Roman Catholic in Quebec	27	54	19	100
No religion	2	27	71	100

– as would be expected – among those who say that they have no religion. However, even 30% of people in that category do not actually reject religion but occupy the middle position between embracing faith and rejecting faith (Table 4.6).

Much publicity has been given to the idea that Canadians and many people elsewhere are increasingly "spiritual but not religious." Individuals who identify with that position are more likely than others to locate themselves in the religious middle, though about 3 in 10 reject religion. Fairly predictably, a majority of individuals who say that they are "spiritual and religious" are inclined to embrace religion and seldom reject it. In the case of people who are "neither spiritual nor religious," close to 6 in 10 indicate that they reject religion, yet 4 in 10 locate themselves in the religious middle (Table 4.7).

These findings suggest that about three in four Canadians in all demographic and social categories are not explicitly rejecting religion. The much more common tendency is for people to either embrace faith or – to a slightly greater extent – opt for a middle position.

It seems to me that the identification of the sizable and understudied religious middle is extremely important. The preference for that position might sometimes reflect ambivalence. But it might also reflect a preference to draw on religion selectively and a reluctance to discard it altogether. The reality that I emphasized in *Fragmented Gods* three decades

Resilient Gods

TABLE 4.7 Religious inclinations by religious/spiritual self-image (%)

	All	Embrace	Middle	Reject	Totals
Canada	100	30	44	26	100
Spiritual but not religious	39	14	59	27	100
Neither religious nor spiritual	27	4	40	56	100
Religious and spiritual	24	74	24	2	100
Religious but not spiritual	10	54	44	2	100

ago seems to continue to characterize a large segment of the Canadian population – not in, not out, but opting for religion à la carte.[6] The religious middle particularly seems to be "up for grabs" when it comes to secularization and desecularization. It therefore needs to be carefully monitored.

Beliefs and Practices
As would be expected, there are considerable variations in one's posture toward religion when it comes to beliefs. Some are predictable; some are not so obvious. The general pattern is for those in the religious middle to show far more commonality with those who embrace religion than with those who reject it (Table 4.8). Consider the following beliefs.

▶ Belief in God or a higher power is high, not only for those who embrace religion (97%) but also for those in the religious middle (81%). Even one in three people who reject religion indicate they are theists.

▶ Similar patterns hold for belief in the divinity of Jesus and belief that one has been protected by a guardian angel. The religious middle continues to be distinct in exhibiting fairly high levels of belief.

▶ As we have already seen, attendance at services is predictably highest among those who embrace faith, modest among those in the religious middle, and extremely low among those who reject religion.

TABLE 4.8 Beliefs and practices by religious inclinations (%)

	Embrace	Middle	Reject	All
Beliefs (definitely, think so)				
God or a higher power exists.	97	81	33	66
Jesus was the divine son of God.	92	63	15	59
I have been protected by a guardian angel.	79	59	19	56
Practices (monthly plus)				
Attend services	56	11	4	23
Pray privately/individually	86	42	14	48
Say table grace	52	16	8	25
Read Bible, Quran, or other sacred text	45	9	6	19

▶ Private prayer, however, while very high among the committed (86%), is also fairly common among those in the religious middle (42%) but relatively rare among those who reject faith (8%). Table grace and scripture reading have similar rankings but at much lower levels.

In March 2016, I worked with Angus Reid on a national survey of prayer. It was of particular interest to Angus since, in his words, "it seems clear to me that the starting point for any assessment of faith in our society must begin with questions about prayer. Prayer is, in many respects, the cornerstone of faith. It assumes there is a God who listens and may intervene in big and small ways."[7] The survey confirmed expected differences in the frequency of prayer by religious inclinations. Still, 23% of those who reject faith said that they prayed at least occasionally in the past year, as did 69% of those in the religious middle and 96% of those who embrace faith.

What stood out are the different purposes of prayer for people in the three categories (Figure 4.2).

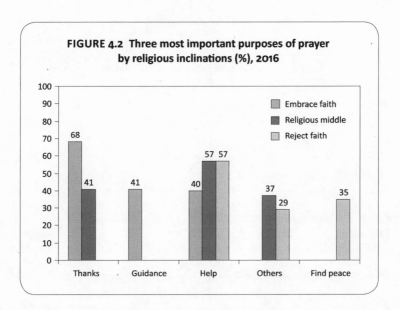

FIGURE 4.2 Three most important purposes of prayer by religious inclinations (%), 2016

- ▶ The pro-faith emphasize giving thanks, seeking guidance, and asking for help.
- ▶ The low faith primarily pray for help and give thanks as well as pray for others.
- ▶ The no faith pray primarily to seek help, find peace, and pursue help for others.

Salience

We asked our survey participants "What is the main thing your religious involvement adds to your life?" Understandably, 56% of those embracing religion offered responses versus only 11% of those in the religious middle and 4% of those rejecting religion. For those who accept faith, God and spirituality stood out as number one, followed by personal enrichment and people.

More generally, 9 in 10 pro-faith Canadians believe that God cares about them personally, as do more than 6 in 10 low-faith and 2 in 10 no-faith individuals. As would be expected, a large number of those embracing religion (79%) report that they feel strengthened by their faith on a

TABLE 4.9 Faith claims by religious inclinations (%)

	Embrace	Middle	Reject	All
Main thing your religious involvement adds to your life				
God and spirituality	33	4	2	12
Personal enrichment	15	4	<1	6
People	5	3	2	3
Other	3	<1	<1	1
Not applicable	44	89	96	78
Believe God cares about you personally				
Definitely/think so	93	64	19	61
Feel strengthened by your faith				
Monthly plus	79	30	12	40
Feel you experience God's presence				
Monthly plus	68	22	9	32

monthly-plus basis. But they are joined by 30% of people in the religious middle and even 12% of those who reject religion.

Close to 70% of the pro-religious tell us that they experience God's presence every month or more. That figure drops to about 20% for the low religious and 10% for the no religious (Table 4.9).

An Overview of the Three Religious Positions

Let's pull everything together into a capsule of the three primary responses to religion in Canada at this point in our history.[8]

Those Embracing Religion: The Pro-Religious

About 30% of Canadians tell us that they embrace religion. That's down from the 45% of Canadians who said that they were religiously committed in 1985.[9]

More than half of the people in this category (56%) report that they attend services at least once a month. Close to 9 in 10 indicate that they pray privately on a regular basis, and about 5 in 10 say that they both say table grace and read the Bible or other sacred texts at least once a month.

For those who embrace religion, faith is more than public and private rituals: 60% indicate that the main thing religious involvement brings to their lives is God and spirituality, while another 30% cite personal enrichment, and the remaining 10% mention the importance of people in their groups.

Of considerable importance, 8 in 10 Canadians who embrace religion say that they feel strengthened by their faith, 93% believe that God cares about them personally, and – beyond mere belief – close to 70% claim that they routinely feel God's presence.

And, contrary to widespread conjecture, Canadians involved in religious organizations do not typically find themselves in churches and temples and synagogues that are crumbling. On the contrary, 35% of those attending services monthly or more report that their congregations have been growing in recent years, while another 42% inform us that their numbers have been staying about the same (Figure 4.3). Only 23% say that their congregations have been declining. These figures are

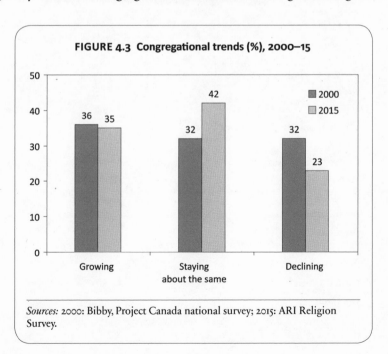

FIGURE 4.3 Congregational trends (%), 2000–15

Sources: 2000: Bibby, Project Canada national survey; 2015: ARI Religion Survey.

more positive than at the turn of the century; in 2000, 32% of the faithful indicated that their congregational numbers were dropping.

One key to understanding the ongoing vitality of organized religion in Canada is to look not at the previously dominant United, Anglican, Presbyterian, and Lutheran denominations but at patterns of immigration. Historically, the lifeblood of those four groups was immigration from Britain and the rest of Europe. Growth depended primarily on immigration. But as patterns shifted in the 1980s, Mainline Protestants – like the rest of Canada – could not sustain their numbers by natural increase. Conversely, as sources of immigration in the past two or three decades have shifted to Asian countries in particular, the big "winners" in Canada have been Roman Catholics, evangelical Protestants, and other major world faith groups, led by Muslims (Table 4.10).

So it is that many observers of the Canadian religious scene have made the mistake of equating the demise of the long-standing Mainline

TABLE 4.10 Religious identification of immigrants to Canada, 2001–11

	Total (1,000s)	Median age
Roman Catholic	478	43
No religion	442	33
Muslim	388	29
Christian, not included elsewhere	162	32
Hindu	154	34
Christian Orthodox	108	42
Sikh	107	33
Buddhist	62	38
Pentecostal	41	36
Anglican	23	51
Jewish	21	45
Presbyterian	17	48
United Church	10	52
Lutheran	7	46

Source: Statistics Canada, National Household Survey 2011.

Protestant "religious companies" with the disappearance of the market for religion. That's not the case. Our findings and those of others suggest that demand persists. What has been changing are some of the dominant suppliers.

Our 2015 survey showed that, as in the past, immigrants to Canada can bring significant vitality to the Canadian religious scene. An examination of the three inclinations toward religion by immigration and age readily makes that point. People born outside Canada are considerably more likely to attend religious services than people born in Canada. Even more striking is that young adults 18–34 and 35–54 – notably people arriving in large numbers from Asian and African countries in particular in recent decades – are much more likely to be active attenders than older immigrants.

Additional analyses reveal that the same pattern holds for the religious self-designations of younger arrivals from other countries: 42% of those 18 to 34 say that they embrace religion, 39% are ambivalent about it, and only 19% reject it. Similarly, 38% of those 35 to 54 born elsewhere embrace faith – well above the level of their Canadian-born counterparts.

Those Rejecting Religion: The No Religious

The proportion of Canadians who say that they are not "into religion" (26%) is very similar to the proportion of those who are (30%). The level is consistent with current census data for people indicating that they have no religion (24%). The figure is up significantly from 4% in 1971 (Figure 4.4).

What is different is that people in this category have become increasingly outspoken about not being religious. The spokespeople for many have tended to be from other places and have sometimes been dubbed "atheist rock stars" – people like Richard Dawkins, Sam Harris, and the late Christopher Hitchens. While Canadians are typically more low key, prominent Canadian organizations promoting life without religion include the Centre for Inquiry Canada and Humanist Canada.

As we will see, not everyone who rejects religion is hostile to it. Some people in this category simply bypass faith. Such sentiments were summed up well by an articulate teenager on a radio panel with me a few years back who, when asked about her faith, calmly informed

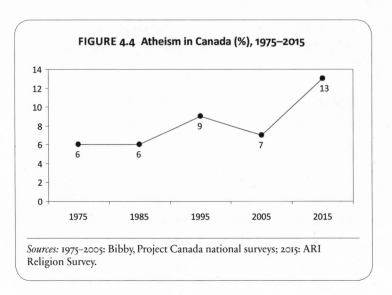

FIGURE 4.4 Atheism in Canada (%), 1975–2015

Sources: 1975–2005: Bibby, Project Canada national surveys; 2015: ARI Religion Survey.

listeners that "our home is religion-free." But the survey found that 63% of people who reject religion acknowledge that they feel somewhat uncomfortable around devout people. For their part, 41% of those who embrace faith express trepidation about being among individuals who have no use for religion.

More than 9 in 10 do not believe that it is necessary to either believe in God or be involved in a religious group "to be moral and have good values." And 70% go so far as to maintain that "the growth in atheism is a good thing for life in Canada."

In sum, about 80% of Canadians who reject religion say that they "prefer to live life without God or congregation," and they believe that "it's important to live life in the here and now, because this is the only existence we will ever have."

For the record, most people in this category are not – at least at this point in their lives – good candidates for religious recruitment: 78% indicate that they are *not* "open to being more involved in religious groups." What's more, recent research by Joel Thiessen and Sarah Wilkins-Laflamme suggests that, increasingly, the no-religion category will grow not only through people disaffiliating but also through no-religion parents begetting no-religion children.[10] Yet, perhaps surprisingly,

22% say that they have not closed the door on organized religion: the big asterisk is that they would have to find involvement "worthwhile."

Those in the Religious Middle: The Low Religious
The largest of the three segments of Canadians – 45% of the population – neither embrace nor reject religion. They see themselves as "somewhere in between the two extremes." Here is a recap of what we have been learning about them so far.

> They are the dominant group in every region, age, and gender category.
> Most are not pro-atheist: the majority (73%) do not believe that the growth of atheism has been a good thing for Canada.
> About 42% say that they are open to greater involvement with religious groups if they can find it worthwhile.
> About 4 in 10 report that they pray privately on a monthly to weekly basis, and 3 in 10 say that they regularly feel strengthened by their faith.
> Most do not need to be introduced to God: 64% inform us that they believe in a God who cares about them personally, and 22% believe that they experience God's presence on a regular basis.

The survey reveals much more about the religious middle (Table 4.11). Relatively few have "dropped out" of organized religion. On the contrary, 87% continue to identify with a religious tradition. These people in the middle comprise around 50% of Catholics, Mainline Protestants, and adherents of other major world faiths, along with about 20% of evangelical Protestants and about 30% of people with no religion.

Looked at in terms of their total, the low religious typically have not abandoned their religious ties (Table 4.11).

> Almost half identify themselves as Roman Catholics, with the Catholic numbers in Quebec equal to the numbers in the rest of the country.
> About one in four is Mainline Protestant, led by people who claim United Church and Anglican links.

TABLE 4.11 The religious middle by identification (%)

Roman Catholic	44
Inside Quebec	22
Outside Quebec	22
Mainline Protestant	24
United	11
Anglican	8
Lutheran	2
Presbyterian	3
Evangelical Protestant	4
Baptist	2
Pentecostal	1
Other	1
Other world faiths	9
Muslim	1
Jewish	2
Other	6
Other Christian	6
No religion	13
Total	100

▶ Most of the remaining quarter of the low religious either have no religion (13%) or identify with other Christian groups and other world faiths (12%).

Here are some brief additional survey findings on the important religious middle (Table 4.12).

▶ The majority (74%) continue to attend religious services at least once in a while. In addition, in the past year, nearly one in two attended a religious funeral and one in four a religious wedding.
▶ Religion is "still in their systems." A full one-third acknowledge that, when they die, they want to have religious funerals. One in

TABLE 4.12 Some characteristics of low-religious, pro-religious, and no-religious Canadians (%)

	Embrace	Middle	Reject	All
Continue to identify with a religion	99	87	56	78
Attend a service at least occasionally	93	74	36	70
Attended a religious funeral in the past year	60	46	28	45
Attended a religious wedding in the past year	37	19	17	24
Want to have a religious funeral	80	34	7	41
Sometimes feel guilty for not being more involved in religion	53	33	8	33
Have a high level of confidence in religious leaders	61	21	6	29
Believe that Pope Francis is having a positive impact on the world	81	78	63	75
"Often" or "sometimes" think about what happens after death	77	79	63	74
"Often" or "sometimes" think about the purpose of life	74	75	69	73

three admits "sometimes feel[ing] guilty for not being more involved."

▸ While only 20% of Canadians in the religious middle maintain that they have a high level of confidence in religious leaders, a rather astonishing 78% think that "Pope Francis is having a positive impact on the world." It's interesting to note that the pope receives "a thumbs up" as well from 63% of those who reject religion.

▸ Finally, the low religious are still asking the proverbial "ultimate questions": some 75% say that they continue to think about issues like the purpose of life and what happens after death.

These findings underline the fact that, contrary to the widespread perception among religious leaders, academics, and other observers, Canadians located in the religious middle certainly have not abandoned faith. On the contrary, they have much in common with people who embrace religion. Most of these people are well known to the devout. They are often brothers and sisters, aunts and uncles, cousins and friends who were raised "in the church" and other religious settings. They are expected to show up for funerals and weddings and baptisms and the like. Many also make cameo appearances at seasonal services like Christmas or Easter. Many want to have religious funerals and burials. Depending on any number of personal, cultural, and religious group factors, these low-faith individuals could readily go in the pro-faith direction rather than the no-faith direction.

Then, again, they might just stay in the middle.

Assessment

The findings help to clarify the nature of religious polarization in Canada. Almost equal proportions of the population are variously embracing or rejecting religion, with a sizable number occupying the middle ground.

Seen against the backdrop of polarization, secularization is conceptually helpful in describing the inclination to move away from religion. However, rather than being a linear reality, it coexists with desecularization – the movement toward religion. In Canada and elsewhere, both inclinations exist and can be expected to persist in the foreseeable future.

An understanding of the role of religion in Canadians' lives begins only with an accurate reading of the religious inclinations of people across the country. Also critical is the "so what?" question. What are the consequences – for both personal life and collective life in the country – of people being religious, not being religious, or being somewhere in between?

People who value faith maintain that religion makes a noteworthy difference in the lives of individuals and societies. They argue that faith elevates the lives of individuals, making them happier, more civil, and more compassionate; addresses their spiritual needs; and enables them to deal with death. While most would not claim that the impact is always unique, faith for them is one important source of enhanced well-being. Beyond the individual level, people who value faith also maintain that it has a positive impact on social life more broadly, in the form of greater civility and social compassion.

That said, the obvious question that arises from religious polarization is what are the implications for personal and social well-being of growing numbers of people not embracing faith? Are there personal and societal losses? Or are people finding "functional alternatives" to religion that enable them to live life and face death and be as civil and compassionate as anyone else? And, if so, then what are some of these alternative sources? In short, we need data on the consequences of embracing, rejecting, or taking a middle position on religion.

To those important questions regarding consequences we now turn.

5

Religious Inclinations and Personal Well-Being

The mind is the source of happiness and unhappiness.

– Buddha

The debate is age-old: does religion contribute to the elevation of life, or do individuals and societies function equally well – or even better – without it?

Virtually everyone has an opinion. Some of the wise men of old, like Marx and Freud, thought that religion is an illusion that helps people to cope with life and death. But it needed to be replaced with real-life solutions – such as altering social conditions (Marx) or adopting rational responses to the quest for happiness and the desire for immortality (Freud). People who value faith have been just as vocal in asserting that religion and spirituality can elevate life for individuals and collectivities – families, communities, nations, and the world.

These days the old questions about religion and well-being continue to be raised. Only the faces have changed.

So it is that critics like Richard Dawkins, the late Christopher Hitchens, and Sam Harris have emphatically decried what religion does to individuals and societies. Dawkins has written that faith isn't "just harmless nonsense" but can be lethal nonsense.[1] Hitchens was similarly hostile in asserting that all religious belief is sinister and infantile, going so far as to say that "religion poisons everything."[2] And Harris has declared that "religious faith remains a perpetual source of human conflict" and that "our enemy is nothing other than faith itself."[3] Pretty strong claims.

Not to be outdone, pro-faith people are not exactly speechless. For decades, prominent American evangelist Billy Graham emphasized that, if people want to experience true and lasting peace and joy, they need "to find Christ." The former head of the Anglican Church of Canada, Michael Peers, said this in a 1996 interview during his time as primate: "I think that if we were not around, the level of meanness would go way, way up."[4] Cardinal Thomas Collins, archbishop for the Toronto Roman Catholic Archdiocese, told worshippers in his 2010 Easter homily that "it is the experience of the risen Lord down through the ages that has made the Church a beacon in a world of darkness, and does so to this day."[5]

A major new report from the Pew Research Center released in the spring of 2016 examines how religion influences the daily lives of Americans. The study found that people who are highly religious are generally happier with their lives and more satisfied with family life than people who are less religious. They also exceed other Americans when it comes to engaging with their families, being involved in their communities, donating resources to the poor, and volunteering. Mind you, Pew also found little difference between the highly religious and others when it came to losing their tempers or telling "a white lie" in the past week.[6]

What about Canada? If this were a public forum and we moved away from the panelists and asked the audience to wade in, I suspect that the lineups at the microphones would be long. Those speaking would appeal to personal experience, history, and the biographies of others in making their cases for and against the contributions of religion to well-being.

Beyond personal and subjective observations, it is crucial that we also have solid research findings that help us to understand some of the correlates of religious polarization. I want to draw on two major sources to address the question. The first is the comprehensive 2015 survey of more than 3,000 people that I carried out in partnership with Angus Reid. The second is my extensive Project Canada national surveys of adults and teens spanning 1975 through 2005. Those surveys – nine in all – provide us with the opportunity to hear from more than 20,000 Canadians, both older and younger, who have been conversing with us over the past four decades.

Of particular importance, the extensive information from our participants makes it possible for us to look at their thoughts, values, beliefs, and experiences from the standpoint of whether or not they personally value religion. It also allows us to explore the important question of the impact of religious polarization on Canadians and Canada.

Obviously, the question of religion's impact is a very broad one. In the next four chapters, I want to focus on four areas that I think provide a good introduction to a conversation about religion's influence: personal life, interpersonal life, spirituality, and life after death.

I have no doubt that these findings and thoughts will be greeted with intense and passionate responses. I also have no doubt that readers will readily cite other important areas of life where the role of religion needs to be explored. Hopefully, future research will be undertaken in response to the latter call.

The Universal Goal

The reality hardly requires research: everyone wants to be happy. The question, of course, is how to find happiness.

Sources of Happiness

Ask ten people, and their ten answers about what makes them happy will invariably revolve around relationships, families, money, health, careers, and leisure activities. One or two might mention religion. Those of us who like to synthesize things might maintain that it comes down to the relative importance that we place on social, economic, physical, achievement, and spiritual factors.

But the sources of happiness can be pretty individualistic. Vancouver leadership consultant Brian Fraser tells the story of "Russell," an African American in his mid-50s. What caught Fraser's attention was "the rhythm of his work. It was like a Gospel two-step, on the 2 and the 4." He says that, "as we were leaving, I asked him what was playing in his head. He smiled, seemed a bit embarrassed at having been noticed, then said, 'Oh, a few tunes really, but they all have to do with love!'"[7]

Resilient Gods

While all of us are walking data and, as such, entitled to our personal takes on what brings us happiness, there have always been people who have packaged themselves as enlightened experts who know what happiness is and know how it can be attained. A title that I like best: *The Zen Commandments*![8]

Religious and spiritual gurus have been and continue to be among the most prominent self-appointed and self-anointed experts. But in recent decades they have been joined by a surprising number of academics, including psychologists, economists, and jurists. Their specialty? "Happiness research."

Chris Barrington-Leigh, an economist at McGill University, has noted that the research dates back to the 1970s and an interest in the relationship between national wealth and individual happiness. He says that the goal is to "learn everything we can and pursue policies" that maximize life. "Measuring progress solely by growth in GDP," he claims, "is an outmoded idea because we have better ways to measure our social objectives." He suggests that the primary sources of happiness for Canadians include social factors – notably interaction with families, friends, and institutions.[9]

Some of the more popular recent works in the burgeoning academic field include *Stumbling on Happiness* by Harvard University psychology professor Daniel Gilbert, *The Politics of Happiness* by former Harvard University president and law professor Derek Bok, and *Happiness around the World* by University of Maryland professor Carol Graham.[10] There has even been a University of Chicago publication, *Behind the Academic Curtain*, that tells people with PhDs how they too can find happiness.[11]

There has also been an increasing call for countries to pursue better understandings of the well-being of their people. In late 2009, a commission appointed by French president Nicolas Sarkozy issued a report calling for new statistical tools to be developed to measure quality of life, including subjective and objective well-being.[12] The report came about from a growing sense that happiness is the product of elements other than a country's gross domestic product.[13] In 2010, the British government followed suit, with Prime Minister David Cameron announcing that the country would start measuring people's psychological and environmental well-being.[14]

In July 2011, a UN General Assembly resolution invited member countries to measure the happiness of their peoples and to use such information to shape public policies. One response has been a series of annual "World Happiness" reports. They have been edited by John Helliwell of UBC, along with Richard Layard and Jeffrey Sachs of Columbia University. The reports have had large readerships that in turn have encouraged local and national experiments in measuring and improving happiness.[15]

Religion and Happiness

People of faith obviously believe that personal happiness – and marital, family, and relational happiness more generally – are enhanced by religion, even if many increasingly distance themselves from that overt term. To varying degrees, religions call on adherents to give of themselves. The costs involved are sometimes substantial.

But in the end one of the most basic rewards that religions promise is happiness. Apart from beliefs, a key component often appears to be social networks within congregations – an idea substantiated in an article by Robert Putnam and colleague Chaeyoon Lim published in 2010 in the prestigious *American Sociological Review*.[16] In a major study of American youth released in 2005, Christian Smith and his associates maintained that organized religion was having a positive impact on young people. Religious ("devoted") teens, for example, were less likely to engage in risk behaviour and sexual activity, more likely to express higher levels of emotional well-being, and more likely to have stronger adult and family ties than non-religious ("disengaged") teens.[17]

That said, religion is hardly without competitors for attaining personal well-being. In the spring of 2010, for example, Pat O'Brien, the president of Humanist Canada at the time, stated on the association's website that "we want people to know that belief in god is not necessary to live a full, moral, and happy life." His thinking is widespread. It's a viewpoint endorsed not only by large numbers of people who are not religious but also by many who are.

In recent years, a prominent advocate for the positive aspects of the so-called secular life has been Phil Zuckerman. In books such as *Society without God* and *Living the Secular Life*, he has provided valuable insights and data concerning what it means to be secular and the implications for morality, social compassion, parenting, spirituality, and dealing with death.[18] Zuckerman writes that "a life lived without religion is not 'nothing.' There are common attributes, characteristics, traits and values one finds among nonreligious people." He adds that such features "directly enhance individuals' ability to cope with life's troubles, allow for fulfillment and existential awe, and even increase societal well-being."[19]

Christel Manning, another colleague and friend, at Sacred Heart University in Connecticut, has carried out extensive qualitative research on how religiously unaffiliated parents are raising their children. Like other parents, she notes, "their ultimate concern is to do what is best for them." In response to the question "is it better to raise your children with or without religion?" Manning writes that the research to date does not offer a definitive answer. In her own case, she notes, "my husband and I are still Nones, and our now thirteen-year-old daughter is a happy, well-adjusted kid who does not believe in God."[20]

In the minds of some individuals, then, religion plays a unique role in the realization of happiness. For others, it is one path but far from the only one.

For a third category of observers, including many researchers, religion is not a source of personal happiness but in fact contributes to strain and pain. An example is the guilt-ridden young woman whom I have mentioned in the past who exclaimed to a counsellor, "My problems began the day I became a Christian."[21] While cognizant of Smith's findings, Manning, for example, notes that there is much "research showing organized religion to put children at risk. Numerous studies have associated religion with psychological and physical abuse of children, with long-term consequences for the victims' lives."[22]

In a fourth category are people who see religion as an illusory source of happiness. They include thinkers like Marx, who concedes that religion, like a drug, soothes symptoms but doesn't deal with underlying causes.

A Canadian Reading

The recent efforts of academics and politicians to measure happiness remind us that it is an extremely elusive concept to tap. Particularly problematic is the common finding that a precarious relationship exists between objective and subjective indicators. People who should be unhappy are often happy; people who should be happy are often unhappy.

Much of the problem lies with the complexity of how people arrive at a state of happiness. To date, at least, objective measures are not exactly known, in methodological parlance, for high levels of either validity or reliability – tapping the concept and doing so with precision. Hampson has aptly described such attempts as similar to "performing surgery with a shovel."[23]

We can line up all kinds of objective measures of happiness and rank individuals and countries. Yet ultimately, it seems to me, happiness lies in the eyes and heart of the beholder. One is happy because one *thinks* that she or he is happy – not because the individual meets some external criteria. We have to go with what people say. Far be it for me as a researcher to inform people who tell me that they are very happy with life or not very happy with their marriages that my objective measures indicate the opposite!

In keeping with that position, we have asked adults and teens for personal assessments of their happiness and well-being in private and school environments, respectively, that hopefully have permitted them to be as honest with themselves and us as possible.

Personal Outlook

Close to 90% of Canadians maintain that they are "very happy" (22%) or "pretty happy" (66%). And while everyone knows that marriages and comparable relationships are not always perfect, people are remarkably positive about their experiences at any single point in time when they are in them. About 45% describe their ties as "very happy," while nearly the same proportion peg them as "pretty happy." Only about 1 in 10 report being involved in unhappy relationships.

We saw earlier that some one in four people who are involved in religious groups say that the main thing participation adds to their lives is personal enrichment; two in four cited God and spirituality. Clearly, for many, faith is viewed as contributing to the elevation of personal life.

People who embrace religion are somewhat more likely than others to maintain that they are "very happy" both personally and relationally. They are also considerably more likely than others to express exuberance about enjoyment from family life and slightly more inclined to indicate that they receive high levels of enjoyment from friends.

These findings suggest that Canadians who embrace religion are somewhat more likely than those in the religious middle or those who reject religion to express happiness and enjoyment both from life as a whole and from relationships more specifically.

That said, the differences are generally not very large. While faith might be playing a role in enhancing personal and relational life for individuals, it is clear that people who reject religion or find themselves in the religious middle are also finding sources that make for happy living, personally and relationally.

In short, religion might be an important source of happiness for some Canadians. But clearly many people who do not embrace faith are finding other pathways to the happiness mountaintop (Table 5.1).

TABLE 5.1 Outlook by religious inclinations (%)

	All	Embrace	Middle	Reject
Happiness				
Very happy	22	29	19	20
Pretty happy	66	62	69	65
Marriage/relationship				
Very happy	45	50	43	42
Pretty happy	46	43	48	49
Family life				
Great deal of enjoyment	55	67	52	45
Quite a bit of enjoyment	32	23	34	38
Friends				
Great deal of enjoyment	43	49	41	41
Quite a bit of enjoyment	38	36	39	38

Source: ARI Religion Survey (2015).

Self-Esteem

It is virtually self-evident that good self-esteem – positive self-worth – is a fundamental component of positive and productive living. It is therefore expected that religions that promote optimum living for individuals also give considerable attention to instilling good self-esteem.

Religions such as Christianity do so but not without introducing a measure of tension. On the one hand, Christianity teaches individuals that they should love themselves precisely because they have worth, having been created by God and being loved by God. On the other, it calls for individuals to downplay an emphasis on themselves in favour of God and others.

If this were a phone-in show, the topic would undoubtedly generate more than a few calls and considerable emotion.

Some Canadians would claim that religion has made significant contributions to their sense of worth. Others would say just the opposite – undoubtedly pointing to the experiences that they and others have had with condemnation, guilt, and maybe even abuse.

Regardless of the role religions play, Canadian culture more generally places considerable value on cultivating positive self-esteem. It is viewed as an essential component of healthy living. Parents and schools, programs and activities, are expected to play roles in instilling and sustaining good self-esteem in children. For adults, it is taken for granted that healthy relationships and environments contribute to positive self-esteem.

So what's the relationship between faith and self-worth?

The Project Canada national teen surveys have been exploring self-esteem for some time. The 2008 survey included a number of items probing how teenagers view themselves. Three statements were aimed at examining virtuousness ("I am a good person"), competence ("I can do most things very well"), and appearance ("I am good looking") – all key components of self-image.

The good news in the findings was that the vast majority of Canadian young people expressed highly positive views of themselves. Incidentally, differences between females and males were minor.[24]

With respect to religion, variations in both attendance and belief in God were small. Religious young people and other young people exhibited very similar levels of self-image (Table 5.2).

TABLE 5.2 Self-image of teens by attendance and belief (%)

	All	Attendance		Belief	
		Weekly	Never	Theist	Atheist
I am a good person.	94	95	94	95	91
I can do most things very well.	80	80	78	82	76
I am good looking.	77	79	76	79	73

Source: Bibby, Project Teen Canada national survey (2008).

Personal Concerns

We are all aware of the fact that we can be very happy with life overall, but that is not to say for a moment that we do not have concerns. Some, of course, are more readily resolved than others.

In the case of adults, the Project Canada surveys have documented the central importance of health, finances, and time.[25] For teens, the surveys have found that the primary personal concern for decades has been the pressure to do well at school, followed by what they are going to do when they finish school. Money and time are also among their foremost concerns.[26]

Our latest national survey findings (2015) suggest that little has changed. However, the top three issues have been joined by a fourth – the feeling among people that they "should be getting more out of life." Predictable additional areas of concern for about one in three adults include getting older and children – the latter obviously a source of joy but also sometimes a source of strain. Loneliness is a concern for about one in four people. Marriage and other relationships trouble one in five adults – also life-enhancing, but not always.

With the aging of the Canadian population, led by Baby Boomers, it is perhaps not surprising that levels of concern about health, getting more out of life, and becoming older have been on the increase.

People in the religious middle are slightly more likely than those either embracing or rejecting religion to express concerns about a number of issues. They include health, money, time, getting more out of life, aging, and loneliness. A tentative hypothesis suggested by this finding is that, when one takes up a clear-cut position either in favour or not in

TABLE 5.3 Personal concerns by religious inclinations (%)

Concerned "a great deal" or "quite a bit" about ...	All	Embrace	Middle	Reject
Health	48	47	52	43
Lack of money	47	43	52	45
Not enough time	44	43	45	42
Getting more out of life	44	38	49	41
Becoming older	36	33	38	35
Children	33	41	31	28
Loneliness	28	28	30	24
Marriage/relationship	19	21	20	14

favour of religion, that posture is associated with a more decisive posture toward life as a whole. That in turn leads to a clearer mindset in dealing with personal issues.

Differences in concerns between the pro-religious and no religious, however, are small. The sole exception pertains to children: people who embrace religion tend to express somewhat higher levels of concern than others. That doesn't mean that the devout have more to worry about than others – just that they are a bit more inclined to worry about their children than others (Table 5.3). As one 19-year-old daughter of Christian parents told me a number of years back, "my parents worry because they want me to turn out OK." She was doing fine, but that didn't stop her parents from worrying – reminiscent of a line from a leadership guru who quipped, "I'm 53, and my mother still worries about how I am going to turn out."

The Global Situation

Large numbers of people in many countries around the world acknowledge that their lives are enhanced by religion. They range from almost everyone in religious monopolies like Saudi Arabia, Iraq, and Iran, through 65% majorities in Ukraine and Canada, to 35% minorities in Britain, Japan, and Sweden.

In a release in late October 2010, the Gallup organization reported that its analysis of more than 500,000 interviews with Americans over the previous two years found that those who are the most religious also have the highest levels of well-being. Religiosity was based on both salience and attendance measures, with well-being probed using subjective and objective indicators. Gallup reported that the relationship held after controlling for numerous demographic variables.[27] However, while the relationships were consistent, the associations were weak. Like the situation in Canada, Americans who are not religious are almost as likely to exhibit high levels of well-being as those who are religious.

When we examine religion and satisfaction with life worldwide, a different pattern is readily evident. To the extent that countries tend to have a relatively high level of affluence, their citizens express high levels of personal satisfaction (Table 5.4). The level of Canadians is among the highest in the world.

Such a pattern for subjective measures of well-being is also apparent when we look at objective measures of standard of living via the UN Human Development Index (Table 5.5).

▶ The dominant pattern is an inverse relationship between the national levels of personal religious importance and place on the Human Development Index.
▶ In Nigeria, 97% of the people say that religion is personally import-ant to them, yet the country ranks 152nd in its standard of living.
▶ Conversely, Norway ranks first according to the index, yet only 23% of its people say that religion is important to them.

In a stimulating synthesis of findings on happiness worldwide, Geoffrey Miller, an evolutionary psychologist at the University of New Mexico, has offered a number of points that help to clarify the context in which religion might be at work:

❶ Almost all humans are happy almost all the time. That's been the case throughout history.
❷ Major life events – like winning the lottery or the death of a spouse – affect happiness for only six months to a year.

TABLE 5.4 Religious salience and satisfaction with one's life in select countries (%)

	Religious salience	Satisfaction*
Senegal	97	35
Pakistan	96	51
Ghana	94	37
Malaysia	92	56
India	*85*	*44*
South Africa	*85*	*49*
Italy	*70*	*48*
United States	*66*	*65*
Poland	64	38
Argentina	*63*	*66*
Israel	48	75
Spain	44	54
Canada	*43*	*71[‡]*
Germany	*40*	*60*
Russia	*34[†]*	*43*
United Kingdom	*29*	*58*
France	*27*	*51*
Sweden	*13*	*72[‡]*

Notes: Italic type indicates a G-20 country; *percent rating personal life 7 or more on a scale of 0 to 10.
Sources: Salience: Stark (2015); *Satisfaction:* Pew Research Center (2014b); [†] Pew Research Center (2007); [‡] Gallup WorldView (2010).

❸ Many alleged factors like age, sex, race, income, education, and national residence have little effect on happiness. Some key exceptions are hunger, health, and oppression. Yet, once minimum standards are met in each case, further increases – greater affluence, for example – do not appreciably increase happiness.

❹ For people who experience very low levels of subjective well-being (e.g., major depression), the most potent anti-depressants are not social or economic but pharmaceutical. The effects of such drugs are stronger than increases in wealth or any other changes in conditions.[28]

Resilient Gods

TABLE 5.5 Religious salience and quality of life in select countries		
	Religious salience (%)	Rank
Nigeria	97	152
Saudi Arabia	97	39
Thailand	97	93
Pakistan	96	147
Philippines	95	115
United Arab Emirates	95	41
Brazil	89	75
India	85	130
South Africa	85	116
Iran	83	69
Poland	73	36
Italy	70	27
Mexico	66	74
United States	66	8
Ireland	54	6
Israel	48	18
Spain	44	26
Canada	43	9
Korea, Republic of	43	17
Switzerland	41	3
Germany	40	6
Iceland	37	16
Cuba	35	67
Russia	34*	50
New Zealand	33	9
Australia	32	2
Netherlands	32	5
Finland	29	24
United Kingdom	29	14
France	27	22
Japan	26	20
Hong Kong	25	12
Norway	23	1
Sweden	16	14
China	–	90

Note: Same ranking indicates a tie.
Sources: Salience: Stark (2015); * Gallup WorldView (2010);
UN Human Development Report (2015).

Given that happiness has something of "a set point," Miller concludes by pointing out that the consumption of products and services marketed as happiness boosters is usually futile. Increasing the gross national product per capita also won't have positive effects on well-being once a minimum standard of living is in place. And runaway consumerism not only fails to make us happier but also can impose high environmental costs on everyone else.

One practical implication: "Every hundred dollars that we spend on ourselves will have no detectable effect on our happiness; but the same money, if given to hungry, ill, oppressed, developing-world people, would dramatically increase their happiness." Miller adds that "the utilitarian argument for the rich giving more of their money to the poor is now scientifically irrefutable."[29]

Recent research carried out by the Pew Global Attitudes Project, for example, has confirmed the findings of various academic studies showing that, in more affluent countries, happiness rises up to a point but not beyond it. Researchers refer to the pattern as the "Easterlin paradox," named after Richard Easterlin, a University of Southern California economist. He concluded that gains in material well-being have little impact on satisfaction with life once a certain level has been achieved.[30]

Those things said, it is also clear that in many parts of the developing world – notably many countries in Africa – such a happiness threshold has not been reached. In such places, people predictably indicate that they are not satisfied with their lives, even though their levels of religiosity might be high.

One area, however, where religion is associated with a difference worldwide is suicide. Both females and males who live in countries characterized by high levels of service attendance are less likely than other individuals to commit suicide. The differences are particularly pronounced in countries like the Philippines, Mexico, Brazil, and Iran, versus China, Korea, and Japan.[31] Gallup has noted the same pattern in a recent examination of 67 countries. The pollster also found that the relationship tends to hold within countries. Gallup's conclusion? Religion might be a factor in reducing suicides that is at least as important as economics.[32]

Assessment

These findings indicate that, according to these measures of personal well-being – outlook, self-esteem, and concerns – there are few differences overall between Canadians who are religious and those who are not. The patterns in Canada are consistent with the patterns worldwide.

This doesn't mean that religion is not an important source of personal well-being for some people. Of course it is. Even in poorer countries, it may help people to deal with economic deprivation.[33] In some circumstances, it also seems to be an important source of elevated self-esteem.

However, it does mean that particularly in more advantaged situations – such as in Canada – people who are not religious or find themselves in the religious middle are almost as likely to find personal well-being through other sources.

This initial reading points to the fact that, without religion, life could be significantly diminished for some individuals. But to the extent that alternatives to religion exist, especially in highly developed countries, including Canada, personal well-being might not necessarily be negatively affected by increasing religious polarization.

There might be good reasons why people seem to find happiness both with and without religion. John Helliwell, a renowned economics professor emeritus at UBC, has been studying happiness for years. As mentioned earlier, he is a central figure in the burgeoning field of happiness research and continues to be a resource for government bodies.[34] In October 2010, he visited Harvard University and summarized happiness research, giving attention to its social contexts.[35] He maintains that, although happiness research is in its infancy, three major findings will ultimately emerge.

❶ *The positive trumps the negative*: Positive outlooks and activities lead to good health and longer life. Two strangers who wave to each other in traffic go home happier than two people who give each other the finger.

❷ *Community trumps materialism*: Relationships enhance life more than the pursuit of things. Research shows that a 1% improvement in a worker-boss relationship improves happiness as much as a 30% increase in salary.

❸ *Generosity trumps selfishness*: People who give away more are happier than those who give away less – regardless of income. Those who did favours for others in the past year felt happier than those who received favours.

If Helliwell is right regarding the three leading determinants of happiness, then one can see where religion might sometimes contribute to each source. But it is clear that other factors contribute as well. Religion can be one source of happiness. Obviously it isn't the only one.

Some people might be surprised by these findings. What might be even more surprising are the findings concerning the impact of religious polarization on how we treat each other – the topic that we turn to next.

6

Religious Inclinations and Social Well-Being

It is doubtful whether men were in general happier
when religious doctrines held unlimited sway than
they are now; more moral they certainly were not.

– Sigmund Freud, *The Future of an Illusion*, 1927

Everyone has heard the argument in one form or another. Are people
who are religious more compassionate than people who are not religious?
Or are they actually less compassionate? Does valuing God result in enhanced interpersonal relations? Even if that's the case, can't people be
good without God?

Old questions, tough questions. Here again, if we were to open up
the mic to people in any audience, we know that the input would be
extremely varied and probably emotional. The data sources would be
extensive.

- We can readily draw on personal experience – and why not? We
  all have known people who are religious and people who are not
  religious. Some of them have been terrific people, others less than
  terrific.
- We can reflect on history. Some people could offer stories of how
  religious groups helped their parents and grandparents when they

arrived in Canada from other countries. Aboriginals in the audience might remind us of what they know about residential schools and decry what religious groups did to children in days gone by. Still others would raise the contributions of religion to wars and conflicts in many parts of the world and even say that the world would have been a far better place without religion.

- A couple of speakers might say that they have been motivated to be better and kinder people because of their faith.
- An academic might try to inform us that research offers mixed reviews regarding the relationship between religion and compassion.
- And then people like Phil Zuckerman's dad might tell us what he told his friendly dental assistant when she asked him, as she polished his teeth, "how can you be a good person if you don't believe in God?" His response? "Remember Jiminy Cricket? I let my conscience be my guide."[1]

The discussion would become even more complex if we tried to carry out the Herculean task of not only comparing things personally and historically but also cross-culturally. What about societies in which religion has been pervasive versus those in which it has seemingly been absent – the United States, for example, versus the Soviet Union prior to the demise of the communist bloc in the late 1980s? Would a person who lived in Chicago in the 1970s have found America a more compassionate place than his or her counterpart in Moscow at the same time? Today, ideology aside, is interpersonal life in a theocratic Iran more civil than it is in a highly secularized Sweden? How about life in predominantly Catholic countries like the Philippines or Ireland versus the Czech Republic or China?

Zuckerman adds an interesting observation to the mix. He writes that we find various versions of the Golden Rule in all of the world's religions. But, he says, "not a single one of these religious articulations of the Golden Rule requires a God. All that is required is basic, fundamental human empathy. Children who grow up in stable, safe, and supportive environments generally develop the capacity to be kind, sensitive, and human toward others." He adds, by way of emphasis, "No philosophical proofs, theoretical arguments, logical axioms, Bible stories, or theistic beliefs are necessary."[2] Who can argue with such an assertion? Actually, lots of people. A Pew Research Center survey released in May 2014 found that "clear majorities" in 22 of the 39 countries examined maintained that "it is necessary to believe in God to be moral and have good values." The view was particularly prevalent in Africa and the Middle East.[3]

Rodney Stark, in his 2012 book *America's Blessings*, emphatically agrees, specifically in the case of the United States. "Americans," he says, "benefit immensely from being an unusually religious people – blessings that not only fall upon believers but also on those Americans who most oppose religion." Stark writes, "In America, militant atheists are far less likely to have their homes broken into or to be robbed on their way to work than they would be in an irreligious society, because of the powerful deterrent effects of religion on crime." He notes that religious people are the primary contributors to charities that benefit everyone, and – for emphasis – he points out that they even "dominate the ranks of blood donors, to whom even some angry humanists owe their lives."[4]

Yet others are not quite as enthusiastic. In 2008, Christian Smith and Michael Emerson wrote a book entitled *Passing the Plate: Why American Christians Don't Give Away More Money*. Their assertion? "All of the evidence points to the same conclusion: when it comes to sharing their money, most contemporary American Christians are remarkably ungenerous."[5] The book provided impetus for establishment of the Science of Generosity initiative at the University of Notre Dame to study the topic, with the help of a $5 million grant from the John Templeton Foundation.[6]

The sources of compassion and generosity prompt very big questions that conjure up very long answers and very little consensus.

New Arguments from Science

Since the 1970s, science has increased its participation in the fray. The burgeoning disciplines of social and evolutionary biology, along with moral psychology, have led the way in giving greater attention to the scientific study of human nature. One area of focus has been morality. In my mind, it is a short path from talking about what is right and wrong to talking about social well-being.

Much of this emphasis on "the new science of morality" has originated at Harvard University with faculty and graduates, including Robert Trivers, Montreal-born Steven Pinker, Edward O. Wilson, Daniel C. Dennett, and Marc Hauser. In 1975, Wilson predicted that "ethics would someday be taken out of the hands of philosophers and incorporated into the 'new synthesis' of evolutionary and biological thinking."[7] Theologians seemingly had little say in the matter.

A 2010 gathering in Connecticut sponsored by the Edge Foundation brought together nine leading thinkers to explore "the new science of morality." John Brockman, the editor and publisher of www.edge.org, noted that "it seems like everyone is studying morality these days, reaching findings that complement each other more often than they clash." In introducing what people had to say, he asked, "What do we have to offer a world in which so many global national crises are caused or exacerbated by moral failures and moral conflicts?"[8]

The participants included Canadian-born Yale University psychologist Paul Bloom, who maintains that humans are born with hard-wired morality and have a deep sense of good and evil bred in the bone; New York University psychologist Jonathan Haidt, who asserts that morality has evolved out of five or more innate foundations: harm, fairness, ingroup, authority, and purity (highly educated people tend to rely on the first two, more religious and lower class people rely on all five); and Florida State University social psychologist Roy Baumister, who cautioned against reductionism, offering the reminder that a focus on the individual and nature needs to be complemented by an emphasis on the interpersonal – nature and culture – in which morality is an attempt to get people to overcome their natural selfish impulses.

One person among the nine was Sam Harris. His ideas are offered in a number of books, one of which is *The Moral Landscape: How Science Can Determine Human Values.*[9] He offered a succinct overview of his views on moral values in the Edge event. The failure of science to address questions of meaning, morality, and values, says Harris, has provided the primary justification for religious faith. Such an abdication has resulted in religious dogmatism, superstition, and sectarian conflict. "We have convinced ourselves that somehow science is by definition a value-free space," he continues, "and that we can't make value judgments about beliefs and practices that needlessly derail our attempts to build happy and sane societies."[10]

Science consequently should not limit itself to merely describing existing moral systems but be engaged in persuading people committed to harmful things in the name of "morality" to change their commitments and lead better lives. Harris sees this as no less than "the most important project facing humanity at this point in time." I'm not exaggerating. He argues that "it subsumes everything else we could care about – from arresting climate change, to stopping nuclear proliferation, to curing cancer, to saving the whales."[11]

"Project Two" for Harris is understanding right and wrong in universal terms. He notes that this is a particularly difficult task because of the pervasive idea that there is no intellectual basis for claiming "moral truth." He uses a poignant illustration to make his point: "In 1947, when the United Nations was attempting to formulate a universal declaration of human rights, the American Anthropological Association stepped forward and said, it can't be done. Any notion of human rights is the product of culture. This was the best our social sciences could do with the crematory of Auschwitz still smoking."[12]

Harris challenges such a relativistic assumption. He maintains that we need to converge globally on the question of how we should treat each other. The point of consensus for him is well-being: "The concept of 'well-being' captures everything we can care about in the moral sphere."[13]

Harris is convinced that there are right and wrong answers to questions of human flourishing, and morality relates to that domain of facts. In his mind, science needs to give top priority to exploring and developing a universal conception of human values.[14]

Rather than questions of meaning, morality, and purpose being outside the limits of science, Harris believes that science alone can uncover the facts needed to enable humans to flourish. Religion, he maintains, not only does not have the answers but is in fact a major source of world problems.

My rereading of this brief exposition leads me to think that I have made Harris sound more charitable toward religion than he is. In a back-cover endorsement of *The Moral Landscape*, Richard Dawkins writes, "As for religion and the preposterous idea that we need God to be good, nobody wields a sharper bayonet than Sam Harris."[15] *Newsweek*'s Jerry Adler sums things up this way: "Dawkins and Harris are not issuing pleas for tolerance or moderation, but bone-rattling attacks on what they regard as a pernicious and outdated superstition."[16]

Clarifying the Question

Undoubtedly, social compassion – concern for others – has a large number of possible sources. A starting point is to agree on that. Let's also be clear on some additional matters, noted below, and save ourselves considerable time and energy by not treating them as issues in question.

- ▶ Neurological or biological determinism can be treated and greeted as a scientific breakthrough. However, it reopens an ancient claim – that nature can explain everything with no recourse to nurture. Sociologists are equally adamant that social environment plays an important role in shaping individuals. A much more productive approach is to combine the insights of both perspectives, as the new area of "social neuroscience" is attempting to do.[17]
- ▶ Religion is one source of compassion for some people in some situations. Religions often and perhaps even typically call on their followers to care about other people. Besides expecting them to adopt such ideals, they expect them to put them into practice. It is therefore hardly a shocker that people taught to "be good" and "be kind" sometimes come through. Former American president Barack Obama recently acknowledged, "I came to my Christian faith later in life and it was because the precepts of Jesus Christ spoke to me in terms of the kind of life that I would want to lead. Being my brothers and sisters' keeper, treating others as they would treat me."[18]
- ▶ Do interpersonal values always translate into behaviour? Of course not. In the parlance of causation, values are not sufficient causes of behaviour. But they are necessary causes: a person who acts compassionately values compassion, even if someone who values compassion is not always compassionate. If the value is in

Resilient Gods

place, then compassionate behaviour is at least a mathematical possibility. Conversely, "no value = no compassion."

▶ Does religion sometimes contribute to the lack of compassion – to the pain, suffering, and even death of another person? Unfortunately, the answer is yes.

▶ Do individuals who are not religious also sometimes treat other people in negative ways, spanning rudeness and exploitation to death? Here again, unfortunately, the answer is yes.

So the question that I want to bring to the Canadian scene assumes all of the above realities. What I want to know is this: at this point in the history of Canada, to what extent is religiousness associated with compassionate values and behaviours?

An important related question, given increasing religious polarization, is how does the level of compassion of those who are religious compare with the level of compassion of those who are not and of those who are in the religious middle?

The answers to these questions will help us to assess the immediate implications of religious polarization for interpersonal life in Canada.

Civil societies require the adoption of values and norms that make for good interpersonal life. Consequently, the question regarding the sources of civility is an extremely important one.

In the fall of 2010, Hockey Calgary, the organization that oversees minor hockey in the city, became the first such organization in the country to require parents to complete a one-hour online course before their children could play. The president of Hockey Calgary, Perry Cavanaugh, explained that cases of unruly parents and violence on the ice required exposure to standards to guide everyone toward mutual respect at the rink. He mentioned hockey parents yelling at referees, climbing the glass, and throwing coffee cups on the ice in addition to a significant number of players being suspended because of illegal hits, fighting, and roughing penalties.

Thinking like a sociologist, Cavanaugh noted that "Calgary has gone through a period of negative activity in terms of violence in the community," with those changes coming "more and more into local arenas. We're seeing less respect to individuals, players, coaches, parents, and we need to send a message that this kind of behaviour is not tolerated."[19]

. By the time the season started, 99% of Calgary's 13,000-plus young hockey players had "Respect in Sport"–certified parents (at least one parent had to take the course). Cavanaugh commented that, even if some parents didn't like the program, they were "putting their egos aside and getting the kids on the ice."[20] The program has subsequently expanded not only within Alberta but also across Canada.[21]

It seems that, when it comes to social well-being, we need all the help that we can get.

A Canadian Reading

Values

Going back to the 1980s, we have been asking adults and teens about the importance that they give to a number of values through our Project Canada national surveys. Some values pertain to goals or objectives, such as a comfortable life, family, and success. Others focus on means or norms for living and relating to other people, including honesty, concern for others, and forgiveness. Findings regarding the latter offer information on the extent to which Canadians of all ages place importance on traits that make for positive interpersonal life.

Our 2015 national religion survey shows that a majority of close to 85% of Canadians place a high level of importance on honesty. Some 55% indicate that concern for others and forgiveness are "very important" to them (Table 6.1).

There are noteworthy differences by age. In all three instances, older Canadians are more likely than younger Canadians to place a high level of importance on these three traits. This is not to say that large numbers of younger adults do not embrace these values – just that they are less inclined to do so than older adults.

Another variable that has predictability is gender.

- ◗ Honesty is highly valued by 89% of women and 79% of men.
- ◗ Concern for others is seen as "very important" by 65% of women and 45% of men.

TABLE 6.1 Interpersonal values by age cohort (% indicating "very important"), 2015

Values	All	Pre–Boomers	Boomers	Gen-Xers	Millennials
Honesty	84	93	90	80	75
Concern for others	55	66	61	49	49
Forgiveness	55	63	60	52	49

Note: Pre-Boomers are those born in 1945 and earlier; Boomers are those born between 1946 and 1965; Gen-Xers are those born between 1966 and 1985; and Millennials are those born after 1985.
Source: ARI Religion Survey (2015).

TABLE 6.2 Interpersonal values by religious inclinations and service attendance (% indicating "very important"), 2015

Values	All	Religious inclinations			Service attendance		
		Embrace	Middle	Reject	Monthly+	Yearly	Never
Honesty	84	87	84	81	84	85	83
Concern for others	55	64	51	52	65	53	52
Forgiveness	55	72	53	42	73	55	44

Source: ARI Religion Survey (2015).

- Forgiveness is highly valued by 64% of women and 46% of men.
- Of considerable importance, this pattern of higher levels for women than men holds within all four age cohorts for each of these traits.

In addition to these age and gender variations, we want to know whether or not religion is associated with differences in the importance given to these values. An examination of these three interpersonal values by religious inclinations shows that Canadians who embrace religion are slightly more inclined than others to place a high level of importance on each (Table 6.2). That's particularly the case with forgiveness, where even those in the religious middle differ somewhat from those who reject religion. Very similar patterns hold for service attendance – seemingly supporting the claim of 95% of those rejecting religion and 91% of those in the religious middle that "it is not necessary to 'go to church' in order to be moral and have good values." By the way, 80% of those embracing faith also agree.[22]

My previous examination of values by a number of measures of religion found noteworthy differences between theists and atheists for both adults and teens.[23] In addition to providing a control for age, the teen data revealed that the relationship between a belief in God and the endorsement of interpersonal values held for both gender and region (Quebec and elsewhere).

An examination of the latest (2015) national religion survey shows similar patterns for today's adults.

- Honesty is seen as "very important" by 91% of theists and 83% of atheists.
- Concern for others is given a similar high ranking by 67% of theists versus 55% of atheists.
- And forgiveness is seen as "very important" by 74% of theists compared with just 40% of atheists.

The fact that the differences in valuing honesty and compassion are fairly modest reminds us that the valuing of interpersonal traits is hardly limited to the devout. It is worth noting that no less than 91% of

Canadians who say that they reject religion maintain that "it is not necessary to believe in God in order to be moral and have good values." Some 86% of those in the religious middle agree. What's more, so do 68% of those who embrace faith.[24]

Still, some differences in values persist.

Civility

Beyond explicit values, we have also been asking adults and young people about some basic ideals related to courtesy and what some would regard as civility. For example, in 2008 we asked teens across the country how they feel about things like people walking on a red light and making traffic wait (apart from getting a ticket), not saying sorry when they accidentally bump into someone, parking in a stall reserved for those who are handicapped when one is not handicapped, and giving someone the finger.[25]

Adults who are cynical about the levels of civility among teens would be wise to take a close look at the results (Table 6.3).

▶ Large majorities of around 80% said that they disapproved of people misusing parking stalls for the handicapped or not apologizing for bumping into someone.

TABLE 6.3 Teens' disapproval of select behaviour by attendance and belief (%), 2008

Behaviour	All	Attendance		Belief	
		Weekly	Never	Theist	Atheist
Parking illegally in a handicapped zone	82	85	79	85	77
Not saying "sorry" for bumping into someone	77	77	77	78	74
Walking on a red light	63	66	61	64	58
Giving someone the finger	45	62	38	53	34

Source: Bibby, Project Teen Canada national survey (2008).

- A two-thirds majority didn't approve of people walking on a red light at the expense of oncoming traffic.
- However, only 45% were troubled about people occasionally giving someone the finger.

Interestingly, differences by service attendance and belief were consistently positive but extremely small – with the exception of extending the famous finger. Clearly, there are various sources of such basic civil attitudes besides religion.

Behaviour
We all know that one shortcoming of surveys is their inability to capture actual behaviour. There is nothing surprising about that limitation. As I often remind my students and others, surveys at their best are simply good structured conversations. As such, they have no equal when it comes to understanding what's going on in people's heads – their thoughts, beliefs, attitudes, values, expectations, and so on. They are indispensable for probing ideas.

When we want to get a good reading on behaviour, however, it can be precarious to simply rely on what people tell us that they do or have done. We can ask them questions about how much money they give to charities, whether or not they have ever used marijuana, how often they work out, the last time they received a speeding ticket, whether or not they ever gamble, how often they have sex, if they ever fib, and on and on.

But – and this is going to sound excessively cynical – we can only put a percentage of certainty on whether or not they have told us the truth. That percentage obviously depends on factors such as how well we know them, how comfortable they feel with us, and the risk of providing the information.

That's my long way of saying that it's difficult to gather reliable data through surveys on how people actually behave. Nonetheless, we try. For example, in our 2000 and 2008 national youth surveys, we asked participants to imagine that they had bought something and received $10 more in change than they were supposed to receive. We asked them if they would be inclined to (a) keep the $10 and keep walking, (b) go back and return the extra $10, or (c) think that what they would do would depend on factors such as the size of the store, whether or not they expected to shop there again, and whether or not they knew the salesperson involved.[26]

It was not behaviour per se but *anticipated* behaviour. In 2008, we found that 4 in 10 teens claimed that they would return the $10, while the remainder were almost evenly divided between those who said "it would depend" and those who admitted that they would probably keep the 10 bucks. However, an examination by our three religiosity variables revealed a consistent, positive relationship among attendance, identification, and belief and the inclination to return the money.[27]

Perhaps the findings reflect what young people *would do.* At a minimum, they reflect what they *thought they should do.* This takes us back to the argument about values functioning like "good intentions." Behaviour doesn't necessarily follow, but the values have to be present for the behaviour to occur.

Our findings so far point to religion at least helping to instill positive interpersonal values and intentions.

As we discussed earlier, a basic hope of almost all parents is that their children will turn out okay. So it is that parents, along with schools, churches, and other institutions, want to see young people stay out of trouble.

Here we have some data that attempted to tap behaviour. The 2008 national youth survey included a number of items that probe both self-image and behaviour with respect to the stereotypical notion of "trying to be good" or "trying to stay out of trouble."

Teens were almost unanimous in claiming that they are "kind to other people." The numbers dropped a bit, as would be expected, when they were asked how well the two statements "I have never got into trouble with the police" and "I try to stay out of trouble" described them personally. Gender differences, by the way, were fairly small in both cases: 86% for females versus 78% for males for not having been in trouble with the police and 83% versus 77% for having stayed out of trouble.

When we looked at these variables through the eyes of religiosity, we found that almost all young people, religious or not, saw themselves as being kind to other people. Religion made a greater appearance in experiences with the police. While the differences weren't large, higher

TABLE 6.4 Good behaviour among teens by attendance and belief (%), 2008

	All	Attendance		Belief	
		Weekly	Never	Theist	Atheist
I am kind to other people.	94	96	93	95	89
I have never got into trouble with the police.	83	90	78	86	75
I try to stay out of trouble.	80	87	75	86	65

Source: Bibby, Project Teen Canada national survey (2008).

percentages of teens who attended services weekly or believed in God said that they tried to stay out of trouble and that they had never had problems with the police (Table 6.4).

Here again religion seems to be having a modest but consistently positive impact on behaviour. Clearly, there are many sources at work, but religion is one of them. Teens can be good without God. But God seems to increase the number of good teens.

Compassion

The Project Canada national surveys have also included numerous items probing the prevalence of social compassion both attitudinally and behaviourally.

For example, we have been asking Canadians for some time if they think that people have the right to an income adequate to live on. We have asked them whether or not they believe that war is justified when other ways of resolving international disputes fail, and we have also probed the extent to which they believe that we should be concerned about people in the rest of the world.

- Our most recent findings reveal that close to 90% of people across the country maintain that individuals have a right to an income that enables them to live, with no noteworthy differences between those who embrace religion and others.

Resilient Gods

▶ Nearly 60% of Canadians maintain that war is not justified, even when efforts to resolve disputes fail. Again, there are negligible differences by religious inclinations.

▶ Almost the same proportion say that we should be concerned about developments outside Canada, disagreeing with the statement that "we need to worry about our own country and let the rest of the world take care of itself." Here again differences by religious outlooks are minor.

As a way of tapping tangible expressions of compassion, in 2015 we borrowed an item from Gallup in asking Canadians whether or not, in the past month, they had (a) helped a stranger, (b) donated money to a charity, or (c) volunteered time to an organization. We found that people who embrace faith, reject faith, or are in the religious middle are equally likely to claim that they helped a stranger in the past month. However, the pro-religious are considerably more likely than others to report that, during the same period, they both donated money to a charity and volunteered time to an organization (Table 6.5).

TABLE 6.5 **Compassion of Canadians by religious inclinations (%), 2015**

	All	Embrace	Middle	Reject
Attitudes: *Agree*				
People have the right to an income adequate to live on.	86	89	85	85
War is not justified.	57	57	58	57
We should have concern for the rest of the world.	54	58	50	56
Behaviour: *In past month*				
Helped a stranger in need	55	57	53	57
Donated money to a charity	53	64	48	50
Volunteered time to an organization	34	46	31	27

Source: ARI Religion Survey (2015).

Coexistence

A central question for social well-being that growing religious polarization raises is this: can people with different positions toward religion coexist?

Our Canadian mosaic is supposed to encompass pretty much everything imaginable. What started out as a cultural mosaic with Pierre Trudeau's unveiling of the federal government's policy of multiculturalism in the House of Commons in 1971 has given birth to a multi-everything psyche in Canada.

The multicultural infant soon left its racial and cultural group cradle. In the course of growing up over the past several decades, it has travelled across the country, visiting our moral, religious, familial, educational, and political spheres. Pluralism is enshrined in our minds and institutions. We now have multiple mosaics in virtually every area of Canadian life.[28]

Pluralism's familiar emphases are on tolerance, respect, appreciation of diversity, and freedom of individuals to think and behave according to their consciences. Ours is a society in which just about everything is possible within the limits of the law and civility.[29]

However, having faced some monumental challenges in areas such as language, race and ethnicity, gender, Aboriginal issues, sexual orientation, disabilities, and age, pluralism is now facing one of its biggest challenges – that of religion. Debates about marriage commissioners and same-sex marriages, Christmas stories and preschool settings,[30] serve as reminders – says journalist Susan Martinuk – that "there are only so many rights to go around. Giving more rights to one group inevitably means taking rights from another."[31] As Rex Murphy wryly notes, that can translate into something like the crucifix being ruled out and beliefs about global warming being ruled in.[32]

In a Canada characterized by growing religious diversity, the question is how can harmony be achieved among the pro-religious, no religious, and those in the religious middle? When the numbers of people involved in certain groups are relatively small – as has been the case with groups like Doukhobors or Jehovah's Witnesses – they can be labelled deviant, dismissed as "sects" and "cults," and have minimal impact on society as a whole. However, when their numbers are sizable, as is the case with Roman Catholics or Muslims in Canada, the potential for

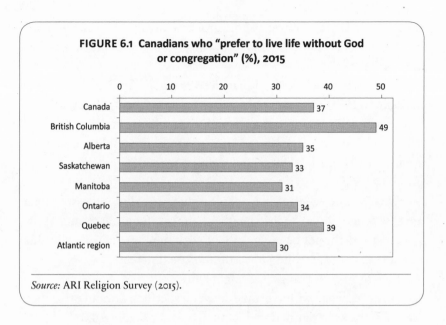

FIGURE 6.1 Canadians who "prefer to live life without God or congregation" (%), 2015

Canada	37
British Columbia	49
Alberta	35
Saskatchewan	33
Manitoba	31
Ontario	34
Quebec	39
Atlantic region	30

Source: ARI Religion Survey (2015).

conflict with everyone else – including conflict with those of other religious persuasions – is very high.

For their part, some atheists and other people who reject religion have become far more vocal in recent years, including in Canada (Figure 6.1). Ted Peters, a Lutheran theologian at the Graduate Theological Union at Berkeley, has noted that "it used to be that atheists didn't bother anybody. They simply stayed home from church on Sunday and avoided praying. The social impact was minimal. But now," he says, "a new breed of atheists is zealously crusading to liberate the world from the chains of religion."[33]

John Allemang of the *Globe and Mail* has summed things up this way: "Proponents of atheism have found their comfort zone in the modern Western world, where penalties for infidelity are few but the residual sense of outrage is still strong enough to propel their attacks on a no-longer vengeful God to the top of the bestseller lists."[34] The "new atheists" are passionate. And they are being widely read, seen, and heard.

So it is that both the range and the elasticity of Canada's mosaic are being severely tested in the case of religion. One issue is polarization involving those who are religious and those who are not. A second important issue is polarization between some groups – notably Muslims but also other groups that sometimes take on culture, such as evangelicals – and everyone else.

The idea that racial and cultural diversity is good for Canada is scarcely in doubt today. Our Project Canada surveys have found that large majorities of people who variously value or dismiss religion endorse the idea.[35] What has been said of the United States seems as applicable or even more applicable to Canada: "Diversity is right up there with progress, motherhood, and apple pie."[36]

What's more, when we ask people if they are willing at least to tolerate how others choose to live their lives, almost all indicate that they are. Canadians might not be excited about what other people do and think. But at least they are willing to accommodate differences.

So far so good. Things just might work.

However, when we pin people down on specifics, we notice that there are a few cracks in our national religious mosaic (Table 6.6).

- Canadians are pretty much split 50-50 on whether or not the decline in religious participation has been a bad thing for Canada. They are also equally divided on the impact of religion on the world.
- Seven in 10 people who reject religion think that atheism is a good thing for Canada, while 9 in 10 who embrace faith disagree.
- Not surprisingly, 8 in 10 people who reject religion say that they "prefer to live life without God or congregation," compared with 1 in 10 people who embrace religion.
- In each case, those in the religious middle own up to their designation: they come in almost right down the middle in their views on the impact of declining involvement, the impact of religion on the world, atheism being good for the country, and preferring to live life without God or congregation.

All right, you say, Canadians with different outlooks on religion would obviously have different views on the merits of religion and its place in their lives. But that's not to say that these differences translate into tension or apprehension when they relate to each other. Good point.

TABLE 6.6 Attitudes toward religion by religious inclinations (%), 2015

Agree	All	Embrace	Middle	Reject
The decline in religious involvement has been a bad thing for Canada.	48	86	44	11
The growth in atheism is a good thing for life in Canada.	33	10	27	69
The impact of religion on the world is positive.	51	80	52	15
I prefer to live life without God or congregation.	37	9	31	79

Source: ARI Religion Survey (2015).

We don't cover everything in our surveys, but we did anticipate this question, so we asked our survey participants to respond to two statements.

❶ Generally speaking, I feel a bit uncomfortable around people who are religiously devout.

❷ Generally speaking, I feel a bit uncomfortable around people who have no use for religion.

What we found is that 43% of Canadians feel uncomfortable around people who are devout (Figure 6.2). Conversely, only about half that number – 22% – indicate feelings of discomfort around individuals who have no use for religion.

It's not as simple as the devout being comfortable around the devout and the non-religious being comfortable around the non-religious. Rather, generally speaking, people feel awkward around the devout more than around the non-devout. The feeling of cross-group discomfort is much more prevalent among the non-religious (63%) than among the religious (41%). Interestingly, people in the religious middle express almost equal levels of ease/unease around both the religiously devout (44%) and those who have no use for religion (41%).

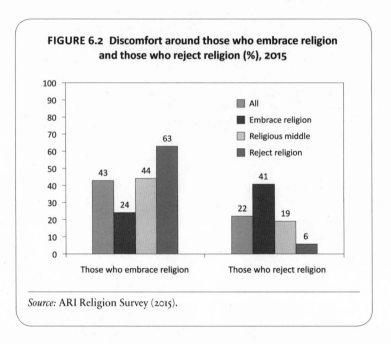

FIGURE 6.2 Discomfort around those who embrace religion and those who reject religion (%), 2015

Legend:
- All
- Embrace religion
- Religious middle
- Reject religion

Those who embrace religion: 43, 24, 44, 63
Those who reject religion: 22, 41, 19, 6

Source: ARI Religion Survey (2015).

Beyond generalities, we got more specific and more personal with our questions. We asked Canadians "how positive, neutral, or negative do you tend to feel?" toward 10 groups, including atheists.

Lest we think that we are even close to full acceptance of all Canadians – especially when it comes to religion – we need to think again. The groups receiving the most positive assessments are Roman Catholics (49%), Protestants (44%), Buddhists (44%), and Jews (39%). But note that no single group receives the positive endorsement of more than 50% of the Canadian population. Further on the downside,

- nearly one in two people say that they have negative feelings about Muslims – a level corroborated by Environics in 2016[37] – with one in three saying the same thing about Mormons;
- about one in four Canadians admit that they have negative feelings about evangelicals, Sikhs, and atheists; and
- Catholics, Jews, Buddhists, and Protestants are the most favoured groups – with each receiving negative expressions from about 1 in 10 Canadians.

Resilient Gods

The 2016 Environics survey of Muslims, by the way, shows that they are well aware of such perceptions. Close to 40% of Muslims think that Canadians have negative views of Islam.[38]

Let's get even a bit more personal. When we look at negative feelings toward certain groups by other religious groups, we find similar rankings (Table 6.7).[39]

▸ Catholics are most negative about Muslims, followed by Mormons and Sikhs (49% to 28%).

▸ Mainline Protestants express negative feelings toward Muslims, Mormons, and evangelicals (39% to 27%).

▸ Evangelicals are often negative about Muslims, Mormons, atheists, Sikhs, Hindus, and Buddhists (56% to 30%).

▸ Other major world faith groups are most negative about Muslims, Mormons, and evangelicals (30% to 26%).

▸ Canadians with no religion are particularly negative toward evangelicals, Mormons, and Muslims, followed by Catholics and Sikhs (44% to 24%). I think here of the poignant comment of Sam Harris in his "letter" to Christians: "Understand that the way you view Islam is precisely the way devout Muslims view Christianity. And it is the way I view all religions."[40]

Canadians who embrace faith differ from others in being considerably less negative about Mormons and evangelicals (Table 6.7). But they are no less likely to be negative about faith groups such as Muslims, Sikhs, Hindus, and Buddhists. Individuals who reject religion tend to be more negative about all religious groups than everyone else – with the exception of Sikhs, Hindus, and Buddhists. Canadians in the religious middle also tend to come down the middle in their feelings about almost all religious groups.

Interestingly, atheists receive the wrath of almost 5 in 10 people who embrace faith but only about 1 in 10 who comprise the religious middle. As noted, those who reject religion return the favour in the case of evangelicals specifically, with 5 in 10 admitting that they have negative feelings about the people whom sociologists commonly refer to as "Conservative Protestants."

TABLE 6.7 Negative feelings about select religious groups by religious group and inclination (%), 2015

		Religious group					Inclination		
	All	Roman Catholic	Mainline Protestant	Conservative Protestant	Other faiths	No religion	Embrace	Middle	Reject
Muslims	44	49	39	54	27	40	45	42	48
Mormons	35	30	27	50	26	44	32	29	48
Evangelicals	27	18	28	6	30	47	12	22	51
Sikhs	26	28	24	40	15	24	31	21	29
Atheists	22	22	25	56	19	5	48	16	4
Hindus	16	13	14	36	7	15	22	11	16
Roman Catholics	13	4	10	16	19	27	8	8	29
Jews	12	13	5	10	9	16	11	9	18
Buddhists	9	8	7	30	3	7	17	6	7
Protestants	8	7	1	6	7	15	7	5	14

Source: ARI Religion Survey (2015).

The reason for getting into these descriptive specifics is by way of calling things the way they are. We have been making considerable progress when it comes to realizing the Canadian dream of a harmonious mosaic. But these findings show that we still have a considerable distance to go when it comes to religion.

Some quick reflections on the high level of negative feelings toward Muslims. Abdie Kazemipur, my close departmental colleague for nearly two decades, has much to say. He is one of Canada's foremost experts on immigration generally and Muslims specifically. In 2014, he wrote an award-winning book entitled *The Muslim Question in Canada*.

Kazemipur maintains that negative sentiments about Muslims are rooted in the belief that they are either unwilling or unable to integrate into immigrant-receiving countries for religious and cultural reasons. He reminds readers that Muslims who come to Canada are not a monolithic group. About 70% who arrived in the early 2000s came from eight different countries – a level matched only by Protestants. This diversity means that their expressions of Islam come from a wide range of different cultures and societies.[41] Far from wanting to confront and challenge life in Canada, most say that they have come to Canada precisely because of its peaceful environment. Their lack of integration, Kazemipur maintains, is the result not of theology and belief but of social factors.

Relationally, the keys to integration are the institutional, media, economic, and social domains. Kazemipur says that his research indicates few problems in the first two instances: there are no major biases against Muslims in public institutions and the media. "However," he notes, "Muslims face major challenges in the economic and social domains. Furthermore, a big portion of the economic challenges seems to be related to the limited integration of Muslims into social spaces."[42]

Kazemipur argues that the mainstream population and institutions "need to genuinely engage with Muslims, and Muslims need to view Canada as their home – as opposed to a temporary place of residence." Barring a violent incident that disrupts the positive flow, "I predict," he says, "that this mutual engagement is what is most likely to occur in Canada."[43]

Environics offers some important relevant findings on Muslims in its *Survey of Muslims in Canada 2016*.[44]

- In 2006, 73% of Muslims said that they were "very proud" to be Canadian; by 2016, the figure had risen to 83%.
- The top sources of pride in both surveys were freedom, diversity, and peace (total of about 60%). The feature liked least? Cold weather.
- Their primary concerns were the economy and unemployment.
- In the October 2015 federal election, 79% said that they voted, with 65% choosing the Liberals, 10% the New Democrats, and 2% the Conservatives.
- The latest survey found that 84% viewed being Muslim as an important part of personal identity; 81% said the same thing about being Canadian. And 41% said that their attachment to Islam has become stronger since they came to Canada; another 52% said that it hasn't changed; just 5% said that it has become weaker.
- As of early 2016, 53% of Muslim women said that they wear a headcovering in public – up from 42% in 2006. The hijab was readily the most common (48%); only 6% indicated that they wear either the chador or the niqab (3% each).
- Finally, 53% think that Muslims want to adopt Canadian customs, while 17% think that they want to remain distinct; in contrast, the corresponding figures for non-Muslims are 34% and 43% respectively.

All in all, Muslims are hardly an alien group of people who differ very much from the general population.

These findings indicate that extensive negative feelings and considerable uneasiness characterize people who value faith and people who don't. In addition, the fact that a significant segment of the population continues to see faith as important does not necessarily mean that they are one harmonious, collective bunch. Quite clearly, a fair amount of negativism also characterizes how people in religious groups see each other.

About 15 years ago, Michael Valpy and Joe Friesen noted that moral issues and other issues pit many religious groups against majority public opinion. They suggested that "faith groups may find more common ground with one another than with secular institutions." They added that there is "growth of a kind of militant secularism among non-believers ...

that treats the religious as unenlightened or backward."[45] Radical though the possibility might sound to some, religious groups would be wise to try to stick together. The evidence to date suggests, however, that they are often at odds with each other rather than exploring and finding commonalities that would enhance their collective clout. That may change, or maybe not.

Confidence in Religious Leaders

In recent decades, confidence in religious leaders has dropped considerably. One reason has been the fact that growing numbers of people have been opting out of religion. But, for some, related factors have included alienation as a result of serious problems relating to things like the legacy of religious group involvement in residential schools, along with sexual abuse, particularly involving Roman Catholic clergy.

The net result has been a serious decline in the confidence of leaders over the past 40 years. What is noteworthy is that the drop-off was particularly sharp in the late 1980s, when there was extensive attention given to scandals that included the Mount Cashel orphanage and the fall of a number of prominent American televangelists. The problems south of the border seemed to have an impact on religion on this side of the border as well.

However, despite the ongoing publicity given to various scandals, confidence in religious leaders has remained about the same since 1990. Smaller declines in recent years would seem to largely reflect growth in the no-religion segment of the Canadian population (Figure 6.3).

What about participation? Have people been staying away as a result of waning confidence in religious leaders? The short answer appears to be "not really." Many people seem to have distinguished between the church and faith that they value versus their very human leaders.

That surprisingly pervasive resiliency was verbalized a few years back by *Toronto Star* columnist Angelo Persichilli:

> I am a Catholic. Even though, I must confess, I'm not a good one ...
> Pedophilia is a crime, and those responsible for that crime must be punished. But at the same time, I cannot approve of the politically motivated posturing over these crimes and the denigration of the entire institution

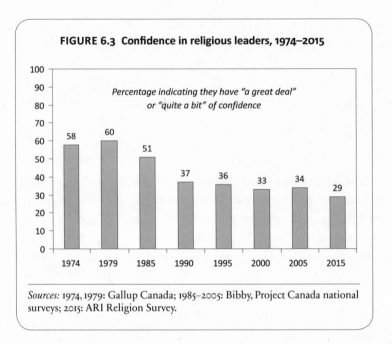

FIGURE 6.3 Confidence in religious leaders, 1974–2015

Percentage indicating they have "a great deal"
or "quite a bit" of confidence

Year	Value
1974	58
1979	60
1985	51
1990	37
1995	36
2000	33
2005	34
2015	29

Sources: 1974, 1979: Gallup Canada; 1985–2005: Bibby, Project Canada national surveys; 2015: ARI Religion Survey.

of the Catholic Church. The Catholic Church will eradicate pedophiles from its ranks ... And today, I'll go to mass.[46]

Some Summary Thoughts

The reality of religious polarization in Canada raises at least two important questions for social well-being. First, to what extent does a society like ours benefit or not benefit from the presence of religion versus the absence of it? As Valpy and Friesen put it, the shift away from religion has raised "profound questions about our social values."[47] Second, to what extent can people with divergent postures toward religion – variously embracing, rejecting, or taking a middle position – coexist?

These illustrative findings on values, civility, and behaviour point to a significant preliminary conclusion: religion is one important source of positive interpersonal life. It is only one source, but a source it is. To the extent that religion is contributing to social compassion in Canada, a decline in the proportion of people who embrace faith will be associated with a decline in social well-being. It's not that the contribution of religion cannot be made up by other sources. But until such sources are located and become operative, social well-being in Canada is going to take a hit.

A second disconcerting finding is that religious polarization is accompanied by considerable discomfort with each other among people who value faith and those who do not. In addition, contrary to the spirit of pluralism, Canadians are expressing a lot of negativism toward a large number of religious groups, notably Muslims.

In short, when it comes to religion, there are more than a few cracks in our hallowed mosaic. Yes, they might always have been there. One has only to think of historical hostility of Protestants toward Catholics, of Protestants and Catholics toward Jehovah's Witnesses, of prejudice directed at Jews, and of punitive responses to those who would dare to practise Aboriginal spirituality.

But this is the 21st century. We are supposed to be exhibiting respect for – or at least tolerance of – differences. When it comes to religion and the lack of religion, we have a considerable distance to go.

The Global Situation

Helping Behaviour

In recent years, Gallup has released extensive survey findings on acts of compassion. Focusing initially on the United States, Canada, and Britain, the pollster's samples now include all regions of the world.[48] Gallup has asked people what we repeated in Canada in 2015 – if they have donated money, volunteered time, or helped a stranger "in the past month." The Gallup surveys show that highly religious people are more likely than others to have engaged in each of the three kinds of behaviour (Table 6.8). What's more, the relationships are consistent not only across global regions but also "across the world's largest faith traditions, including Christianity, Islam, Hinduism, and Judaism." For example, Gallup researchers report that "differences for helping a stranger" range "from 7 percentage points among Buddhists to 15 points among Jews."[49]

More detailed analyses of the Gallup data have found that a key factor is attendance at religious services. They have suggested that such a finding points to the importance of community – and not just beliefs or the subjective importance of religion – to individuals.[50]

TABLE 6.8 Helping behaviour globally by level of religiosity (%), 2006–8

| | Those who have in the past month ... | | | | | |
| | Donated money | | Volunteered time | | Helped a stranger | |
	Highly religious	Less religious	Highly religious	Less religious	Highly religious	Less religious
Europe	43	28	24	17	42	36
Asia	41	26	24	19	46	37
Americas	39	28	29	18	56	49
Africa	23	15	27	17	52	43

Note: Gallup defines "highly religious" people as those who report that religion is important to their daily lives and report having attended a religious service in the week prior to being surveyed. All others are categorized as "less religious."
Source: Gallup World Poll analyses by Pelham and Crabtree (2008).

Development Assistance

On a national level, to what extent do relatively affluent countries show generosity to countries in need of assistance?

The results are mixed. According to recent figures provided by a key monitoring body, the Organisation for Economic Co-operation and Development (OECD), in absolute terms the top 10 donors are the United States, Britain, Germany, France, Japan, Sweden, the Netherlands, Norway, Australia, and Canada. The overall correlation between service attendance and giving in real dollars is both positive and appreciable. However, if giving is computed as a percentage of gross national income, then the correlation between attendance and giving is actually negative. One's conclusion here is based on one's judgment about whether appropriate and significant giving is "how much" versus "what proportion" based on capabilities. Attendance gets a B on the former, a D on the latter (Table 6.9).

Trust and Crime

Still other measures of positive interpersonal life might be trust and crime. An examination of attendance, trust, and crime in a sample of 29 countries reveals that a modest positive relationship exists between trust

TABLE 6.9 National development assistance for select countries, 2015

Country	Religious service attendance (%)	Donations for development assistance ($US billions)	Donations as a percentage of gross national income
Poland	64	0.44	0.10
Ireland	56	0.72	0.36
Italy	*48*	*3.84*	*0.21*
United States	*46*	*31.1*	*0.17*
Portugal	39	0.4	0.16
Austria	35	1.2	0.32
Greece	33	0.3	0.14
Spain	31	1.6	0.13
Germany	*30*	*16.6*	*0.52*
Japan	*29*	*9.3*	*0.22*
Switzerland	28	3.5	0.52
Luxembourg	27	0.4	0.92
Canada	*27*	*4.3*	*0.28*
New Zealand	*26*	*0.4*	*0.27*
Netherlands	23	5.8	0.76
Belgium	23	1.9	0.42
Australia	*21*	*3.2*	*0.27*
United Kingdom	*20*	*18.7*	*0.71*
France	*19*	*9.2*	*0.37*
Denmark	16	2.6	0.85
Norway	15	4.3	1.05
Finland	13	1.3	0.56
Sweden	13	7.2	1.40

Note: Italic type indicates G-20 countries. As of early 2016, there were 34 OECD member countries.
Sources: Attendance: Stark (2015); *Contributions:* OECD (2016).

and a lower crime rate. But attendance by itself is not positively related either to trust or to a low crime rate.

In countries such as South Africa, Mexico, and Brazil, for example, service attendance is fairly high – well above the levels in places like

TABLE 6.10 Attendance, trust, and crime in select countries

	Attendance in prior seven days (%)	Trust (%) ("most people in society are trustworthy")	Crime rate per 100,000 population
Nigeria	90	32	1.3
India	67	54	2.8
Malaysia	67	56	2.3
Philippines	65	–	6.4
Poland	64	48	1.2
Mexico	58	46	11.6
South Africa	58	42	36.5
Pakistan	56	54	6.8
Palestinian Territories	52	34	3.9
Brazil	49	35	22.0
Italy	48	41	1.2
Iran	47	–	2.9
United States	46	58	5.2
Israel	35	42	2.4
Korea, Republic of	35	46	2.3
Spain	31	43	0.9
Germany	30	56	0.8
Japan	29	43	0.5
Canada	27	71	1.7
Ukraine	24	47	6.3
Australia	21	–	1.2
United Kingdom	20	65	1.4
France	19	45	1.4
Norway	15	–	0.6
Russia	15*	50	14.2
Czech Republic	14	42	2.0
Sweden	13	78	0.9

Sources: Attendance: Stark (2015); * Gallup WorldView (2010); *Trust:* Pew (2008); *Crime rate:* UN Office on Drugs and Crime (2010).

Canada, Britain, and Sweden. Yet crime rates in those settings are significantly above those of Canada and the other two countries, and – predictably – levels of trust are much lower (Table 6.10).

These global findings underline the complexity of whether or not religion has an impact on both trust and crime in every social or geographical setting around the world. In some settings where cultures of crime, violence, and corruption have been rampant historically – such as the Philippines, Africa, Latin America, and the Middle East – religious devotion by a variety of measures has been high. However, religion all by itself has hardly turned around the quality of life in those places. Conversely, countries such as Canada and the United States along with European countries – including Britain, France, Poland, Germany, and Sweden – seemingly have come to know high levels of safety and civility, with religion at best being only one of the contributors.

In short, the global portrait shows that religion is sometimes an important source of enhanced interpersonal life; in other instances, it has little effect.

The findings remind us that religion typically has an impact on individuals and societies to the extent that it can work with and through other institutions – such as families, schools, governments, private industry, and media – positioned to influence personal and collective life. Without that kind of social reinforcement, religion finds it difficult to have a significant, unique impact in any setting.

Coexistence

As I have been arguing throughout the book, religious polarization is found everywhere. Globally, there are currently more than 2 billion Christians, 1.5 billion Muslims, and 1 billion Hindus – easily the three largest religions. Together, they comprise some 70% of the world's 7 billion people (Figure 6.4). Other religions account for another 15%. A further 15%, just over 1 billion people, are unaffiliated – the global "religious nones."

In any given country, those numbers are associated with Christian, Muslim, and Hindu monopolies or minorities, who are joined by varying numbers of people with no religion. Consequently, the question of how

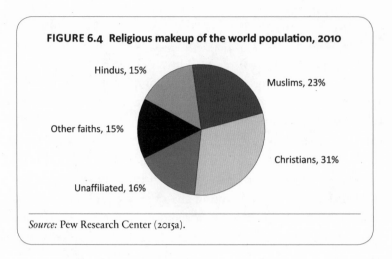

FIGURE 6.4 Religious makeup of the world population, 2010

Hindus, 15%

Muslims, 23%

Other faiths, 15%

Christians, 31%

Unaffiliated, 16%

Source: Pew Research Center (2015a).

well people with diverse postures toward religion and each other can coexist is being raised right across the planet.

The question has become all the more important in recent years because of two significant developments. The first is the historically unprecedented number of Muslims who have been migrating from predominantly Muslim countries to other parts of the world (Table 6.11). The second is the alarming amount of violence and terrorism associated with some militant Muslim organizations, notably al-Qaeda and, more recently, the Islamic State in Iraq and Syria (ISIS).

As Michael Lipka of the Pew Research Center has recently pointed out, migration and the impact of acts of violence carried out by groups in the name of Islam "have brought Muslims and the Islamic faith to the forefront of the political debate in many countries."[51] We have already seen that more than 44% of Canadians express negative feelings toward Muslims. In the United States, a similar item run by the Pew Research Center in 2014 found that 41% of Americans also expressed negative feelings toward Muslims.[52]

In Europe, anti-Muslim sentiments have been highly publicized in recent years. Here again the survey work of the Pew Research Center is informative.[53] Pew asked people in 10 European countries in 2016 whether they held favourable or unfavourable views of Muslims in their respective countries (Figure 6.5).

TABLE 6.11 Muslim populations in select countries (millions), 2010, 2030, 2050

	2010	2030 (projected)	2050 (projected)
World totals	1,599.7	2,209.3	2,761.5
Canada	0.7	1.4	2.3
United States	2.8	5.2	8.1
Indonesia	209.1	245.0	256.8
India	176.2	249.0	310.7
Pakistan	167.4	230.4	273.1
Nigeria	77.3	139.6	230.7
Iran	73.6	84.5	86.2
Iraq	31.3	53.2	80.2
China	24.7	30.8	35.3
Syria	18.9	26.2	31.2
Russia	14.3	17.7	20.9
Philippines	5.2	7.5	9.4
Germany	4.8	6.1	7.0
France	4.7	6.1	7.5
United Kingdom	3.0	5.1	7.8
Italy	2.2	3.6	5.3
Spain	1.0	2.3	3.9
Greece	0.6	0.7	0.8
Australia	0.5	0.9	1.4
Sweden	0.4	0.9	1.4
Japan	0.2	0.2	0.3
Poland	<0.1	<0.1	<0.1
Brazil	<0.1	<0.1	<0.1

Source: Pew Research Center (2015a).

- Negative sentiments were expressed by about 70% of respondents in Hungary, Italy, Poland, and Greece, and 50% in Spain. As Table 6.11 shows, relatively few Muslims live in these five countries.
- In the Netherlands and Sweden, negative attitudes dropped to 35%, falling further to around 30% in France, Germany, and the United Kingdom.

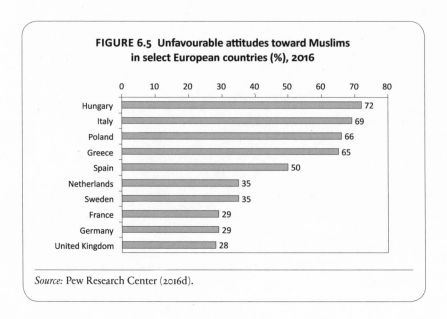

FIGURE 6.5 Unfavourable attitudes toward Muslims in select European countries (%), 2016

Source: Pew Research Center (2016d).

Obviously, negative and positive responses to Muslims will fluctuate and need to be monitored. Ongoing acts of violence, as well as mixed reactions to new developments such as the recent influx of large numbers of Syrian refugees, will undoubtedly affect public attitudes pretty much everywhere.

As might be expected, in national settings where religious monopolies exist, people are more likely than those in other countries to think that "most faiths" make positive contributions to their societies.[54] But religious monopolies in particular don't seem to be conducive to promoting religious tolerance.

Predictably, in countries where Islamic monopolies exist, attitudes toward Muslims are positive. Those sentiments are somewhat more restrained toward Christians, except in Lebanon. Attitudes toward Jews are extremely negative. In India, the dominance of Hinduism is associated with fairly positive opinions of Christians, somewhat less positive views of Muslims, and very negative attitudes toward Jews.

In European and North American settings characterized by religious polarization, including Canada, there is a tendency for positive views of all three groups to be far higher than elsewhere.

Resilient Gods

TABLE 6.12 Views of Christians, Jews, and Muslims
of each other in select countries (% indicating "very"
or "somewhat" favourable opinion), 2005

	Christians	Jews	Muslims
Religious monopoly			
Indonesia	58	13	99
Jordan	58	0	99
Morocco	33	8	97
Pakistan	22	5	94
Lebanon	91	0	92
Turkey	21	18	83
India	61	28	46
Polarization			
United States	87	77	57
Poland	86	54	46
Germany	83	67	40
Canada	83	78	60
Netherlands	83	85	45
Spain	80	58	46
Secular monopoly			
Russia	92	63	55
United Kingdom	85	78	72
France	84	82	64
China	26	28	20

Source: Computed from Pew Research Center (2005).

In countries where secular monopolies exist after years of Christian dominance, a "shadow effect" seems to contribute to very positive attitudes not only toward Christians but also toward Jews and Muslims. In China, where all three groups have known a limited presence historically, favourable attitudes are low (Table 6.12).

In the immediate future, religious polarization might turn out to be subsumed under the umbrella of pluralism in Canada and other places. In fact, somewhat ironically, there is reason to believe that the current religious polarization we are experiencing might actually be a plus for pluralism. The fact that Canada is characterized by neither a religious monopoly nor a secular monopoly might contribute to an enhanced capacity to handle religious and non-religious diversity. Balance might be best. We'll see.

One important cause for pause. We have already seen that immigration, on balance, is currently functioning as a plus in Canada for the pro-religious camp. Yet immigrants – led by Catholics and Muslims – while religiously zealous are also inclined to hold more conservative views of sexuality and family life than other Canadians (Table 6.13).

Here the "balance may be best" argument gains strength. In light of the national enshrinement of diversity, one could argue that any excesses on the part of conservative immigrants may well be offset, in particular, by people in the no-religious camp. Put pointedly, in a pluralistic Canada, if religious folk fail to honour diversity, the call for diversity will be invoked by people who are not religious.

Here Canada may provide something of a case example for what may well be true in other countries around the world.

TABLE 6.13 **Attitudes toward same-sex marriage by religious inclinations and birthplace (%), 2015**

	All	Embrace	Middle	Reject
All				
Approve and accept	63	40	70	78
Disapprove but accept	21	29	21	13
Disapprove and do not accept	16	31	9	9
Born in Canada				
Approve and accept	65	43	72	80
Disapprove but accept	21	29	20	12
Disapprove and do not accept	14	29	8	8
Born outside Canada				
Approve and accept	47	29	54	68
Disapprove but accept	24	25	26	18
Disapprove and do not accept	29	46	20	14

Source: ARI Religion Survey (2015).

Incidentally, the question of how religious polarization can coexist with religious pluralism in the United States has been raised explicitly by Robert Putnam and David Campbell. They maintain that, for all the attention given to existing and potential division, "America peacefully combines a high degree of religious devotion with tremendous religious diversity – including growing ranks of nonreligious Americans." The fluidity of American religion, they say, means that nearly all Americans are acquainted with people of different religious backgrounds. "All of this religious churn produces a jumble of relationships among people ... which keeps religious polarization from pulling the nation apart."[55]

In recent years, one of the more articulate, influential, and strident spokespersons for the potential of religion to contribute to society has been Karen Armstrong. A former nun and self-proclaimed "freelance monotheist," she has maintained that Christianity, Islam, and Judaism share a common basic bottom line that can be summed up in the proverbial Golden Rule – treating others the way that we would want them to treat us. With the help of the TED Foundation, she unveiled a "Charter of Compassion" in November 2009 that attempts to inspire "worldwide community-based acts of compassion."[56] What will evoke such compassion, she said in a March 2009 interview with journalist Bill Moyers, is "basically a sense of urgent need."[57]

Assessment

These findings point to a fairly consistent pattern in both Canada and around the world: people who are religious are more likely than others to endorse positive interpersonal values and exhibit positive interpersonal behaviour. Put far more succinctly and provocatively, for all the bad publicity, religion appears on balance to be making a noteworthy contribution to social well-being.

Religion typically has a positive influence to the extent that it is associated with other institutions that have positive impacts on interpersonal life. American political scientist Walter Russell Mead comments that, in various parts of the world, one can readily uncover "young Muslims who have only a narrow and sectarian education, and young Pentecostals who know very little outside of their Bibles. God may have a special love for the poor," he says, "but that does not mean that the poor get sophisticated religion. They get strong religion and hot religion more than they get subtle religion and sophisticated religion." The result can be a dangerous world.[58]

The findings also make it clear that religion is not the only source of civility. Far from it. Without question, people can be good without God. Nonetheless, religion, for all its dark sides, is one important source of civility.

Such a finding should hardly come as a surprise. When we stop to think about it, it is fairly readily apparent that few institutions and organizations have the enhancement of interpersonal life as one of their foremost goals. Religions typically have such a goal. It is a central part of what they are about.

Some might argue that Canada and much of Europe benefit from the aforementioned shadow effect of Christian legacies – sort of like the after-effects that our parents and grandparents have on our lives long after they are gone. Historian Mark Noll, for example, has suggested that Canada has not abandoned its "communal social order" – just "the Christian presence that did so much to build" it.[59]

Those claims undoubtedly carry some truth. But one can also argue that shadows disappear with time – that some semblance of their sources needs to exist if they themselves are to live on. Such would seem to be the case with religion in Canada.

Toronto Star journalist Carol Goar pointed out a short time ago that "faith-based organizations are the bedrock of Canada's charitable sector." She noted that they run homeless shelters and transition homes for abused women; offer asylum to refugees and settlement assistance to immigrants; set up after-school programs for kids in troubled neighbourhoods; organize soup kitchens; open their doors to seniors, community groups, and service clubs; raise millions of dollars "for good works"; and mobilize thousands of volunteers. But, Goar wrote, "as their membership rolls shrink and their collection plates lighten, they are struggling to maintain this network of charitable activities." She concluded with these strong words: "It is fine to say – as the majority of Canadians do – that you prefer to explore your own spirituality, practise your religion privately and ponder metaphysical questions in solitude. But look around. There's a world in need out there. Church members are on the front lines, putting their faith to work. They could use some help."[60]

The concerns raised by Goar received considerable support from an important analysis released in 2009. Ray Pennings and Michael Van Pelt of Cardus – a think tank that examines cultural, social, and religious intersections in Canada – note that the crucial civic sector, with its array of charitable and non-profit organizations, accounts for just under 10% of Canada's gross domestic product. This "third sector," distinct from the public and private sectors, is driven disproportionately by a small core of citizens: about 20% of adults donate 80% of the money given to charities, while about 10% of adults provide 80% of the hours volunteered.[61] The imminent problem raised by Pennings and Van Pelt is that the vast majority of people in this "civic core" are older and often religious. As they pass from the scene, many organizations and charities will feel the effects.

An ongoing Statistics Canada survey series on giving and volunteering corroborates such an assertion. The latest survey in the series, conducted in 2013, found that Canadians who attend weekly religious services were more likely than other people to be among the top donors and volunteers.[62]

Maclean's has offered this provocative take on the findings over the years: "If religion is simply a license for bad behaviour, how does one explain the mammoth gap between the charitable acts of those who believe and those who do not?" The magazine then posed this important question: "If organized religion continues to fade from mainstream practice, how will society ever replace the massive contributions of time and money that believers currently provide?" *Maclean's* concluded that "spirituality and altruism share an obvious and welcome concern for humanity and its future. Do atheists?"[63]

In the midst of our debates on whether or not religion contributes more or contributes less to optimum social life, perhaps we would be wise to recognize that it has the potential to be one important source of social well-being. But given that significant numbers of Canadians are choosing not to embrace religion, including opting for the religious middle, it is also extremely important to give greater attention to identifying emerging sources of social well-being that can complement the best that faith has to offer. We'll keep the camera running.

The alleged "death of the gods" has been accompanied by a fascinating development – a largely unanticipated explosion in interest in spirituality. To that important development we now turn.

7

Religion versus Spirituality

Spirituality is about what we do with the fire inside of us. The opposite is not a person who rejects the idea of God. It is to have no energy, to have lost all zest for living.

– Ron Rolheiser, *The Holy Longing*, 1999

One of the anomalous features of life in an era of post-religious dominance in Canada has been the high profile and privileged status of spirituality. While religion has been scorned and stigmatized and rejected by many, spirituality has known something of celebrity status. Until recently, it seems, spirituality was strongly associated with religion – something like a family member. But now it seems to have moved out of the house. Spirituality has received fairly remarkable treatment.

▶ It is assumed to be something that exists apart from religion, as in the frequent comment "I am spiritual but not religious." In fact, the phrase has spawned the acronym SBNR and a large number of books, websites (e.g., SBNR.org), and Facebook and Twitter entries.[1]
▶ Spirituality is typically viewed as superior to religion. "I'm spiritual but not religious" is often said and heard as a triumphant

declaration – greeted on the talk-show circuit with a positive nod from the host and even a polite ovation.

▶ It doesn't carry any of the negative baggage of religion. When one says "I'm spiritual," the slate is clean. People who say "I'm Catholic," or "I'm Muslim," or "I'm born again" hardly receive the same response.

Some pro-religious individuals who link spirituality to religion decry the growing lack of religion in people's lives and fear a future of unmet spiritual needs. Those who place importance on spirituality but not religion have few such concerns.

The Autonomy of Spirituality

In his best-selling book *The Holy Longing*, Ron Rolheiser asks the question "What do Mother Teresa, Janis Joplin, and Princess Diana have in common?" His answer? All were spiritual. More precisely, all three had spiritualities.[2]

Rolheiser argues that the term "spirituality" is badly understood today. It's not about certain activities like going to church, praying, or engaging in a spiritual quest, he says. Rather, all of us are born with a restlessness like a fire. "We have to do something about the fire that burns within us," he writes. "What we do with that fire, how we channel it, is our spirituality."[3]

The dominant choices that the three women made were very different, with life-giving versus life-destroying consequences. But, Rolheiser explains, how they directed their energies comprised their spiritualities.[4] While he attempts to clarify what spirituality "really" is, the meaning of the term in everyday life is pretty much up for grabs. One can seemingly be spiritual in ways limited only by one's imagination. Few other concepts get such a definitional exemption. A tree is a tree; a puck is a puck; but spirituality – well, in our culture, it's whatever a person says it is. Spirituality is seemingly in the eye of the beholder.

The result is that we have spiritualities of every shape and make. The "About Us" statement on SBNR.org declares that it "serves the global population of individuals who walk a spiritual path outside traditional religion." The website notes that "the SBNR community is very diverse" and that "there is no single SBNR belief system." Visitors to the website are invited to "share your opinions and convictions as you might at a dinner party, with good manners and a measured demeanor."[5]

When we have asked Canadians "what do you mean by spirituality?" about the best that our coders have been able to do is classify the responses into "conventional" and "less conventional" categories and then add subcategories. The first refers to expressions of spirituality that have fairly traditional religious connotations. The second refers to, well, essentially everything else. What stands out about the less conventional responses is how subjective and individualistic they tend to be. One searches largely in vain for threads of commonality (Table 7.1).

If we were to group 100 people at a conference into tables of five and ask them to discuss their views of spirituality, I think we would quickly

TABLE 7.1 **What Canadians mean by "spirituality"**

Classification of response	What spirituality means
Conventional (52%)	▸ Living in fellowship with Christ ▸ Believing in God and the Bible ▸ Believing that God is there for us, hears our prayers, and answers them ▸ Needing God's spirit to guide, protect, and support us in good times and bad ▸ Building a personal relationship with Jesus Christ ▸ Nourishing our souls so that we can be closer to God
Less conventional (48%)	▸ A matter relating to our inner selves or souls ▸ Peace of mind ▸ A feeling of oneness with the Earth and everything within us ▸ The existence of an immortal soul that has to be cared for ▸ Positive thinking and excitement ▸ Appreciation of the beauty of nature ▸ The love of family and friends ▸ Inner awareness

Source: Adapted from Bibby (2006, 186).

discover that about all they have in common is the word. Incidentally, my research does not indicate that things are changing very much: the responses to "what do you mean by spirituality?" are as diverse today as they have ever been.

Charles Taylor cautions that, while the expressions are highly varied, many young people today are "following their own spiritual instincts" in looking for a direct experience of the sacred. He writes that the search "often springs from a profound dissatisfaction with a life encased entirely in the immanent order," where people sense "that this life is empty, flat, devoid of higher purpose."[6]

Perhaps. But the diversity of what is available in what Wade Clark Roof calls "a spiritual marketplace"[7] makes one wonder where the cutting points are between meaning and marketing, searching and selling. A simple website search for "spirituality online Canada," for example, includes a link to Walmart Canada with the heading "Buy Religion and Spirituality Online"![8]

The choices seem unlimited – and they are growing. A cursory look at book offerings, websites, and conferences provides a sense of the varied "takes" on spirituality.

▸ The conventionally religious can find titles like Henri Nouwen's *A Spirituality of Living*, Phyllis Tickle's *Spiritual Practices*, William Young's novel *The Shack*, Brian McLaren's *Naked Spirituality*, or Richard Rohr's *What the Mystics Know*, as well as titles offering Islamic, Buddhist, Jewish, Hindu, and Sikh takes on spirituality.[9]

▸ For those who want something a bit different, there are books like *The Secret, Aboriginal Spirituality and Biblical Theology, Celtic Spirituality, Mormon Spirituality, Wiccan Spirituality, The Spirituality of Sex, The Spirituality of Wine,* and *The Spirituality of Pets.*[10] Additional titles treating topics like crystals, spirit guides, and channelling have exploded through new self-publishing options that include Amazon's Kindle Direct Publishing.

▸ The burgeoning choices of titles also include many that explicitly omit gods from the equation. They include offerings like *God without God, Parenting without God, The Little Book of Atheist Spirituality, Spirituality without God, The Christian Atheist,* and *The*

Homemade Atheist, with the subtitle *A Former Evangelical Woman's Freethought Journey to Happiness.*[11]

▶ *Vancouver Sun* columnist Douglas Todd notes in the introduction to his edited volume on spirituality in the Pacific Northwest that his contributors "agree that one does not have to adhere to a religion to be spiritual." He adds that "contributors to the volume may go one step further: we assume that atheists, who live in record numbers in Cascadia, can and are making profound contributions to this region's particular sense of spirituality and place."[12]

▶ As of early 2016, a Google search of "spirituality websites" provided about 2,450,000 results. Websites were offering material on everything imaginable. There were also many attempts to make sense of it all through "experts" identifying the "Best Spiritual Sites," "The World's Top 10," and religion and spirituality "Webby Winners."

▶ Companies are aggressively marketing a wide range of spirituality products. For example, a spiritual resource company known as Body Soul and Spirit "showcases products, services, and resources" and "fosters the individual quest for wholeness and self-understanding." It holds both large and small expos with exhibits, speakers, and workshops in cities, including Calgary, Edmonton, Ottawa, Regina, Saskatoon, Vancouver, and Winnipeg.[13]

▶ But one doesn't have to leave one's computer. Online spiritual information and practices abound. One can learn how to be "a spiritual atheist" or engage in "computer spirituality."[14] There's a website that provides instructions on how to raise "your frequency" so that you can access "the Guidance that is always here for you."[15]

▶ A Jewish website, http://www.aish.com, recently featured a thought-provoking article entitled "Spirituality without God," by Sara Yoheved Rigler. "The advantages of spirituality without God are obvious," she wrote. "One can choose one's own direction, methods, and goals without the intrusions of the Divine. The 'inner voice,' which functions as the CEO of most New Age enterprises, rarely tells one what one doesn't want to hear." She reminded readers that a faith like Judaism speaks of a God who not only creates and sustains the universe but also issues orders about things like stealing and adultery. "Little wonder," she said, "that most people resist such encroachments on their personal lives."[16]

▸ Sam Harris, the best-selling atheist author, has displayed what John Allemang of the *Globe and Mail* has called "a mystic streak that allows a little too much room for spiritual fuzziness."[17] By his own admission, Harris finds inspiration in Eastern religions, and he told *Newsweek* in 2010 that his next project was a spiritual guide explaining "how we can live moral and spiritual lives without religion."[18] True to his word, in late 2014 his book, *Waking Up: A Guide to Spirituality without Religion,* appeared.[19]

These days the relationship between religion and spirituality is anything but clear-cut. As Trisha Elliott of the *United Church Observer* has put it, "spirituality in on the rise, yet religion is on the wane. Are we living in a paradox, or in the midst of seismic cultural change?"[20]

The complexity of the religion/spirituality issue has been underlined by the results of our research in Canada. Hopefully, it has also been clarified.

A Canadian Reading

Across the country, 67% of adults acknowledge that they have spiritual needs. So do over 50% of teens.[21] More than 9 in 10 adult Canadians who embrace faith say that they have spiritual needs. But so do about 7 in 10 of those in the religious middle and 4 in 10 of those who reject religion. A check by religious service attendance reveals similar, predictable patterns. Regardless of religious inclinations or attendance levels, women are consistently more likely than men to express spiritual needs (Table 7.2).

A common response by those who value faith is that the findings signal both need and opportunity. The needs are there, and therefore – so the thinking goes – religious groups are well positioned to respond. However, here the caution flag needs to go up.

As we saw earlier with the individualistic and subjective expressions of what Canadians mean by spirituality, what large numbers have in mind when they think of spirituality is not necessarily what the religious groups have in mind or have to offer. It might be analogous to people saying

Resilient Gods

TABLE 7.2 Acknowledgement of spiritual needs by inclination, attendance, and gender (%)

	All	Inclination			Attendance		
		Embrace	Middle	Reject	Monthly +	Yearly	Never
Canada	67	92	68	38	93	69	45
Females	73	94	71	49	94	75	55
Males	61	89	64	30	91	64	35

Source: ARI Religion Survey (2015).

that they are hungry, but what they want to eat is not necessarily what the restaurants – even the specialty venues – have to offer. In an episode of *The Big Bang Theory*, no less, Amy Farrah Fowler verbalizes potential dissonance with this line: "I don't object to the concept of a deity. But I'm baffled by the notion of one that takes attendance."[22]

The SBNR in Canada

Things get a bit more complicated with a growing number of people maintaining that they are spiritual but not religious. Their presence has been acknowledged with the popularization of the designation SBNR, the birth of organizations, and the attention that has been given to them by the media, academics, and religious leaders. Increasingly, they are being more closely studied.[23]

One Canadian researcher who has been taking a close look at the category is Siobhan Chandler. She has examined the prevalence of people identifying as SBNR and some of the category's social engagement correlates.[24] She has further attempted to delineate a variety of SBNR types.[25]

On the religious group front, Gary Paterson, the 41st moderator of the United Church of Canada, recently summed things up this way: "The church in Canada exists in a changed world, a society that is increasingly secular with many 'Nones' (no religious affiliation); 'Dones' (who have a church background, but are no longer interested); 'SBNRs' (Spiritual But Not Religious); and those who are fervently atheist, anti-religion."[26]

As we have already seen, that is a good summation regarding the religious middle and those who reject faith. But it underestimates the numbers and the impact of people who continue to embrace faith. It also leaves us with the need to make sense of the SBNR segment of the population. Given the widespread assertions and assumptions about SBNRs, there is considerable value in obtaining data that help to bring things into focus.

First, to what extent do Canadians actually see themselves as spiritual but not religious? Second, how religiously autonomous are they? Are they, for example, primarily rejecting religion, forming part of the religious middle, or still embracing faith? Third, who exactly are they beyond the common claim that they are disproportionately young? Fourth, to be candid, just how spiritual are they? And fifth, how are they faring when it comes to personal and social well-being?

Prevalence of the SBNR
Our extensive 2015 national survey has found that about 40% of Canadians currently claim that they are "spiritual but not religious." Another 25% or so tell us that they are "religious and spiritual." About 10% indicate that they are "religious but not spiritual," while the remainder – about 25% – report that they are "neither religious nor spiritual" (Figure 7.1).

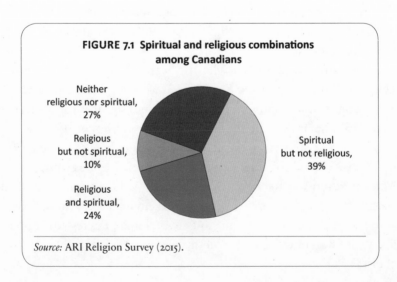

FIGURE 7.1 Spiritual and religious combinations among Canadians

Neither religious nor spiritual, 27%

Religious but not spiritual, 10%

Religious and spiritual, 24%

Spiritual but not religious, 39%

Source: ARI Religion Survey (2015).

Autonomy of the SBNR

It is interesting and important to note that those who are SBNR have not necessarily said goodbye to organized religion. On the contrary, while 3 in 10 never attend services, a majority of 6 in 10 show up on occasion, and a minority of 1 in 10 is equally divided between monthly and weekly attenders.

Looked at as part of the entire Canadian population, some patterns are striking (Table 7.3).

▶ Slightly more females (43%) than males (35%) see themselves as SBNR.

▶ Only 17% are Millennials because even higher proportions of the SBNR are "recruited" from the Gen-X and Boomer ranks, in contrast to the pre-Boomer cohort (born before 1946, 70 and over).

▶ The SBNR self-designation characterizes about 40% of never attenders and 50% of yearly attenders but also 30% of monthly attenders and 15% of weekly attenders.

▶ While the idea that people who have no religion might be inclined to be SBNR, only about 37% are; that percentage is matched or exceeded by the percentage of people in almost every religious group – and is even only slightly above the 30% figure for Conservative, evangelical Protestants.

▶ There is little variation in the presence of SBNR individuals across regions of the country, with the levels ranging from just above 40% in British Columbia and Quebec to a low of 34% in Saskatchewan.

In short, the term "spiritual but not religious" might be largely a misnomer. Just because people describe themselves that way doesn't make it true. The empirical reality is that many have religious links. There is also no truth to the stereotype about SBNRs being top-heavy with Millennials. And what is still unclear is just how spiritual they really are.

It's illuminating to locate SBNRs in the broader context of Canadian religious orientations – relative to those embracing, rejecting, and taking a middle position on religion (Table 7.4). That "peek" at things reveals that the majority of SBNRs (about 60%) are located in the religious

TABLE 7.3 Demographics of those claiming to be SBNR

Demographics		% claiming to be SBNR
Canada		39
Gender	Female	43
	Male	35
Age	Millennials	37
	Gen-Xers	42
	Boomers	41
	Pre-Boomers	29
Attendance	Never	41
	Yearly	48
	Monthly	30
	Weekly	16
Religious group	Roman Catholic: Quebec	44
	Mainline Protestant	39
	Other faith	37
	None	37
	Roman Catholic: outside Quebec	33
	Conservative Protestant	30
Region	British Columbia and Quebec	42
	Alberta	40
	Ontario and Atlantic provinces	37
	Manitoba	36
	Saskatchewan	34

Source: ARI Religion Survey (2015).

middle, with about 25% rejecting faith and about 15% embracing it. Significantly, they are disproportionately located in the religious middle.

The finding that only 25% of SBNRs have not rejected religion suggests that most aren't really that far from "home." Such an assertion is further supported by their responses to two pointed statements: (1) "I sometimes feel guilty for not being more involved in religion," and (2)

Resilient Gods

TABLE 7.4 The spiritual-religious matrix by inclinations (%), 2015

	Embrace	Middle	Reject	Totals
Nationally	30	44	26	100
Spiritual but not religious	14	59	27	100
Religious and spiritual	74	24	2	100
Religious but not spiritual	54	44	2	100
Neither religious nor spiritual	4	40	56	100

Source: ARI Religion Survey (2015).

"I'd be open to more involvement with religious groups if I found it worthwhile."

Of those who are SBNR, 28% admit that they feel a measure of guilt for not being more involved in religion. Further, 39% indicate that they would be open to greater involvement *if* they could find it to be worthwhile. Hardly the responses of people who have shut the door on organized religion.

Practices, Values, and Beliefs of the SBNR

A comparison of SBNR individuals with other Canadians reveals few distinct characteristics.

Data on religious and spiritual salience and practices provided by Statistics Canada's General Social Survey are helpful here. These data permit an examination by service attendance, thereby allowing us to get an indirect reading on many SBNR Canadians who tend to be located in the "yearly" to "never" brackets.

The analysis shows that about 80% of Canadians who are actively involved in religious groups also engage in religious and spiritual activities on their own. That figure drops to about 40% for people who attend services less than monthly and to just under 20% for individuals who never attend services (Figure 7.2). Further, our 2015 national survey found that only about 10% of SBNRs practise spiritual activities online – raising the question of the extent to which SBNR "practices" are either private or public.

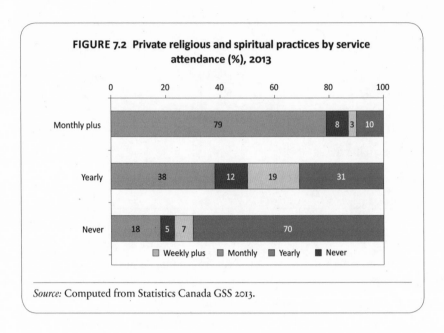

FIGURE 7.2 Private religious and spiritual practices by service attendance (%), 2013

Monthly plus	79	8 3 10
Yearly	38 12 19 31	
Never	18 5 7 70	

Legend: ☐ Weekly plus ☐ Monthly ☐ Yearly ■ Never

Source: Computed from Statistics Canada GSS 2013.

How Spiritual Are the SBNR?

Our 2015 survey findings also raise some important questions about how spiritual SBNRs actually are. Despite describing themselves as spiritual, they are no more likely than those who define themselves as "religious" to acknowledge that they have spiritual needs. They are far less inclined than the "religious and spiritual" to indicate that they actually highly value spirituality – but considerably more likely not to value religion. And, contrary to stereotypes, SBNRs are only marginally more inclined than the "religious and spiritual" to embrace alternative beliefs such as the possibility of having special psychic powers, precognition, or contact with the spirit world (Table 7.5).

When all is said and done, people in Canada and elsewhere who say that they are "spiritual but not religious" may genuinely believe what they are saying. But as social scientists and other onlookers, we have difficulty knowing to what extent the claims are accurate. It appears that many SBNRs are more religious than they think. They are also frequently not as spiritual as they think. Further research is needed to verify and clarify these findings.

TABLE 7.5 Practices, values, and beliefs by the spiritual-religious matrix (%)

	Spiritual but not religious	Religious and spiritual	Religious but not spiritual	Neither religious nor spiritual
Weekly plus				
Reflect on things	81	88	62	52
Practise spiritual activities online	9	19	7	2
Spirituality and religion				
Have spiritual needs	78	94	77	23
Highly value spirituality	30	64	16	2
Highly value religion	5	54	20	<1
Believe in ...				
Psychic powers	62	58	46	31
Contact with the spirit world	61	63	43	25
Precognition	60	53	37	33

Source: ARI Religion Survey (2015).

Well-Being of the SBNR

Apart from the distinct and non-distinct characteristics of people who are spiritual but not religious, how do they fare when it comes to personal and social well-being?

We have already seen that there are only small differences in personal well-being between Canadians who value faith and others. This lack of variation is also apparent when we look at reported levels of happiness for SBNRs and other people. Marginally more individuals who are both religious and spiritual report being personally and relationally happy. SBNRs are somewhat more likely than others to indicate that they should be getting more out of life.

With respect to social well-being, the SBNR are just as inclined as others to highly value honesty. But they lag slightly behind the religious and spiritual in the value that they place on concern for others as well as donating money and volunteering time (Table 7.6).

TABLE 7.6 Personal and social well-being by the spiritual-religious matrix (%)

	All	Spiritual but not religious	Religious and spiritual	Religious but not spiritual	Neither religious nor spiritual
Personal well-being					
"Very happy"					
Personal life	22	22	27	21	20
Marriage/relationship	45	41	49	49	45
Concerned "a great deal" or "quite a bit" about					
Lack of money	47	49	46	52	45
Getting more out of life	44	47	39	47	42
Social well-being					
"Highly value"					
Honesty	84	87	88	82	78
Concern for others	55	59	66	44	45
In past month					
Donated money	53	50	67	51	46
Volunteered time	34	33	45	30	28

Source: ARI Religion Survey (2015).

In short, this cursory look suggests that the well-being edge goes to those who are religious and spiritual over those who are spiritual but not religious.

The Global Situation

It is difficult to find global data on spirituality akin to the data on religion that we have been accessing. Gallup has been inclined to conceptualize spirituality in terms of religion. In fairness to Gallup, much of the world has likewise not made a sharp dichotomy. In fact, only in recent years have academics and others who observe religion noted that average Americans, Canadians, and Europeans, for example, are now making such a distinction.

Significantly, the distinction has been closely tied to the recognition that secularization has not eliminated the sense among many people that they have needs that outlive their involvement and interest in organized expressions of religion. So it is that, in some settings where secularization is seen as fairly rampant, increasing attention has been given to exploring how people continue to pursue ways of addressing their spiritual needs versus focusing only on involvement in religious groups.

One might argue that, if spiritual needs are fairly pervasive, then to the extent that interest in organized religion in any society declines individuals would be expected to seek more specific, personal, and customized ways of having such needs addressed. Sociologist Wade Clark Roof, for example, has written extensively on how the American Baby Boomer era has seen a major shift from involvement in organized religion to highly individual spiritual quests. Moreover, he has described how a burgeoning spirituality industry has emerged in response to such interests, resulting in lively "spiritual marketplaces."[27]

For Roof, three features stand out in the United States. First, the number of people involved in pursuing spiritual needs is significant. Many who have lost traditional religious groundings are looking for new and fresh moorings. Others who are still religiously grounded are looking for further enrichment. Second, a dominant theme is self-understanding. Consequently, Roof speaks of questing, seeking, and searching. Third, somewhat paradoxically, spiritual yearnings are leading many beyond the theme of self-fulfillment of the 1960s and 1970s. Now, he says, that quest has moved beyond consumption and materialism. "Popular spirituality may appear shallow, indeed flaky," Roof writes, but it also "reflects a deep hunger for a self-transformation that is both genuine and personally satisfying." His reading is that the current religious situation among American Boomers "is characterized not so much by a loss of faith as a qualitative shift from unquestioned belief to a more open, questing mood."[28]

Princeton University sociologist Robert Wuthnow has been giving research attention to post-Boomers, focusing on people between the ages of 21 and 45. In his book *After the Baby Boomers,* released in 2007, he reminds readers that the availability of choices and the inclination to engage in seeking spiritual fulfillment have never been greater.

In exploring the extent to which young adults are spiritual but not religious, Wuthnow notes that 55% of his sample attended religious services less than once a month. Of that number, 6 in 10 indicated that spiritual growth was important to them, and 3 in 10 said that they had devoted some attention to their spiritual lives in the previous year. Many were what Wuthnow calls "spiritual tinkerers" who, like their Boomer parents, "piece together ideas about spirituality from many sources."[29]

Consistent with the findings of Roof and Wuthnow, the National Opinion Research Center's poll data spanning 1998 to 2014 have documented a shift toward an SBNR outlook. A majority of people of all ages describe themselves as equally spiritual and religious. But as the centre's long-time director, Tom Smith, noted, growing numbers are reporting that they are more spiritual than religious. The latter include about 30% of Americans under 30 – double the figure for those over 70 (Figure 7.3).[30]

Reflecting on these SBNR inclinations of Americans, Mark Chaves offers this cautionary observation: "It is difficult to know what people mean when they say they are spiritual but not religious. The most obvious interpretation is that such people consider themselves to be generally concerned with spiritual matters (whatever *that* means) but are not interested in organized religion." Chaves goes on to say that, if this is the case, "then this growing segment of the population is unlikely to re-energize existing religious institutions or new religious movements." They

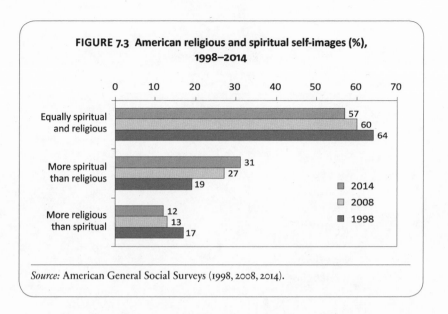

FIGURE 7.3 American religious and spiritual self-images (%), 1998–2014

Equally spiritual and religious: 57 (2014), 60 (2008), 64 (1998)

More spiritual than religious: 31 (2014), 27 (2008), 19 (1998)

More religious than spiritual: 12 (2014), 13 (2008), 17 (1998)

■ 2014
□ 2008
■ 1998

Source: American General Social Surveys (1998, 2008, 2014).

might contribute to "a growing market for certain products, such as self-help books with spiritual themes," but they will probably not result in stable forms of organizational expression. The SBNR orientation, he claims, "is too vague, unfocused, and anti-institutional for that."[31]

With respect to Europe, Smith notes that the argument for the movement toward personal spiritual expression has been summed up in Grace Davie's phrase "believing without belonging."[32] Other European observers going back almost 50 years ago to Thomas Luckmann have spoken of "invisible religion,"[33] while the concept of "implicit religion" has become increasingly popular in recent decades, in large part through the efforts of Edward Bailey.[34]

A recent survey of European Common Market countries shows that interest in spirituality extends well beyond the parameters of conventional religion. As expected, there is a fairly strong relationship between attendance and spirituality, but there are also many exceptions.[35] In all but one instance (Poland), levels of interest in spirituality fairly readily exceed levels of attendance (Table 7.7).

As we look at the data for Canada, the United States, and elsewhere, it seems clear that any movement away from organized religion will typically not result in the demise of spiritual interest. On the contrary,

TABLE 7.7 Attendance and interest in spirituality in select European countries (%)

	Attendance	Spirituality*
Poland	64	52
Ireland	56	63
Slovak Republic	44	54
Spain	31	50
Portugal	38	59
Germany	30	36
Greece	33	57
Hungary	20	45
Switzerland	28	56
Netherlands	23	61
Luxembourg	27	53
Belgium	23	47
Ukraine	24	68
France	19	42
Bulgaria	16	53
Denmark	16	40
Czech Republic	14	32
Russia	15†	40
Finland	13	47

* Measurement: "Whether or not you think of yourself as a religious person, how spiritual would you say you are: that is, how strongly are you interested in the sacred or the supernatural?" (% indicating that they are "very" or "somewhat" interested).
Sources: Attendance: Stark (2015); † Gallup (2010 WorldView); *Spirituality:* European Values Survey 2008.

"religious defection" will see many individuals move toward highly personal forms of spirituality, and cultures will respond with increasingly lively "spiritual marketplaces."

A Prominent Journalist's Take
In looking for a current informed overview of developments in spirituality worldwide, we have the thinking of an acclaimed Canadian journalist

and author, Douglas Todd of the *Vancouver Sun*. He has been keeping a careful eye on developments relating to spirituality in Canada and abroad. His books on the topic include *Brave Souls* (1996) and *Cascadia: The Elusive Utopia: Exploring the Spirit of the Pacific Northwest* (2008). His many awards include the Templeton Reporter of the Year Award twice as the top reporter on religion in North America.

In January 2009, he penned a stimulating piece entitled "Five Spiritual Trends to Watch for in 2009." A year later he reaffirmed the trends: "I'm coming to the conclusion the five trends have real staying power, which could see them sticking with us to 2020 and beyond."[36] So, let's look at them again.

❶ Eastern spirituality will flower.
❷ Religious terrorism will be the new normal.
❸ Religious liberals will build on advances.
❹ The religious right will regroup.
❺ Secular spirituality will strengthen.

Eastern Spirituality

Eastern spirituality, Todd says, has gone mainstream in the West. Once an East-West topic of dialogue for a small number of intellectuals, Asian spirituality is being embraced by growing numbers of people around the world. "Small spiritual armies of young Buddhists, calling themselves Dharma Punx, are spreading around North America." But Todd says that "it's not only whites jumping on the Eastern spirituality train." Growing numbers of Asians, inspired by the Dalai Lama, Thich Nhat Hanh, and Thailand's Sulak Sivaraksa, are transforming Eastern spiritual traditions with a commitment to an "engaged Buddhism" that emphasizes justice. He notes that the Taiwan-based Chi Tzi movement has millions of followers in 40 countries, including Canada. It downplays religious rites and zealously pursues international charity projects.

Religious Terrorism

Todd draws on Pew Forum findings in noting that 9% of countries are experiencing some form of terrorism – "not only from Muslims, but from Christians, Hindus, atheistic leaders and others." Surveys show that Islamic anger is based largely on a sense that Muslims are being oppressed by Western financial, political, and military powers. But anger is also being felt much more widely.

Religious Liberals

Spiritual searchers are yearning for alternatives to conservative versions of Western religion. Todd notes that they are finding it in progressive Christian and other writers, including Marcus Borg, Jim Wallis, Tariq Ramadan, and Ron Rolheiser. He suggests that, as civil rights, South African apartheid, and the Vietnam War brought religious progressives together in the 1960s and 1970s, "possible environmental disaster now galvanizes them."

The Religious Right

The religious right, in Todd's words, "has been hit some body blows," including the rise of Obama, the failure of the Iraq War that it backed, the defeat of Sarah Palin, and – in both the United States and Canada – legislation allowing same-sex marriages. Nonetheless, its passion, anger, money, followers, and political and media connections will continue to make it a societal force.

Secular Spirituality

The inclination for people to dichotomize between religion and spirituality will persist. It is becoming increasingly common to reject organized religion yet embrace a host of spiritual practices and beliefs. Todd sees "secular spirituality" manifesting itself in mainstream publishing, academia, reverence of nature, and pop culture figures, including Oprah Winfrey, Eckhart Tolle, and Deepak Chopra.

Todd adds that polls – as we saw with Wuthnow's work – show that more and more people are becoming "spiritual tinkerers" who "mix and match an often dizzying variety of beliefs and practices." Secular spirituality is also appearing in movies. Todd cites the example of *Avatar*, with its ecospiritual theme, in which the Na'vi humanoid heroes "practice a powerful indigenous form of nature spirituality that holds the potential to heal the universe." He notes that Canadian director James Cameron took the title of his movie from Indian religion – "an 'avatar' is an incarnation of a Hindu god."

A Prominent Academic's Take

A few summary thoughts from Harvey Cox of Harvard University. In his book *The Future of Faith* (2009), this respected observer of religious developments maintains that religion has done more than re-emerge as an important component of 21st-century life. What it means to be "religious," he says, is shifting considerably across the globe. In the case of Christianity, he sees this shift as "its most momentous transformation since its transition in the fourth century CE from what had begun as a tiny Jewish sect into the religious ideology of the Roman Empire."[37] After its previous Age of Faith (first three centuries) and Age of Belief (next 15 centuries), Christianity, he says, is now experiencing its Age of the Spirit.

Cox reminds us that, as in the past, the term "spirituality" can mean different things. "At a minimum, it evokes an ambiguous self-reflection void of content. For some it can become mere navel gazing. For others [it] can mean a disciplined practice of meditation, prayer, or yoga that can lead to deepened engagement in society." He adds that "it is evident different forms of 'spirituality' can lead to either self-indulgence or a deepened social engagement, but so can institutional religion."[38]

Cox offers an insightful summary of what people have in mind when they use the term:

"Spirituality" can mean a host of things, but there are three reasons why the term is in such wide use. First, it is still a form of tacit protest [against] the preshrinking of "religion." Second, it represents an attempt to voice the awe and wonder before the intricacy of nature that many feel is essential to human life without stuffing them into ready-to-wear ecclesiastical patterns. Third, it recognizes the increasingly porous borders between the different traditions, and looks more to the future than to the past.[39]

Widespread use of the term "spirituality," says Cox, "constitutes a sign of the jarring transition through which we are now passing from an expiring Age of Belief into a new but not yet fully realized Age of the Spirit."[40]

Assessment

These findings document the fact that spiritual interest and needs are widespread. That said, how spirituality is conceptualized varies considerably across the population. Large numbers of Canadians of all ages express spiritual needs. But this does not necessarily mean that they are looking in the direction of conventional religion to have them met. In fact, many are finding alternatives to religion when it comes to both conceptualizing and nurturing spirituality. It seems clear that, as religious polarization intensifies in Canada, spiritual needs and responses will persist – with and without the presence of religion in people's lives.

Because of the subjectivity associated with spirituality, its nature will probably be understood best with the help of some adjectives. We can think, for example, of Catholic spirituality, Baptist spirituality, Buddhist spirituality, Islamic spirituality, and so on. But we will also find that a variety of atheistic and agnostic spiritualities exist, along with an array of more generic forms of theistic and non-institutional spirituality.

To the extent that spirituality finds expression both within existing religions and apart from them, there is no doubt that it will persist on a global basis. We can expect that its expressions will only become more diverse as it moves outside the parameters of formal religion in an increasing number of cultural settings around the world. And, like products of every kind, we can expect those expanding expressions to be exported, further expanding spirituality marketplaces pretty much everywhere.

Growing religious polarization in Canada will do little to reduce the apparent fascination that most people have with spirituality. That's not to say that all expressions of spirituality "are born equal" when it comes to functionality. Many expressions of spirituality, for example, along with "civil religions" and "implicit religions," have little or nothing to say about death.

On a number of occasions, Todd has reflected on the extent to which something like hockey has been said to be a Canadian "religion" – an idea actually posited by some academics.[41] Obviously, hockey – like sports such as soccer in many parts of the world – can call forth personal and collective emotions and bind people together. Sports are also replete with symbols and rituals.

But let's not get carried away. Whatever the functions of sports and other potential "invisible religions" to which we direct our energies – like careers, materialism, or family life – they fall far short of being substitutes for religions that can address the "big questions of our existence." Such a reality was underlined after the tragic death of NHL executive Brian Burke's son, Brendan, in early 2010. *Hockey News* writer Sam McCaig commented that it "makes things like trade deadlines, NHL playoff berths and Olympic tournaments seem like little more than surreal, meaningless pastimes."[42] In the face of things like tragedy and death, most of us need much more.

Dating back to *Fragmented Gods* some three decades ago, I have been among those arguing that religion is only one source of meaning. People find ways of making life meaningful without exclusively or even necessarily turning to religion. In the words of Bertrand Russell that I cited back then, "I do not think that life in general has a purpose. It just happened. But individual human beings have purposes."[43]

In a recent poll of 84 countries, Gallup confirmed that meaning does not require religion. Only 2% of all respondents worldwide said that they were secular or non-religious. Nevertheless, 83% of these same people indicated that their lives have an important meaning or purpose – up to 10% below Christians, Hindus, Muslims, Buddhists, and Jews but still extremely high.[44]

Spiritual needs and expressions, if necessary, will readily outlive religion. The always stimulating Phil Zuckerman, for example, doesn't even use the word "spirituality" as he talks about living life with "aweism." In contrast to someone who is religious, he says, "an aweist just feels awe from time to time, appreciates it, owns it, relishes it, and then carries on – without any supernatural or otherworldly baggage."[45]

Spirituality or something like it will always be with us. The extent to which its varied expressions will add to people's lives or come up short remains to be seen.

* * *

A closing thought. I have found that the news about various conceptions of spiritual needs that in turn are widely being met brings a fairly predictable response from religious leaders in particular. "People might be into spirituality," they protest. "But what they are embracing is not 'real' or 'genuine' spirituality." I myself might be teetering on that precipice in my fairly harsh critique of people who say that they are "spiritual but not religious."

The critics of contemporary expressions of spirituality might be right. But the job of the sociologist is not to tell people of faith what "true" spirituality looks like. If the wide range of spiritualties is not viewed as bona fide, then the onus is on those who think that way to get the word out to the growing number of people in Canada and elsewhere who think otherwise.

The research suggests that large numbers are not only finding alternatives to conventional expressions of spirituality but are also finding those alternatives to be highly functional. Many of them are happy with both their paths and their destinations. Consequently, if they are travelling up the wrong mountains, then they need to hear from some persuasive and credible guides.

The gods are not indispensable to finding purpose. But it's not at all clear that the same can be said when it comes to addressing with certainty a question of universal importance – what happens when we die.

8

Dealing with Death

If mortals die, will they live again?

– Job 14.14, RSV

Baby Boomers increasingly have had to come to grips with mortality in recent years, while people following behind them have been pondering the strain that they will put on health-care and social services. The oldest in the cohort were born in 1946 and turned 65 in 2011. The youngest, who arrived in 1965, hit 45. As a "borderline Boomer," I know how many of them have been feeling.

We all know the folk wisdom, but most of us ignored it when we were younger. "Life is short." "Take time to smell the flowers." "If you've got your health, you've got everything." "Enjoy people while you can." Those things all sounded so trite.

But in the last while, many Boomers have had to deal with aging and ailing grandparents, parents, and other relatives and friends. There have also been quite a few deaths. It's not just the older people. Friends and acquaintances who were supposed to be around are no longer here, reduced to memories far too early. What has been particularly difficult to deal with has been the loss of the very young, whose lives were just beginning.

There is something so random, unpredictable, and surreal about it all. One year or one day people are with us. The next year or the next day they are gone. Knowing that aging and death are facts of life provides little comfort. Watching such things unfold as an inevitable part of the life cycle does not make them any easier to accept. Few things underline limits, helplessness, and finality with more vividness than death.

So it is, writes Tom Harpur, that "surely the most momentous personal question of our day – or indeed any other – is, having once died, is that the end or do we somehow live again?"[1]

The Problematic Question of Death

Boomers have been problem solvers. They have been a generation that has worked hard, pursued a good education, set challenging goals, and achieved many of them. In Canada and the United States, they have been part of social and technological revolutions that have elevated the quality of life for millions of people. Few things have been beyond what's doable.

Contrary to excessively enthusiastic commentators, the Boomers haven't done it all, and they haven't achieved it all. They have accomplished much and provided a rich legacy upon which post-Boomers can build.[2]

But as they come to grips with death, they don't appear to have any particular advantages over generations before them. As one provocative Boomer, Michael Coren, has put it, death as "the great egalitarian blade comes to us all. We can shout and moan and complain, but in the end we can do nothing. We slide and slip into the beyond."[3] In a Stanford University commencement address in 2005, Steve Jobs summed things up this way: "No one wants to die. Even people who want to go to heaven don't want to die to get there. And yet death is the destination we all share. No one has ever escaped it."[4]

The Limits of Science
The information explosion has not resulted in our knowing much more than earlier generations about death. When we think about it, it's rather strange. Science can enable us to explore the universe. It can provide us with miraculous technologies for carrying out our work, performing life-saving medical procedures, and transmitting copious amounts of music, images, and messages. Yet, while science and technology can combine to

equip us, inform us, entertain us, and prolong our lives, the mighty duo have few trustworthy product lines to offer when it comes to understanding death, the reality from which no one gets an exemption. It remains as much a mystery as ever.

The difficulty, of course, is that we as humans have to rely on what we can know. And as long as the rules of science limit the knowable to what we can see, touch, hear, smell, and taste, we remain remarkably clueless about death. There could be something more. But science throws up its hands and declares, "There is no way of knowing."

It might not be an exaggeration to say that, rather than being less troubled by death, Boomers find it all the more frustrating to accept. They have been a generation accustomed to finding solutions to problems, including physical deterioration. Much has been written about their age-defying outlook and their co-opting of technology to enable them to deal with declining looks, hearing, sight, mobility, and sexual ability. Their generation has also been replete with forecasters who can tell them what the weather will be like next month and, allegedly, what social life will look like decades from now. Why should death be any different?

Alas, with death, Canada's Boomers have met their match. And the fact that many of them have decided to take a pass on religion along the way doesn't exactly help. To borrow the poetry of songwriter Randy Newman, they won't have any God to greet them, having already taught their children "not to believe those lies."[5]

Efforts to go lightly with death do not help much. *Globe and Mail* columnist Margaret Wente has put things this way: "I hate the modern loss of ritual and solemnity surrounding death. Something's lost when people get together and have a party and pretend the loved one has done nothing more dramatic than move to Cleveland." She adds, "These are serious matters, and we shouldn't pretend they're not."[6]

Death and Religion
If science can't help us with the question of death, what options do we have?

Option 1 would be to take the advice of someone like Freud.[7] He reminded us that it would be great to be able to believe that there is something out there after we die – that there is life after death.

Unfortunately, he said, there isn't. Consequently, we have to take a deep final breath and realize that's it. No more. It's over. It's not great. But things are what they are.

Christopher Hitchens found out in 2010, at the age of 61, that he had cancer. Somewhat stoically, he told Noah Richler of *Maclean's* that he had been "looking forward to some good sixties. I really didn't want more than a decade" when "I'd cash out a bit. And now I'm not going to get that."[8]

Phil Zuckerman writes, "Everything dies. Everything. And that's just how it works." The virtue of accepting such a fact, he says, is that it fosters "a greater appreciation for life," and it makes "living all the more urgent, love all the more important, authenticity all the more warranted, and time with friends and family all the more precious."[9]

Option 2 would be to plead ignorance – to take an agnostic position toward death and declare that we just don't know. Maybe there's life after death; maybe there isn't. This option doesn't necessarily do much for morale. But, for some people, "maybe" is better than "no" – akin to something being better than nothing.

Option 3 would be to believe that death is not the end, that there actually is life after death. Obviously, this is the option that many religions have posed. The difficulty here for the empirically minded is that we don't have much, if any, reliable scientific data on which to base such a possibility. Lots of people have claimed that they have had near-death experiences that have allowed them to observe first-hand what life after death is like. A religion such as Christianity, of course, claims that Jesus died and was raised from the dead, providing a concrete example of what can be experienced.

The choices come down to this: is one going to rely exclusively on what is known scientifically, or is one open to the possibility that faith is also a way of knowing? Since science cannot speak to the non-observable, it is really unable to address the question of life after death. Religions, to varying degrees, claim to have insight into what happens after we die.[10] In lieu of being accompanied by observable evidence, those claims have to be taken on faith.

The first option goes with science, the third option with religion. The second option is the choice of the undecided. As we will see, these are more than just belief choices. The directions that people choose to go have important consequences in terms of both their emotions and their outlook.

A Canadian Reading

A while back I sat in a food court in the West Edmonton Mall reflecting on the extent to which young people reflect. To my left were two buoyant teenage girls ostensibly having lunch together. What intrigued me was that both were texting the whole time. As they got up from their table, they were still texting, taking a few seconds out to simultaneously pop in earbuds as they returned to the mall. I thought to myself, "Are my surveys really capturing what's going on in the world? When would two people like that possibly give time to thinking about life's 'big questions'? They barely give time to each other."

I can almost hear someone saying that "those teens were multitask-ing." I'm not so sure. Ron Rolheiser's observation seems more apt: multi-tasking is really the ability to be inattentive to more than one thing at the same time.[11]

Actually, my West Edmonton Mall data reflected a number of realities beyond multitasking. The percentage of teens who admit that they seldom or never take time to "sit and think" doubled from 13% in 1984 to 26% in 2008. Consistent with that pattern, the percentages of those who say that they *never* think about issues like death, suffering, and purpose rose slightly.

Still, these "ultimate questions" seem to get squeezed in – maybe because they sometimes simply force themselves in. Dating back to our first surveys in the 1970s and 1980s, we have found that a consistent 9 in 10 Canadians of all ages say they wonder about meaning and purpose, suffering and death.[12]

Undoubtedly, the reflections are typically periodic – often the result of teens and the rest of us having to come to grips with illness and death, other times the results of events that receive extensive media attention. But either way the questions are raised, regardless of how full lives might be.

What *has* changed slightly over the past few decades is the inclination among adults in particular to put these questions aside a bit faster. It's not because they think they have found the answers, because most acknowledge they have not. Some go so far as to say that it isn't possible to find answers. As a result, many people have simply moved on to more tangible and doable things – led by the pragmatically minded Boomers.[13]

In the case of the question of life after death specifically, more than 9 in 10 adults and teens say that they have raised it. Needless to say, good answers have been hard to come by. Our research dating back to the mid-1980s has found that close to 5 in 10 adults admit that "dying" concerns them at least "somewhat." Perhaps surprisingly, concern about dying also differs little by age group.[14]

Belief in Life after Death

Currently, 66% of Canadian adults indicate that they believe in life after death, 12% that they definitely do not (Table 8.1). The comparable figures for teenagers in 2008 were 78% and 8% respectively. The adult numbers are virtually unchanged from the mid-1980s. In fact, the 12% figure for disbelief in 2015 is identical to what Gallup found when it first put the question to Canadians way back in 1945.

Our polls since the mid-1970s have documented the ongoing reluctance of people to rule out life after death. But they are showing increasing levels of ambivalence about it. Such a lack of clarity should hardly come as a surprise. After all, we don't know anything more now about the chances of a hereafter than we did in the past.

TABLE 8.1 Belief among adults in life after death (%), 1985 and 2015

Do you believe in life after death?	1985	2015
Yes, I definitely do.	36	29
Yes, I think so.	29	37
No, I don't think so.	20	22
No, I definitely do not.	15	12

Sources: 1985: Bibby, Project Canada national survey (1985); 2015: ARI Religion Survey.

Those things said, if religion offers some "market entries" on the topic, then we would expect differences in belief to vary by religiosity. For starters, we would expect noteworthy differences by religious inclination, and, yes, they are readily apparent.

▶ Some 57% of Canadians who embrace religion say that they "definitely" believe in life after death – far above the levels for those in the religious middle (20%) and those who reject religion (12%).
▶ Those who "definitely do not" believe in life after death include only 3% of those embracing faith, and just 6% of those occupying the religious middle, compared with 34% of those rejecting faith.

As we saw earlier, both attendance at religious services and belief in God are highly correlated with the three religious inclinations. It is therefore not surprising that attendance and theism in turn are highly correlated with belief in life after death (Table 8.2).

Related Beliefs

Large numbers of Canadians continue to believe in heaven and angels (around 60%), and about half the population maintain that we can have contact with the spirit world, including being able to communicate with the dead. Some 40% believe in hell. No fewer than 6 in 10 people tell us that they "have been protected from harm by a guardian angel."

Consistent with expectations, active attenders and theists are considerably more likely than others to believe in all of these phenomena. Yet it's intriguing to note that these beliefs are hardly limited to the conventionally devout (Table 8.3).

▶ Many who are infrequent attenders and ambivalent about the existence of God also endorse these ideas.
▶ Not surprisingly – given that they are typically in those two categories – SBNRs tend to reflect the responses of occasional attenders and ambivalent theists but are more inclined than others to endorse contact with the spirit world and communication with the dead.

TABLE 8.2 Belief in life after death by attendance and belief in God (%), 2015

Do you believe in life after death?	All	Attendance			Belief in God		
		Monthly+	Yearly	Never	Theist	Ambivalent	Atheist
Yes, I definitely do.	29	57	24	15	62	7	3
Yes, I think so.	37	30	44	32	29	51	12
No, I don't think so.	22	9	25	27	7	35	21
No, I definitely do not.	12	4	7	26	2	7	64

Source: ARI Religion Survey (2015).

TABLE 8.3 Beliefs related to life after death by attendance, belief in God, and SBNR (%), 2015

	All	Attendance			Belief in God			SBNR
		Monthly +	Yearly	Never	Theist	Ambivalent	Atheist	
Heaven	63	92	67	36	92	54	5	64
Angels	62	89	64	39	92	51	7	66
Protected by a guardian angel	56	78	59	36	83	46	10	52
Contact with the spirit world	50	58	51	43	64	47	15	61
Hell	42	72	41	20	68	30	1	35
Communication with the dead	42	41	47	38	52	42	13	52

Note: Response options were "Yes, I definitely believe" or "Yes, I think so" versus "No, I don't think so" or "No, I definitely do not believe."
Source: ARI Religion Survey (2015).

The beliefs of Canadians are not always predictable. For example, if a person believes in heaven or hell, that must mean that he or she believes in life after death, right? Well, usually, but not always.

- No less than 91% who "definitely" believe in hell also "definitely" believe in heaven; however, among those who are certain that there is a heaven, a much lower 53% are also certain that there is a hell. Who said that we have to take the bad with the good?
- About 7% who are certain that there is a hell don't think that there is life after death. If hell is associated with some kind of non-existence, then I guess that makes sense.
- But about 7% who believe in heaven don't believe in life after death. Presumably, heaven is something else.

One interesting pattern that is somewhat more pronounced among younger adults is the inclination to believe in life after death without necessarily believing in God (Figure 8.1). Among pre-Boomers, 94% who say that they "definitely" believe in life after death express the same certainty about the existence of God. In the case of Gen-Xers and Millennials, close to 85% who are certain that there is an afterlife express the same certainty about God (Figure 8.1).

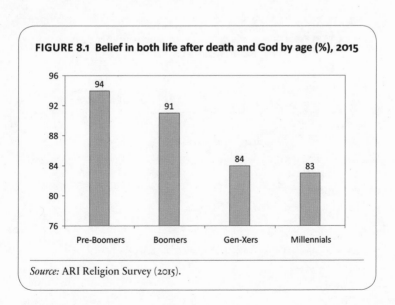

FIGURE 8.1 Belief in both life after death and God by age (%), 2015

Source: ARI Religion Survey (2015).

Such findings point to the fact that our culture – notably the music and video game industries – gives credence to supernatural phenomena generally, including spirits, angels, demons, and the like. God? Not so much. Sara Yoheved Rigler sums up the situation this way: "The popularity of angels, psychic phenomena, faith healing, meditation, and near-death experiences testifies to a paradigm shift in our concept of reality. But somehow God has gotten lost in the shuffle."[15]

Beliefs about What Happens after Death

We put this blunt question to Canadians: "What do you think will happen to you after you die?" Their responses reflect the religious polarization that characterizes the country (Table 8.4).

▶ About 3 in 10 people say that they "really don't know," while another 3 in 10 maintain that they will "go to heaven or another good place."
▶ Just over 2 in 10 think that they will simply stop existing.
▶ The remaining 2 in 10 are almost evenly divided between those who believe that they will go "somewhere else" and those who think that they will be reincarnated.

TABLE 8.4 Views of adults of what happens after death, by attendance (%), 2014

What do you think will happen after you die?	All	Attendance		
		Monthly+	Yearly	Never
I really don't know.	32	13	34	38
I will go to heaven or another good place.	29	67	31	10
I will simply stop existing.	23	9	17	37
I will go somewhere else.	9	7	9	10
I will be reincarnated.	7	4	9	5
Totals	100	100	100	100

Source: Project Canada/Vision Critical 2014 Easter Survey.

Resilient Gods

Responses to Death

We all are well aware that death brings with it an array of emotional responses. Foremost, initially at least, is sorrow. A life has been lost. A family member, a friend, an acquaintance, perhaps a stranger with whom we empathize is gone. If a partner or child is involved, then maybe it's the thought of the pain experienced by the ones we leave behind that troubles us the most. In his book *The Last Lecture*, Randy Pausch writes that, as much as he was troubled by the fact that he wouldn't be able to see his three young children grow up, what disturbed him more was that they would grow up not having a father.[16] A survey respondent summed up another dimension of parental pain when he said that he'd be troubled most by having any of his children die before him.

The prospect of our own death brings forth so many additional emotions: simply not being able to live, laugh, love, all the things that we want to do. Even someone as confident and enthusiastic about life after death as the Apostle Paul wrote that he nonetheless struggled with the fact that he needed to live life and therefore, on balance, preferred to live a little longer.[17]

In our Project Canada surveys, we have put a tough question to Canadians beginning in 1980 that we asked again in 2015: "What would you say your primary response is to the reality of death?" We have offered five responses: fear, sorrow, mystery, hope, and no particular feeling (Table 8.5).[18]

TABLE 8.5 Responses to life after death by attendance (%), 2015

	Mystery	Sorrow	Hope	Fear	No particular feeling	Totals
All	23	20	16	16	25	100
Monthly plus	17	20	44	9	10	100
Yearly	29	22	13	14	22	100
Never	20	20	5	21	34	100

Source: ARI Religion Survey (2015).

- The 2015 survey found rankings very similar to those of the past: mystery (23%), sorrow (20%), and no particular feeling (25%) were mentioned most often, followed equally by hope (16%) and fear (16%). The one in five who said that they didn't have any particular feeling seemingly have an array of emotions.
- What stands out when we look at the survey results by religiosity is the inclination of weekly attenders to cite hope (44%) far more frequently than anything else.
- Yearly attenders are the most likely to mention mystery, those who never attend that they have no particular feeling.

Clearly, funerals and funeral homes reflect the varied ways in which Canadians are understanding and responding to death. A perusal of death announcements provides a reminder of the range of choices involved – from people requesting that nothing be done, through a gathering of celebration, to a traditional funeral. One local Alberta funeral home has run an ad in recent years showing an endearing father-son picture with the caption "Dad Wasn't Really a Churchgoer" and emphasizing that "there are many options available ... for whatever you think is best."[19]

Today's Canadians are certainly familiar with religious funerals. Almost half indicate that they have attended a religious funeral in the past year. They are led by those who embrace faith (60%), followed by individuals in the religious middle (46%) and those who reject faith (28%).

Asked "When you die, do you want to have a religious funeral, a non-religious service of celebration, or no service?" their responses once again reflect the reality of religious polarization.

- Almost equal portions of 4 in 10 say that they anticipate having a religious funeral or a celebration of their lives.
- The remaining 2 in 10 tell us that they do not want to have a service of any kind.
- It comes as no surprise that most people who embrace faith envision having a religious funeral, but those in the religious middle vary considerably with respect to the three possibilities.

TABLE 8.6 Funeral ceremony preferences by inclinations (%), 2015

	Religious funeral	Non-religious service of celebration	No service	Totals
All	41	37	22	100
Embrace	80	10	10	100
Middle	34	42	24	100
Reject	7	59	34	100
SBNR	28	49	23	100

Source: ARI Religion Survey (2015).

Suspecting that many readers are curious, I have also looked at the end-of-life ceremony preferences of the "spiritual but not religious." Their diversity is reflected in the finding that half prefer to have a non-religious ceremony. However, the remaining half are almost equally divided between wanting a religious funeral or no service at all (Table 8.6).

A Fascinating Footnote

In March 2014, I partnered with my colleague Andrew Grenville of Vision Critical in exploring some additional questions about life after death in three settings: Canada, the United States, and Britain.[20]

Over the years, I've had the sense that many people who attend funerals don't really think "this is it" – be they religious or not. We put the question to our survey participants, and the surveys confirmed the hunch. Close to 60% of Americans said that they "definitely" or "possibly" will see the deceased again. The levels for Canada and Britain were about 40% and 30% respectively. In all three settings, about 30% said that they don't know.

One can confidently say that there is no concrete empirical evidence for such expectations. And about one in two people in Britain, one in three in Canada, and one in five in the United States don't have them. Nonetheless, somewhat remarkably, in the two North American countries in particular such people are in the minority (Table 8.7).

TABLE 8.7 **Belief one will again see people who have died,**
United States, Canada, and Britain (%), 2014

	United States	Canada	Britain
Will definitely see them again	30	18	11
May possibly see them again	27	21	18
Will never see them again	18	32	46
Don't know	25	29	25

Source: Project Canada/Vision Critical 2014 Easter Survey.

I have also been interested in the extent to which people think that interaction continues to take place between those who are alive and those who have died. In probing that topic, we posed three questions to survey participants.

❶ Do you think that people who have died could be aware of what is taking place in our lives?
❷ Do you think it's possible to communicate with people who are no longer alive?
❸ Have you ever felt that you were in touch with someone who has died?

We were taken aback by the extent to which people in the three settings offered affirmative responses to each item.

▶ More than 6 in 10 Americans and about 5 in 10 Canadians and Brits said that they "definitely" or "think" that the deceased can see us, know what we are up to, and share in our lows and highs.
▶ But people don't just play a passive role when it comes to contact with those who are no longer with them. Some 4 in 10 – led slightly by North Americans – also claim that they themselves "have been in touch with someone who has died." The levels for the three settings are up from about 25% in 1980.

TABLE 8.8 Belief in contact with the deceased, Canada, United States, and Britain (%), 2014

	Canada	United States	Britain
People who have died could be aware of what is taking place in our lives.	54	66	46
It's possible to communicate with people who are no longer alive.	42	50	37
Believe that you have been in touch with someone who has died.	37	44	33

Note: Table includes those who responded "yes, I definitely do" or "yes, I think so."
Source: Project Canada/Vision Critical 2014 Easter Survey.

Those hefty numbers represent a lot of seemingly average people whom we see and talk to every day. Contrary to common stereotypes, they are hardly an eccentric minority. What's intriguing is the extent to which people haven't given up on the possibility that life continues after death. What's startling is the extent to which they believe that people who have died continue to follow what is taking place in their lives and – even more – remain in contact (Table 8.8).

The various responses to the findings are fairly predictable, we think, perhaps falling into three main categories.

The first is a *cultural response.* Observers confronted with the data will say that people interpret death and possible interaction with the dead through cultural lenses, including religious subcultures. Some individuals obviously believe that they will see people again because they've been taught that there is life after death, often replete with rewards and punishments. In some settings, the dead are believed to make contact with the living through dreams. And, as we have seen, some 55% of Canadians believe that they have been protected by a guardian angel. The beliefs and alleged experiences have been culturally instilled.

The second is a *clinical response.* Some researchers see beliefs about the afterlife as not only functioning to help people deal with trauma surrounding death but also having been created to do so. One classic expression of such a view, of course, is that of Freud, who argued that immortality is "the universal wish of mankind" but unfortunately will not happen.[21] Similarly, Marx – as we all know – saw religion as a response to deprivation.

The third, which we think needs to be included, is an *empirical response*. When one person says that something is happening, we might not take it seriously. When five people say that it's happening, we find the claim a bit more credible. When 100 people say that it's happening, it's hard to ignore. And if several thousand people say that it's happening, well, the claim warrants a serious look. Such is the case these days with respect to at least some claims about what happens after death.

Currently, the questions of life after death and interaction with people who have died are largely ignored by academics. Even religious groups often have little to say. There is an incredible lack of credible answers. The extensive market is left largely to channellers and charlatans, with the predictable result that claims are trivialized and claimants stigmatized.

The result is that most people remain largely in the dark. Obviously, clear-cut answers are extremely elusive. Nonetheless, much more attention needs to be given to the life after death issue, beginning with far more open discussion and, yes, even more exploratory research.

The topic is far too important to be treated as taboo. And the claims are far too common to be trivialized and stigmatized. At this time in history, when we take pride in drawing on unlimited information to address unlimited questions, the question of death should not be ignored. There is a vast market for persuasive responses. But unlike virtually every other area of interest and inquiry, the life after death market is dramatically underserviced.

It's time to take a closer look.

The Global Situation

The reality of death and its social and emotional impacts are obviously felt worldwide. Every culture since the beginning of time has had to find ways of responding to death. Every individual has had to find ways

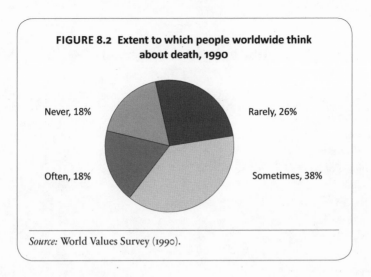

FIGURE 8.2 Extent to which people worldwide think about death, 1990

Never, 18%

Rarely, 26%

Often, 18%

Sometimes, 38%

Source: World Values Survey (1990).

of coping with the loss of others and the fact that one's own life will eventually end. It therefore should surprise no one that reflecting on death is a universal phenomenon.

Just before the end of the 20th century, people in almost 50 countries were asked in the World Values Survey "Do you ever think about death?" Some 80% indicated that they do – about 20% saying "often," 40% "sometimes," and the rest "rarely" or "never" (Figure 8.2).

The countries in the survey with the highest numbers of people indicating that they "never" think about death were China (46%), Slovenia (36%), and Brazil (35%). Many countries with low attendance at religious services still had relatively few people who said that they never thought about death, including Great Britain (14%), Sweden (11%), and Norway (7%). The level in Canada was only 9%, in the United States 8%. The same survey found that a solid majority of people (77%) took the position that, because "death is inevitable, it is pointless to *worry* about it."

Levels of reflection and anxiety aside, a majority of people around the world are inclined to give credibility to the idea of life after death. Another World Values Survey in 2000, involving people in 75 countries, found that 61% said they believed in life after death, while 28% indicated they did not; the remaining 11% were unsure (Table 8.9).

Table 8.9 Belief in God, life after death, and heaven in select countries by attendance (%)

	Attendance	Belief in God	Belief in life after death	Belief in heaven
Nigeria	90	99	86	99
India	67	99	59	66
Saudi Arabia	70	99	97	98
Philippines	65	99	81	95
Poland	64	96	70	70
Mexico	58	97	67	85
South Africa	58	99	66	87
Ireland	56	96	69	77
Pakistan	56	99	100	100
Iraq	51	99	95	98
Italy	48	83	61	50
Iran	47	99	95	94
United States	46	88	75	84
Turkey	49	98	89	93
Singapore	44	95	68	75
Spain	31	92	43	42
Japan	29	87	32	22
Chile	33	90	76	75
Germany	30	77	27	23
Greece	33	97	47	38
Canada	27	85	65	70
Netherlands	23	74	47	36
Ukraine	24	85	29	29
Australia	21	83	53	56
France	19	80	38	28
United Kingdom	20	86	43	45
Sweden	13	70	39	28
Finland	13	91	45	50
Czech Republic	14	57	29	17
Russia	15*	91	26	25

Sources: Attendance: Stark (2015); * Gallup WorldView 2010; *Belief in God:* computed from World Religion Database in Smith (2009, 284–87); *Life after death and heaven:* World Values Survey 2000; *Australia, life after death, and heaven:* Nielsen (2009).

- Here again what's interesting to note is the tendency for people in countries where levels of conventional religiosity are fairly low not to rule out the possibility of life after death.
- Significant numbers either expressed belief in life after death or said that they didn't know – Sweden at 39% and 15% respectively, Japan at 32% and 38%, and Russia at 26% and 28%.
- About 58% said that they believe in heaven – just above the 50% who believe in hell.
- As with Canada, we would expect fairly high correlations between service attendance and belief in God, life after death, and heaven.
- A statistical look at the relationships bears out those expectations (see details in notes).[22]
- But the fact that the correlations are far from perfect points to these beliefs also being fairly common among people not involved in religious groups.

Reincarnation – the idea that one's spirit or soul will return in another life form after death – is, of course, particularly associated with Hinduism. Accordingly, it has been a widely held belief in countries such as India.

The most recent information suggests that, to varying degrees, belief in reincarnation extends to countries throughout the world (Table 8.10).

- Nine in 10 people in Turkey believe in the idea, as do about 6 in 10 individuals in countries such as Taiwan, Japan, Israel, and the Philippines.
- In European settings as well as the United States and Canada, the belief levels range from around 4 in 10 to 2 in 10.
- Slightly less than one in five Scandinavians also indicate that they believe in reincarnation, and they are joined by similar proportions of other Europeans, including Brits, Belgians, Greeks, and Poles.

These findings on heaven, hell, and reincarnation illustrate the fact that people have highly divergent ideas concerning the nature of life after death. But what the majority of people on the planet have in common

TABLE 8.10 Belief in reincarnation by select countries

Country	% who believe in reincarnation
Turkey	91
Taiwan	64
Israel	58
Japan	56
Philippines	54
Chile	47
Mexico	47
South Africa	47
Dominican Republic	44
Venezuela	43
Austria	38
Portugal	36
Russia	36
Uruguay	34
United States	33
Ireland	32
Switzerland	31
Ukraine	31
New Zealand	29
Canada	27*
Italy	27
United Kingdom	27
Netherlands	26
Australia	25
Poland	23
Slovak Republic	22
Spain	22
Germany	21
Sweden	21
Denmark	20
Finland	20
France	20
Northern Ireland	20
Norway	18
Czech Republic	16
Belgium	14

Sources: International Social Survey Programme (2008);
* Association for Canadian Studies (2010).

is a sense that they will continue to exist somewhere, in some form, after they die.

Some additional global findings further illustrate how extensive the belief in life after death actually is.

The item about being in touch with a person who has died that Andrew Grenville and I repeated in 2014 in Canada, the United States, and Britain was originally administered in the World Values Survey in 1981. The item literally read "Have you ever felt as though you were really in touch with someone who had died?"[23] The results were intriguing.

▸ Slightly over a fifth (22%) said that they had – not exactly a small number of people.
▸ The levels ranged from about 4 in 10 in Iceland, through 3 in 10 in the United States, Britain, and Canada, to about 1 in 10 in the Netherlands and the three Scandinavian countries.

If these reports have seemed like fodder for supermarket tabloids because they sounded bizarre and extremely rare, there was a need to think again. The fact is that many Canadians back in the early 1980s were keeping such experiences to themselves. I've suspected for some time that sizable numbers of people these days are doing the same thing.

That's why we repeated the item in 2014. In Canada, the numbers were up from 25% to 37%; in the United States, from 29% to 44%; and in Britain, from 23% to 33% – not decreases but noteworthy increases in each case.

One reason that belief in life after death appears to readily outlive involvement in organized religion is because the belief that we have souls is so pervasive. A World Values Survey item, administered in 33 countries as the new century began, asked "Do you believe that people have a soul?"[24]

▸ Eighty-five percent said "yes," 10% responded "no," and 5% indicated they didn't know.
▸ The levels ranged from highs of 100% or so in countries like Pakistan and Saudi Arabia; through 90–95% in places such as Iran,

the United States, Iraq, and Mexico; to 75% in India, 50% in Japan, and 35% in Vietnam.

▶ Canada came in at 87%.

These diverse probes into the hereafter point to a clear overall conclusion: the market for answers to the universal question of what happens after we die remains vast. As we have seen, in his classic work *The Future of an Illusion,* Freud acknowledged that everyone wants to believe that there is life after death, stating in the language of his day that it represented the universal wish of all mankind. But because it is an illusion, Freud expected that, in time, we would "learn to endure with resignation" such "great necessities of fate, against which there is no remedy."[25]

People worldwide have continued to defy Freud's prediction. Frankly, his assumption that one day we would put such hopes behind us was wrong. Survey after survey has demonstrated that the belief in something "out there" after we die – as nebulous as that "something" might be – simply persists.

It's axiomatic: as long as people die, most of us will contemplate what, if anything, happens next. Actually, that's an understatement. The majority of people around the planet do more than simply contemplate what's next. They don't believe that death is "the end" (Table 8.11).

TABLE 8.11 Belief that death is not the end by select countries, 2004	
	% who believe that death is not the end
Nigeria	79
Lebanon	75
United States	74
Indonesia	64
South Korea	57
Mexico	55
Russia	54
United Kingdom	54
India	51
Israel	50

Source: BBC (2004).

Resilient Gods

Assessment

The age-old questions about meaning and purpose, suffering and purpose, continue to be raised in our time. A few years back I received word that my best friend during the late 1970s and early 1980s had died. They said that it was surprising. Around the same time, a student had to withdraw from my class. His beloved one-year-old son was undergoing life-threatening brain surgery. That was more than surprising.

Journalist Margaret Wente writes, "I envy people of faith. By all accounts, they are happier, healthier and more emotionally secure than the rest of us. They give away more money and do more good works. They are kinder, more generous and more community-minded." She wryly adds that "we secular humanists, by contrast, tend to be stingy, lonely folks" still in search of some larger purpose. "I wouldn't choose to be a nonbeliever if I could help it, but I can't."[26]

The question about purpose can be set aside; the question about death cannot (Table 8.12). The emotions felt when loved ones die, as well as the awareness that we too will live only so long, awaken it over and over in our lifetimes: "What happens when we die? Is this all there is?"

TABLE 8.12 Believing in life after death and knowing the meaning of life (%), 1975 and 2015

	1975	2015
Do you believe in life after death?		
Yes	48	49
No	17	20
Uncertain	35	31
How sure are you that you have found the answer to the meaning of life?		
Very certain	11	12
Quite certain	24	20
Rather uncertain	22	27
Don't think there is an answer	43	41

Sources: Bibby, Project Canada national survey (1975), ARI Religion Survey (2015).

To the extent that we see increasing religious polarization in Canada and around the world, we will not see a decrease in the inclination of people to ask the question about life after death. Reflective people *have* to raise it – and not answer it prematurely. There is too much at stake. However, our findings also make another conclusion clear: without religion, hope will be hard to find.

We are wary of people who seem to know too much – of titles like *What Happens When I Die?*[27] or *Everything You Ever Wanted to Know about Heaven.*[28] Yet we would love to have some solid, authoritative assurances. At the end of his book *Life after Death,* published in 1991, Tom Harpur hinted that he believed in life after death. Two decades later, in 2011, his update appeared – with the title *There Is Life after Death.*

We want some clarity on this critical issue. That widespread desire guarantees a permanent place for religion.

9

The Resilience of Religion

Our souls are restless until they find their rest in Thee,
O God.

— St. Augustine

Prophecy is not exactly a social science virtue. We can do a reasonably good job of explaining what happened after the fact. But we haven't been known for our ability to accurately foresee economic slowdowns, the rearranging of nation-states, or the arrival of the World Wide Web with its transformative powers. For years, I have taught students in research methods classes that the three great goals of social science are description, explanation, and prediction. To date, we don't have much success to show in long-range social forecasting.

It's not that we never try. When it comes to religion, we have had a good share of would-be social prophets. People like Auguste Comte (1798–1857), Karl Marx (1818–83), and Sigmund Freud (1856–1939) saw the disappearance of religion as inevitable. Comte said that scientific thought would replace religious thought, Marx believed that resolving social and economic inequities would eliminate the need for religion as a pain-killing drug, and Freud maintained that science and personal resolve would combine to allow us to abandon our child-like fantasies about a father-like God and a future existence in heaven.

We now know that such thinkers were too quick to write off religion. In settings where religion is currently flourishing, a measure of secularization will undoubtedly take place. The historical precedents of Europe and North America suggest that such a trend will be closely associated with heightened levels of development. But in other places where religious polarization is prominent, or where secularity is pronounced, comebacks are in the works.

The Religious Comeback

Not every social science prophet has declared that religion is doomed. In 1912, French sociologist Emile Durkheim (1858–1917) offered many stimulating thoughts about the nature, functions, and future of religion in his classic work *The Elementary Forms of the Religious Life.* Durkheim believed that, theoretically speaking, one day science would answer all of our questions. However, he maintained that religion would continue to have an important speculative function because science "is fragmentary and incomplete; it advances but slowly and is never finished; but life cannot wait."[1] In the foreseeable future, religion would continue to exist.

Durkheim's point about the gap-filling role of religion is important. However, the problem lies not only with the speed with which science progresses but also with the nature of science itself. Put bluntly, science is not equipped to say much about many religious claims. The reason is that scientific knowledge is based on verifiable observations. The problem with such an empirical method is that important questions about the existence of God and life after death cannot be addressed through observation. They consequently stand outside the grasp of science. This second limitation is not one of speed but one of capability. Science simply cannot address everything.

Precisely because of such limitations, other meaning makers have stepped forward to fill the market void. That's why religion and other such initiatives have had a significant presence throughout the world in the past and present. That's also why they – and their market successors – will have a place in the future.

So it is that social scientists beyond the classic high-profile positivists have taken quite a different position on the future of religion.[2] For example, three prominent 20th-century Harvard University sociologists offered some stimulating ideas about what happens to religion over time.

The Views of Sorokin, Davis, and Bell

The first was Russian-born Pitirim Sorokin (1889–1968), who founded the Department of Sociology at Harvard. The second was Kingsley Davis (1908–97), Sorokin's student, who spent most of his career at the University of California at Berkeley. The third was Daniel Bell (1919–2011), a renowned social forecaster at Harvard who wrote extensively on the emerging post-industrial world.[3]

Sorokin maintained that societies oscillate or swing between "rationality" and "irrationality," between a moving away from religion and a moving toward it. History more generally, he said, has consisted of pendulum-like fluctuations between "ideational" and "sensate" cultures. The ideational period is characterized by ideals and spiritual concerns, while the sensate period is a time when a society emphasizes material values.

Davis picked up on Sorokin's thinking in arguing that there is "a limit to the extent to which a society can be guided by illusion." But "there is also a limit to which a society can be guided by sheer rationality." Secularization, he wrote, will therefore "likely be terminated by religious revivals of one sort or another," complete with new sects. But religion is unlikely to be replaced by secular substitutes.[4]

In like manner, Bell saw people in post-industrial societies as experiencing the limits of modernism and alternatives to religion. He wrote that "a long era is coming to a close. The theme of Modernism was the world beyond ... We are now groping for a new vocabulary whose keyword seems to be limits."[5] Bell predicted that new religions would arise in response to the core questions of existence – death, tragedy, obligation, and love.

This "oscillation" argument became increasingly popular in the last two decades of the 20th century. Social analyst Jeremy Rifkin, for example, claimed that it accounted for the emergence of the charismatic movement and the accelerated success of evangelical Christianity.[6]

Intentionally or not, American research in the late 1980s and early 1990s suggesting that Baby Boomers were heading back to churches fed the idea that the religious pendulum was swinging once again.[7] Even prominent futurist John Naisbitt proclaimed in 1990 that the world was on the verge of a massive return to spirituality.[8]

The Views of Parsons and Greeley

Some observers – standing alone for the most part –claimed that the notion that a major religious shift had taken place was a gross exaggeration. Among the most prominent was still another Harvard sociologist, Talcott Parsons, along with American sociologist, priest, and – later in his career – best-selling novelist Andrew Greeley.

In a very influential essay published in 1964, Parsons maintained that it was a mistake to equate either the decline of the church's authority over life or the individualistic approach to religion with a loss of religious influence. Christianity, he said, continued to have an important place in the Western world, particularly in the United States. While there had been a decrease in the direct control of religion in a number of societal spheres, its legacy was nonetheless being felt. Values emphasized by Christianity, such as tolerance and decency, Parsons claimed, had been institutionalized: "I suggest that in a whole variety of respects, modern society is more in accord with Christian values than its forebears have been."[9]

Parsons argued that increasingly prevalent personal expressions of religion were consistent with both "the individualistic principle inherent in Christianity" and the emphasis on differentiation in modern societies. The result? Religion was a highly "privatized," personal matter, differing from earlier expressions in being less overt and less tied to formal group involvement.[10]

For Parsons, Christianity was not in a state of decline. Rather, it had been both institutionalized and privatized. Similar to the traditional family, Parsons wrote, religion "has lost many previous functions and has become increasingly a sphere of private sentiments." But, he insisted, "It is as important as ever to the maintenance of the main patterns of the society."[11]

One might conclude from reading Parsons that all was well on the religious front. Individuals were still taking religion seriously but keeping their commitments to themselves. Religious groups hadn't lost influence. They were helping to shape cultural values and, if anything, in a better position than ever before to concentrate on religion.

Greeley went even further than Parsons. He argued that secularization was a myth.[12] He acknowledged that religion was facing significant secular pressures and was not important to everyone. However, he insisted, such realities were not unique to our time.

Greeley explicitly addressed a number of common claims about the decline of religion. He maintained that

❶ Faith was not being seriously eroded by science and education and that religion was no less significant in daily life than in the alleged great ages of faith.
❷ Levels of participation were not down relative to periods of time beyond the immediate past.
❸ The impact of religion was continuing but in less obvious ways.
❹ Private commitment was having an impact on the public sphere.
❺ The sacred remained highly visible in everyday life.

According to Greeley, religion was continuing to flourish. Rumours of its decline and death simply weren't warranted. For some time, Greeley – always the unflappable individualist – stubbornly stood his ground. These days he doesn't lack for company.

Stark and Market Demand
As we saw earlier, since the late 1970s Rodney Stark has played a major role in championing the idea that secularization actually stimulates innovation. Ironically, the decline of existing religious forms actually triggers the appearance of new ones. The process has always been in place. The reason is that the demand for religion has been and continues to be constant. What has changed is not the demand for religion but its "suppliers."

Such an argument clearly goes back at least as far as Durkheim. While he observed that Christianity in late-19th-century Europe was in decline, he believed that religion more generally would persist because of its "gap-filling" role. Science and religion had coexisted since the birth of the former and would continue to do so. Religious explanations might be forced to retreat and reformulate and give ground in the face of the steady advance of science.[13] But, as Kingsley Davis noted in summing up Durkheim's point, "religion retreats. But it never surrenders."[14]

Stark and his colleagues have maintained that religion is guaranteed an indispensable role when it comes to meaning. Only ideas grounded in the supernatural, they say, can provide plausible answers to the "ultimate questions" pertaining to the meaning of life and death. As carriers of explanations based on such supernatural assumptions, religions play a unique and irreplaceable role in human affairs (Table 9.1).

Religious activity, they argue, is dynamic. Some religions and some groups are always losing ground. But because the market for religion persists, the activity only increases and the competition only intensifies as old groups and new groups struggle to gain, retain, and increase market shares. The never-ending human quest for meaning ensures the viability of religion.[15]

Writing in 2015, Stark reiterated his long-time argument that "people want to know *why* the universe exists, not that it exists for no reason, and they don't want their lives to be pointless." He added that "only religion provides credible and satisfactory answers to the great existential questions."[16]

The Religious Marketplace

The good news that such thinking brings to religious groups is that the future of religion is not in question. Ongoing spiritual needs guarantee that it will always have a place in the lives of large numbers of people in Canada and around the world – not for everyone, but for very large numbers.

That said, the sobering news for religious groups everywhere is that their own specific futures are anything but guaranteed. Quite the opposite. To the extent that they can effectively address the needs of people relating to ultimacy – led by the question of life after death – they have a future. But the success of any given group – measured by size and vitality – will depend on how well it performs.

TABLE 9.1 Reflections on meaning and purpose in selected countries (%)

	Think about meaning and purpose*	Life has meaning and purpose[†]
Nigeria	92	98
Philippines	92	97
Ghana	91	99
South Korea	90	81
Turkey	89	85
Zimbabwe	88	93
Pakistan	83	82
Jordan	88	90
Canada	82[‡]	92[‡]
Chile	81	93
Mexico	81	94
Hong Kong	81	62
Brazil	80	97
New Zealand	80	88
Germany	80	88
Japan	79	77
United States	78	94
Australia	78	88
Singapore	77	90
Ukraine	77	82
South Africa	73	97
Russia	71	85
Netherlands	71	73
Poland	70	84
Sweden	69	89
India	56	91
Argentina	62	96
China	50	–

* "How often do you think about the meaning and purpose of life?"
= "often" or "sometimes."

† "Do you feel your life has an important purpose or meaning?" =
"yes" or "no."

Sources: World Values Survey Wave 6 (2010–14); ‡ Canada, Meaning and purpose: World Values Survey (2005).

As Stark and his associates have pointed out, the viability of religious groups over time in the United States, for example, has been determined by how well they have addressed the needs of Americans. They argue that the same pattern holds for the entire planet. The demand is universal; the question is which suppliers will emerge to meet that demand.

Stark and his colleagues maintain that sects and revivals, cults and innovations, can contribute to lively religious marketplaces. But typically they face stiff competition from well-established groups that, to varying degrees, reinvent themselves in the light of social change and changing demographics. The Church of England did not disappear just because upstart groups such as Methodists and the Salvation Army came into being. Southern Baptists did not shrivel up just because Nazarenes and Pentecostal groups arrived on the American scene. Canadian Catholics are not going to limp to the sidelines just because Muslim franchises are springing up across the country. We would expect no less of Mainline Protestants.

Apart from performance, however, there are no guarantees as to which "religious companies" will thrive and which will be headed toward "insolvency." All we know for sure is that universal and national market demand means that there will be both winners and losers.

The Canadian Situation

As we look at Canada, some general observations about the immediate future of some of the religious groups here can be made with a high level of confidence.

Roman Catholics

Catholicism is the big player in Canada. The 2011 National Household Survey revealed that close to 13 million Canadians (44%) viewed themselves as Catholic – about 7 million outside Quebec (24%) and 6 million inside Quebec (20%). The median age of Catholics is 42.9, close to that of the Canadian population as a whole (40.6).

In our new book *Canada's Catholics*, Angus Reid and I have taken a thorough look at the current Catholic situation in the country.[17] We have confirmed some central features (Figure 9.1).

Resilient Gods

FIGURE 9.1 Eight facts about Canadian Catholics

① They have an enormous number of people.

② They benefit immensely from immigration.

③ Their people are slow to defect.

④ Large numbers are enriched by their faith.

⑤ Many are open to greater involvement.

⑥ The less involved are looking for ministry.

⑦ The onus is on the shepherds.

⑧ The shepherds need the help of the sheep.

Source: Bibby (2010).

▶ Without question, Catholics continue to be no. 1 numerically by a large margin.

▶ They aren't going anywhere in Quebec or elsewhere; they stick like glue.

▶ Beliefs remain strong, and practices like private prayer are pervasive. At worst, Catholics are seasonal attenders. But they value faith.

▶ Their Catholicism is an important personal resource that enhances their lives.

▶ Yes, when it comes to personal morality, they are individualists, but they are Catholic individualists.

There is no question that things have changed. In Quebec, for example, the provincial government plays no religious favourites.[18] The lack of concrete commitment and involvement understandably troubles leaders. But widespread defection isn't on the horizon. Religion à la carte, for better or worse, is part of contemporary Canadian Catholic life.[19]

Catholicism is experiencing new vitality that is fuelled in large part by new arrivals from other countries. But that's only part of the story. Faith remains important for earlier generations of people raised in Canadian homes. Large numbers might show up only for seasonal services or rites of passage or because they think that they are overdue for a Mass. But they still show up. And they are still Catholic.

Reid and I have found that significant numbers also remain open to greater involvement if they can find it to be worthwhile. The challenge lies with the supplier. If the Catholic Church comes through, then who knows what could happen?

Of particular importance, as the Catholic Church goes, so goes organized religion in the nation. Because of Catholicism alone, religion has a bright future in Canada.

Mainline Protestants

As I look at the four primary "firms" in this group – United, Anglican, Lutheran, and Presbyterian – I see far more than cold numbers. I see many people whom I have known who value faith and have been working hard to resuscitate their denominations. Minus their formal titles, they have included people like Lewis Garnsworthy, Ted Scott, Gord Turner, Ralph Milton, Muriel Duncan, Christopher White, Vince Alfano, Mardi Tindal, Tony Plomp, Wayne Holst, Michael Pryse, and Susan Johnson.

Yet the research findings point to a reality that would not surprise any of them: it is difficult to see much hope for viable futures (Table 9.2). The poetic line that Durkheim used to describe the demise of Catholicism in 19th-century Europe comes to mind: "The old gods are growing old or are already dead."[20]

The problems have been evident for years. Kenneth Bagnell, in an astute article in the *Observer* in 2011, wrote that he saw hope for the United Church. He was not clear, however, as to why. As we have seen, there are some readily identifiable reasons why Mainline Protestant groups have been declining numerically since the 1960s (Figure 9.2).

TABLE 9.2 Mainline Protestants in Canada (%), 1931 and 2011

	Mainline Protestant	United	Anglican	Presbyterian	Lutheran
1931	48	20	16	8	4
2011	15	6	5	2	2

Source: Statistics Canada census data.

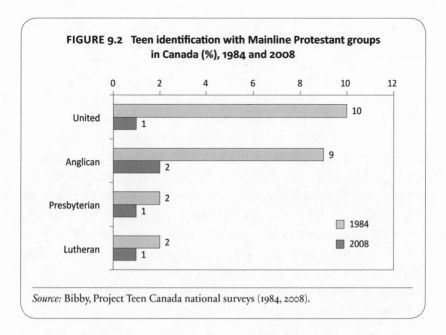

FIGURE 9.2 Teen identification with Mainline Protestant groups in Canada (%), 1984 and 2008

Source: Bibby, Project Teen Canada national surveys (1984, 2008).

▶ Growth via their once potent immigration pipelines has dropped off considerably from pre-1960s levels.
▶ They have not been successful in retaining their children.
▶ They have not been inclined to emphasize aggressive evangelism, with the result that they have been adding relatively small numbers of "outsiders."

In short, the demographics have not been good. Limited growth through immigration, migration, and birth, coupled with mortality, add up to an obvious result: zero or negative growth. Given their global nature, Anglicans could be helped considerably by immigration. But to date their potential global gains have been neutralized considerably by divisive issues regarding homosexuality and gender.[21]

There is an additional problem. To the extent that Stark and others are right in maintaining that people will be drawn to groups who address questions that "only the gods can answer," it's not clear that Mainline Protestants have particularly strong ultimate answer "product lines." Tom Harpur doesn't mince his words. In the case of life after death, he says that many groups simply "avoid the topic completely."[22] And he's not talking about evangelicals.

Unlike Catholics, for example, who give a fair amount of attention to things like heaven and the importance of "last rites" so that people are ready for life after death, a group like the United Church – rightly or wrongly – is seen by many as focusing almost exclusively on life. Perhaps Anglicans, Presbyterians, and Lutherans are different.[23]

Recently, two important works have appeared that provide informative "takes" on what happened to the United Church specifically in the post-1950s and why. One was written by an insider, Phyllis Airhart, a history professor at the University of Toronto's Emmanuel College. The other was written by an evangelical historian, Kevin Platt, of Redeemer University College in Ancaster, Ontario.[24] Airhart is inclined to see the evolution of the United Church as largely a product of social and cultural changes. Platt thinks that the downfall of the United Church was largely the result of its abandonment of evangelical emphases.

Respected American historian Mark Noll has provided a valuable exposition and critique of the positions of both Airhart and Platt. He agrees that "the United Church once embodied liberal evangelicalism; in the 1960s and early 1970s it became simply liberal." Yet he sees "the failure" of the United Church "as essentially cultural rather than primarily theological. It advocated a form of Protestantism well adapted to Canada's historical development." But with the major cultural shifts of the 1960s and 1970s, "the United Church found itself unwilling or incapable of presenting a vital Christian vision for the nation." Noll concludes that "the problem had less to do with its liberal evangelical character or its attempt to Christianize Canada, but lay rather with how that attempt at Christianization was carried out. It was too much commitment to Canada ca. 1925 for what Canada had become by 1970."[25]

Apart from the causes, the reality is that Mainline Protestant numbers are down dramatically, with significant resource implications: good ministry is all the more difficult to accomplish.[26]

Still, Diana Butler Bass could be right: it might yet be possible for Mainline Protestant churches to be renewed "by weaving personal spiritual quests" with a primary strength – their "more traditional forms of religious life."[27] For all the gloom and doom, affiliate numbers are still relatively high. David Harris, publisher of the now-defunct *Presbyterian Record,* comments that "the church desperately needs to find a way to move forward." But he cautions that flexibility and creativity can be hard to come by. In the self-disparaging words of one former moderator, "Zacchaeus was not a Presbyterian."[28] More than Mainliners sometimes realize, the future remains largely in their own hands.

Conservative Protestants

The evangelicals, as they are commonly known, are characterized by considerable vitality.[29] Their major demographic accomplishment has been their ability to sustain a market share of approximately 8% (7% Baptist) from the first census in 1871 through to the present day.

Religious intermarriage alone should have decimated the Conservative Protestants. Yet, because of factors that include immigration, their emphasis on tight-knit communities, and strong youth and family ministries, they have been able to sustain their market share. The thesis of Mainline Protestant executive Dean Kelley, put forth in the early 1970s, also has increasing support. In his book *Why Conservative Churches Are Growing,* Kelley maintained that two key factors of central importance were (1) the demands that evangelicals placed on their members, in the form of expectations like participation, tithing, and lifestyle, and (2) the provision of answers to ultimate questions, including life after death.[30]

My examination of evangelical church growth in Calgary dating back to the late 1960s has shown that, contrary to popular myth, Conservative Protestants know only modest growth through the recruitment of outsiders. Their numerical stability and growth are tied primarily to their ability to retain their own people – their children and their geographically mobile members – now increasingly global as well.[31] To the extent that they add outsiders, the key factor is relationships: they tend to either befriend or marry them.

Those patterns are consistent with Kelley's argument. The emphasis on a faith that has value and addresses life's big questions helps to explain the vitality and significance that contribute to evangelicals' high level of retention.

Somewhat paradoxically, while Conservative Protestants tend to stay with their "Believers' Church" denominations, they move fairly freely

TABLE 9.3 Select Conservative Protestant groups as percentages of the Canadian population, 1901–2011

	1901	1921	1941	1961	1981	2001	2011	Membership in 2011 (in 1,000s)
Baptist	5.9	4.8	4.2	3.3	2.9	2.5	1.9	636
Pentecostal	0.0	0.8	0.5	0.8	1.4	1.2	1.5	479
Mennonite	0.6	0.7	1.0	0.8	0.8	0.6	0.5	176
Evangelical Missionary	0.0	0.0	0.0	0.0	0.0	0.2	0.2	80
Christian Reformed	0.0	0.0	0.0	0.3	0.3	0.3	0.2	76
Adventist	0.0	0.2	0.2	0.1	0.2	0.2	0.2	67
Salvation Army	0.2	0.2	0.3	0.3	0.5	0.5	0.2	67
Christian and Missionary Alliance	0.0	0.0	0.0	0.1	0.1	0.2	0.2	51
Non-denominational	0.0	0.0	0.0	0.0	0.0	0.1	0.1	44
Brethren in Christ	0.0	0.0	0.0	0.1	0.1	0.1	0.0	23
Church of Christ	0.0	0.2	0.2	0.1	0.1	0.0	0.0	16
Free Methodist	0.0	0.0	0.1	0.1	0.1	0.0	0.0	11
Church of Nazarene	0.0	0.0	0.0	0.0	0.0	0.0	0.0	9
Christian: not indicated elsewhere	–	–	–	–	–	2.6	3.0	986

Sources: 1901 and 1921: computed from Kalbach and McVey (1976, 230); 1921–61: Hiller (1976, 360); 1981, 2001: census; 2011: National Household Survey.

between individual evangelical groups.[32] As a result, no single denomination in this "family" makes up even 3% of the Canadian population, nowhere near the 7% who identified themselves as "Baptist" when the first
census was conducted in 1871 (Table 9.3). Many increasingly prefer to go
simply by "Christian"[33] – or even, as we saw earlier, as SBNR.

Evangelicals, who are typically younger than Mainline Protestants,
will continue to be small players on the Canadian religious scene. But
their steady market share of 8% through the end of the 20th century is
finally edging upward – about 11% as of 2011. Why? The explosive growth
of evangelicals in many parts of the world will result in an increasingly
robust immigration pipeline – and an increasingly multicultural church
with a greater concern for social justice.[34]

Other Religious Groups

Historically, as people came to Canada from an array of countries, they
obviously brought with them religions other than Christianity. At the
time of Confederation, Jews made up about one-tenth of 1% of the population. With the arrival of increasing numbers of people from outside
Europe and the United States, additional faiths also took root.

Through about 1981, the number of people identifying with faiths
other than Christianity remained very small. Much of the difficulty such
groups had, of course, was tied to the difficulty of holding on to their

---

**TABLE 9.4 Identification with other religious groups as percentages
of the Canadian population, 1921–2011**

	1921	1941	1961	1981	2001	2011	Membership in 2011 (1,000s)
Muslim	–	–	–	0.4	2.0	3.2	1,054
Jewish	1.4	1.5	1.4	1.2	1.1	1.0	330
Buddhist	0.1	0.1	0.1	0.2	1.0	1.1	367
Hindu	–	–	–	0.3	1.0	1.5	498
Sikh	–	–	–	0.3	0.9	1.4	455
Jehovah's Witness	0.1	0.1	0.4	0.6	0.5	0.4	138
Latter Day Saints	0.2	0.2	0.3	0.4	0.3	0.3	105

Source: Statistics Canada census data.

---

children: many married Protestants and Catholics. The net result was that, by 1981, less than 3% of Canadians indicated that they were Jewish, Muslim, Buddhist, Hindu, or Sikh. Another 1% were either Jehovah's Witnesses or Mormons (Table 9.4).

Over the past three decades or so, immigration has seen the percentage of people who identify with other major world religions double to about 8%. The largest of these is Islam at around 2%.

The historical track records of a number of these faiths – Judaism, Buddhism, Hinduism, and Sikhism, along with Latter Day Saints and

TABLE 9.5 Identification with religious groups in Canada, 2011		
	N	%
Total population	32,852,320	100
Christian	22,102,745	67
Roman Catholic	12,810,705	39
United	2,007,610	6
Anglican	1,631,845	5
Baptist	635,840	2
Orthodox	550,690	2
Pentecostal	478,705	2
Lutheran	478,185	2
Presbyterian	472,385	2
Christian (not included elsewhere)	1,475,575	4
Other	1,561,205	4
Other faiths	2,768170	8
Muslim	1,053,945	2
Hindu	497,965	2
Sikh	454,965	1
Buddhist	366,830	1
Jewish	329,495	1
Aboriginal spirituality	64,940	<1
Varied other	130,800	<1
No religion	7,850,605	24

Source: Statistics Canada, National Household Survey (2011).

Jehovah's Witnesses – suggest that they will continue to be parts of the Canadian religious scene. But similar to the once-dominant four Mainline Protestant groups, they won't be among the major religious firms.

Islam is another story. The number of Muslims is now fourth behind Canadians who identify as Catholic, United, and Anglican (Table 9.5). They might well be on the verge of attaining the proverbial "critical mass" – such as evangelicals have experienced – whereby they can cut down on losses through intermarriage. Moreover, Islam obviously is a powerful multinational religion. In light of the diverse countries in which it is prominent, the immigration pipeline that has been such a critical component of religious group growth over the years will continue to produce large numbers of new Muslims for some time to come.

In addition, a relatively high birth rate and an emphasis on the retention of children will further contribute to the viability of Islam. The median age of Muslims as of the 2011 census was 28.9, compared with 42.9 for Catholics, 51.1 for Anglicans, and 52.3 for those identifying as United. Additions through proselytism – or what many social scientists call "switching" – can also be expected.

Finally, the two traits that observers such as Kelley and Stark see as essential to success – an emphasis on demands and rewards and the ability to speak to ultimate questions – are major features of Islam. Recent data

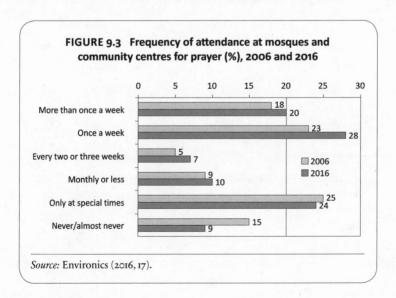

FIGURE 9.3 Frequency of attendance at mosques and community centres for prayer (%), 2006 and 2016

Source: Environics (2016, 17).

on attendance at mosques and community centres for prayer generated by Environics are impressive (Figure 9.3).

In short, as we look to the future of religion in Canada, we can anticipate that the Roman Catholic Church will continue to be the dominant player. Other key market members will be Conservative Protestants and Muslims. The marketplace won't lack for other players, both old and new. But those groups will have to work hard just to retain – let alone expand – their market shares.

The Global Situation

As in Canada, there are and will continue to be people all over the world who are not in the market for religion, old or new. But they will be in the minority. Today, about 6 billion of the planet's 7 billion people identify with a religion. They are led by Christians (2.2 billion), Muslims (1.6 billion), and Hindus (1 billion). Like auto multinationals, including Toyota, General Motors, Volkswagen, Ford, and Hyundai, these religious powerhouses will continue to lead the way as the most prominent religious "suppliers."

TABLE 9.6 Major religious groups worldwide, 2010 and 2050

	2010 population		2050 projection	
	N	%	N	%
World totals	6.9 billion	100.0	9.3 billion	100.0
Christians	2.2 billion	31.4	2.9 billion	31.4
Muslims	1.6 billion	23.2	2.8 billion	29.7
Unaffiliated	1.1 billion	16.4	1.2 billion	13.2
Hindus	1.0 billion	15.0	1.4 billion	14.9
Buddhists	488 million	7.1	486 million	5.2
Folk religions	405 million	5.9	449 million	4.8
Sikhs	25 million	0.3	25 million*	0.3
Jews	14 million	0.2	16 million	0.2
Other	33 million	0.5	36 million	0.4

* Based upon a growth rate of 0.5%.
Source: Pew Research Center (2015a).

Collectively, the major religious companies have been performing very well of late. The projections through 2050 of the highly reputable Pew Research Center point to ongoing vitality and growth, with Muslims in particular increasing their market share (Table 9.6).

In the words of Harvey Cox, "Instead of disappearing, religion – for good or ill – is now exhibiting new vitality all around the world and making its weight widely felt in the corridors of power."[35] In 2015, Rodney Stark exuberantly proclaimed that "the world is more religious than it has even been. Quite simply," he wrote, "a massive religious awakening is taking place around the world." Beyond rhetoric, he backed up his claim with extensive global data, dealing in detail with Europe, Latin America, Africa, Japan, China, Taiwan, Hong Kong, Singapore, South Korea, and the United States. In the process, he gave specific attention to the new global vitality being experienced by Christianity, Islam, and Hinduism.[36]

The Growth of Christianity

In recent years, Christianity – along with Islam – has experienced phenomenal worldwide growth (Table 9.7). Word of the faith's global prosperity will come as news to many people. After all, as Philip Yancey noted

TABLE 9.7 **Ten countries with the largest Christian populations, 2010**

Country	Christian population (in millions)
United States	243
Brazil	173
Mexico	108
Russia	105
Philippines	86
Nigeria	78
China	68
Democratic Republic of the Congo	63
Germany	57
Ethiopia	52

Source: Pew Research Center (2015a).

recently, it's not making the headlines of CNN.[37] *Globe and Mail* columnist Neil Reynolds similarly wrote in 2010 that "you could call it the greatest story never told."[38]

Reynolds drew on two prominent observers of the global religious scene, American political scientist Walter Russell Mead and British scholar Scott Thomas. Their thoughts are worth retrieving in detail,[39] with some invaluable 2015 global data produced by the Pew Research Center worth splicing in.[40]

The flamboyant Mead has noted that Christianity is now "on its biggest roll" in its 2,000-year history.[41] Its absolute numbers and market share are at all-time highs. In the past 50 years, Mead says, "it has surpassed Islam as the most popular religion in sub-Saharan Africa and as the leading Abrahamic religion in China."[42] The Pew Forum's global data released in April 2015 show that Christians outnumber Muslims, but Islam is growing faster. By 2050, there will be close to 3 billion Christians and about 2.8 billion Muslims.[43] Here are some additional observations and numbers.

> ▸ Roman Catholic commentator John Allen notes that, between 1950 and 2000, the number of Catholics worldwide grew from just under 500 million to over 1 billion. The church suffered serious losses in the global North (Europe and North America) but grew dramatically in the global South (Africa, Asia, and Latin America).[44]
> ▸ In a country like Russia, Orthodox Christianity is enjoying a revival after 70 years of communist suppression.[45]
> ▸ Of particular significance, says Mead, Pentecostals have experienced the fastest growth of any religious movement in history, "from zero to something like half a billion members in the last 100 years." Growth has been pronounced in Africa, Asia, and Latin America (Table 9.8).[46]

Thomas likewise maintains that, "around the world, religion is on the rise," and he notes that "the most dramatic religious explosion is the spread of evangelical Protestantism, led by Pentecostalism." After Catholics, he says, Pentecostals represent the largest single group of Christians worldwide.[47] It typically crosses class lines.

TABLE 9.8 Regional distribution of Pentecostals, 2010

	% of region that is Pentecostal	% of world's Pentecostal population
World total	4	100
Sub-Saharan Africa	15	44
Americas	11	37
Asia-Pacific	1	16
Europe	2	4
Middle East–North Africa	<1	<1

Source: Pew Research Center (2011).

Perhaps startling is not only that evangelicals now number close to 700 million people worldwide but also that they have achieved strategic masses in places like China, Indonesia, India, Nigeria, the Philippines, South Africa, and Brazil (Table 9.9). For example, the Pew Research Center estimates that, by 2050, there could be more than 70 million Christians in China – about 5% of the population.[48] Thomas, along with Stark and Wang, believes that the numbers will be even higher.[49] In many instances, Thomas notes, Christianity is "returning to its roots by becoming a post-Western religion dominated by the peoples, cultures, and countries of the global South."[50] While having a strong personal focus, it has also become increasingly politically active, especially in Latin America.[51]

These patterns of expansion, of course, have not been without conflict. Thomas points out that "three countries with substantial Muslim communities – India, Indonesia, and Nigeria – also have large Pentecostal populations and sizable minorities of Christians more broadly." Tensions have been rising, resulting in violence like the conflict in Nigeria in 2010 that left over 500 people dead.[52]

In addition, competition with Catholicism in various parts of the world is frequently intense. John Allen writes that, as "Pentecostals march across the planet," they have been "siphoning off significant numbers of Catholics." He notes that "the Catholic Church is itself being 'Pentecostalized' through the Charismatic movement."[53]

A massive shift in population growth from the developed countries of the global North to the developing countries of the global South will result in a changing religious landscape worldwide. Thomas points out that the developed countries of the global North accounted for 32% of the world's population in 1900 and 18% in 2000. By 2050, that figure will drop to just 10%.[54] "A new kind of world is in the making," he says, "and the people, states, and religious communities that compose the global South are making it."[55]

In the case of Roman Catholics, Allen notes that the church was dominated in the past century by the global North. Today two in three Catholics are found in Africa, Asia, and Latin America.[56] One obvious result is that an unprecedented number of Catholic leaders are coming from all over the world[57] – often, in the case of Canada, to a parish near you.

Both Mead and Thomas draw attention to the fact that the rise in evangelical Christianity in particular can be expected to bring with it an increase in Protestant ideals such as the work ethic, entrepreneurial aspiration, and personal freedom.[58] Thomas sees global Christianity as becoming more conservative than it is in Europe but more liberal than Catholicism, which will be replaced, in some Latin American settings, by evangelicalism. Sometimes it will be a hybrid with Catholicism, sometimes not.[59] In addition, Mead and Thomas maintain that the spread of evangelical Christianity will have important social consequences. Globally,

TABLE 9.9 Number of Christians in China (estimates and projections), 1980–2040

Year	Population (in millions)
1980	10.0
1990	19.7
2000	38.7
2010	76.1
2020	149.7
2030	294.6
2040	579.5

Source: Stark and Wang (2015, KL 1416).

"evangelicals will be a major religious, social, and political force in the coming century," Thomas writes.[60]

In China, for example, he points out that the government tacitly allows the established religions of Christianity and neo-Confucianism "to operate relatively freely, believing that they can promote social harmony amid rapid social changes." Thomas suggests that if Christianity achieves the cultural permeation in China that it has in South Korea – at about 25% – it could fundamentally alter China's political fabric (Table 9.9).[61]

The Growth of Islam

As we have seen, observers say that Islam is also experiencing a revival that extends well beyond the more extreme Islamic fundamentalist movements. We noted in Chapter 6 that Muslims are migrating from predominantly Islamic countries to the rest of the world in unprecedented numbers (Table 9.10). Moreover, we saw with the global Gallup data that Muslims value faith: large proportions say that religion is an important part of their daily lives. In reminding readers that Islamic renewal is extending far beyond the Arab world, Thomas writes that "more Muslim women are wearing the veil, more Muslim men are growing beards, and more Muslims are attending mosques more often."[62] These findings are also worth noting.

- Russia now has more Muslims than any country in Europe.
- Northwestern China "is home to over 20 million Muslims and is in the grip of an Islamic reawakening."[63] Many young Chinese Muslims are studying across the Middle East.
- Numbers alone mean that Christian-Islamic relations will, in Allen's words, "be a major driver of world history in the twenty-first century."[64]

It's important to recognize the role that the Internet is playing in connecting Muslims, Christians, and people of other faiths. In the past, geographical separation meant that they were isolated religious diasporas. No more. Yet, ironically, Thomas observes, globalization is producing "a more unified and yet more fragmented world."[65]

TABLE 9.10 Ten countries with the largest Muslim populations, 2010

Country	Population (in millions)
Indonesia	209
India	176
Pakistan	167
Bangladesh	134
Nigeria	77
Egypt	77
Iran	74
Turkey	71
Algeria	35
Morocco	33

Source: Pew Research Center (2015a).

To sum up and underline the important numbers here, both Christianity and Islam are showing dramatic worldwide growth. Currently, there are more Christians than Muslims. But Muslims are closing the gap. By 2050, each group will have about 3 billion people spread across the world. A hint of polarization globally? The unaffiliated will number about 1.2 billion.[66]

Assessment

Obviously, the levels of receptivity to religion vary considerably around the world. In Stark's parlance, settings are religiously "regulated" and "deregulated."[67] They have open as well as closed markets, robust competition as well as long-standing monopolies.

But because of both the ongoing demand for and the ongoing availability of global suppliers, one thing is clear: religion will persist as far as the social scientific eye can see, individually and organizationally. The market for religion is so vast that, apart from the gods, entrepreneurial human beings would find its potential too great to ignore.

Religions, major and minor, well established and freshly minted, will continue to be at work, attempting to increase their local, national, and global market shares. Individuals will continue to explore the options and will usually opt for one – or more. After all, for some, religion enriches life. For all, it offers market entries when it comes to death. And as for the gods, if they actually exist, and people ignore them for too long, they can be expected to shake things up from time to time.

It is significant, I think, that Thomas concludes his recent overview of global religious developments by underlining the importance of religion for the vast majority of people around the world. Precisely because "faith informs the daily struggles of millions in confronting" life, he says, countries like the United States need to understand the worldwide resurgence of religion. If they fail to do so, Thomas maintains, then "the potential for religiously motivated violence across the globe may increase dramatically over the next century."[68] At a time when the debate about secularization has become something of a spectator sport for academics, the scale of the resurgence of religion is affecting the entire planet – including Canada.

Conclusion

When people believe that the future will be different,
it transforms the way they feel about the present.
– Harvey Cox, *The Future of Religion*, 2009

This brings me back to where I began. In trying to make sense of religious developments in Canada, many of us have been pretty myopic. We've looked at what is happening to our dominant religious groups and assumed that, if they are not doing well, religion in the country is doomed.

One of the great things that has happened in the late 20th and early 21st centuries is that our eyes have been opened regarding our place on the planet. Never before have so many of us been aware of what is happening around the world and how events and developments elsewhere might impact us.

So it is that we watch as Canadian and American television networks tell us how market changes in places like Toronto and New York, Tokyo and Beijing, affect the value of the Canadian dollar. We see how a terrorist attack in New York or Paris, Syria or Bali, results in heightened security alerts. Significantly, the alerts affect us not only as we fly to distant countries but also as we line up for short domestic trips from places ranging from Lethbridge to Winnipeg to Toronto. Our sources of entertainment no longer have geographical boundaries as we watch the Olympics in Russia or Rio or see our hockey players and tennis stars

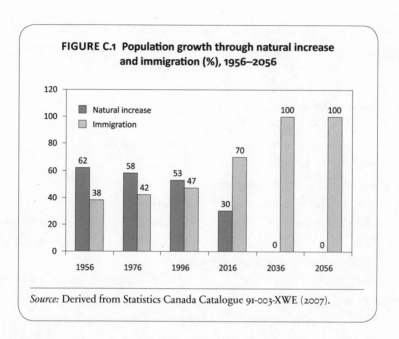

FIGURE C.1 Population growth through natural increase and immigration (%), 1956–2056

Source: Derived from Statistics Canada Catalogue 91-003-XWE (2007).

compete anywhere in the world. Through television and the Internet, Facebook and Twitter, we are connected to people around the globe.

Then there is the ongoing reality of immigration. Yes, most of us – probably almost all of us – had great-grandparents, grandparents, and parents who came to Canada from other parts of the world. Maybe we ourselves arrived here from another country. But we are in the midst of a new era of immigration in which the population of Canada will be dependent in the foreseeable future on immigration for growth. Our birth rate has not been keeping up with our death rate. As a result, as Statistics Canada reminds us, the math is simple: if our population is going to increase, then it is going to have to increase through net international migration. And this means that increasingly the world will be coming to Canada. *There is no single factor that is going to be more important in determining the future of life in Canada than immigration.*

The Impact of Immigration on the Religious Continuum

Religion is anything but an exception. As the global data demonstrate conclusively, people around the world haven't abandoned religion. And when they arrive in Canada, religion is going to be in their luggage. Groups led by Roman Catholics, evangelical Protestants, and Muslims in particular will feel the effects. One prominent world religious organization has referred to Filipinos, for example, as "God's secret weapon."[1]

But the impact of immigration will also be felt by Canadians who prefer to live life without religion. Their already hefty ranks will be bolstered by significant numbers of immigrants who feel the same way.

Polarization among the Arrivals

In short, the people who come to Canada will resemble the rest of us who are already here. Not all who self-identify as religious will be devout. Similarly, they will be variously comprised of the pro-religious, the no religious, and those in the religious middle.

But given the high levels of religiosity characteristic of many of their homelands, on balance immigration – at least in the short run – is going to give religion a significant shot in the arm. Our 2015 national survey shows that individuals born outside Canada are considerably more likely than those born here both to attend services and to embrace faith (Table C.1).

TABLE C.1 Attendance and religious inclinations by birthplace and age (%), 2015

	Age	Born in Canada	Born elsewhere
Monthly-plus attendance			
All	23	21	35
18–34	25	22	49
35–54	19	17	34
55+	24	24	27
Inclined to embrace religion			
All	30	29	38
18–34	28	27	42
35–54	25	24	38
55+	36	35	36

Source: ARI Religion Survey (2015).

Particularly noteworthy is the fact that the differences are most pronounced among younger adults. For example, 49% of adults under 35 who were born outside Canada maintain that they attend services at least once a month. The level for their counterparts who were born in Canada is less than half – 22%. The same pattern holds for middle-age adults.

The directions that immigrants will be inclined to move along the religion–no religion continuum will depend to a large extent on how religious groups perform. That leads to a very important question.

Will the Children of Immigrants Remain Involved?

I am frequently asked if the children of immigrants – the second generation – will continue to be as involved in religious groups as their parents. My sense is that many people who ask the question are doubtful.

I believe that the key suggested by our research over time is that religious groups must do everything they can to ensure that involvement is significant for the children of people coming to Canada. If young people can find that participation in such groups adds to their lives and, in turn, those of their children, then there is nothing written in the stars to say that they will cease to value and practise involvement.

A wild-eyed observation: contemporary religious groups that are homes to immigrants need to learn an important lesson from their Mainline Protestant predecessors – United, Anglican, Presbyterian, and Lutheran Churches. What many people fail to realize is that demographic profiles don't lie: those four denominations were also predominantly "ethnic churches" at one point. Their memberships were top-heavy with people who had come from England, Scotland, and western Europe. A key reason that these Mainline "ethnic" denominations faltered in the post-1960s was because they weren't able to convince younger people that involvement was worth their while.

The new influx of immigrants gives today's latest religious group entries a chance to succeed where the Mainline ethnic groups largely failed. It is not a new problem, but it does require some new, creative, and life-enhancing solutions.

However, those cheering for the intergenerational retention of "the Nones" also need to keep a close eye on their daughters and sons. Sheer numbers make it difficult for people with no religion to retain that status.

As I have playfully put it for years, "Nothings often befriend and marry Somethings." And when that happens, the odds in the past at least have favoured the latter – especially when it comes to how the children are raised.[2] Things are ever changing along the polarization continuum.

The Myth of Demise

In early 2011, I was contacted by a journalist who asked for my response to research that had just been presented at professional meetings in Dallas. A team of American physicists had proclaimed that census data from nine countries – including Canada – pointed to religion in those settings being en route to extinction.[3] Perhaps those physicists had been spending too much time in their labs.

Global data are decisive: religion in Canada and elsewhere is not headed for demise, contrary to what many prominent early social scientists thought and some current scientists think. Because of the eternal quest for meaning – the need to make sense of life and death – there will always be a significant market for religion in Canada and around the world.

That's not to say that everyone will be part of the market. Clearly, significant numbers of people in Canada and elsewhere are choosing to live life without religion. Polarization is a reality everywhere. But the polarization continuum is just that: it consists of the pro-religious and the no religious at the extremes, with lots of people in the religious middle.

Demise and Rise

In speaking about "the demise and rise of religion in Canada" in the past, what I had in mind was that a significant core of people value faith, in contrast to generalizations about its relegation to history.[4] Religion was never really in demise; it's just that many people thought that it was because they confused the problems of some of our historically prominent religious groups with the problems of religion.

In the proverbial "big picture," religion is far more than human organizations, which rise and fall for any number of reasons. Seen from the vantage point of the organizational analyst, religious groups are like businesses trying to make headway in the religious market. Some succeed, some fail. But, regardless, the market continues to exist, awaiting new and more effective entries. History tells us that any number of religious groups come and go. But the gods, as far as we can tell, seem to last forever.

And as the world comes to Canada in growing numbers during the 21st century, religion – and polarization – will feel the invigorating and sometimes debilitating effects. Today about 65% of Canadians – led by Catholics – identify with the Christian faith. So much for all the rhetoric about this being a post-Christian Canada. Another 10% look to other faiths to have their religious needs met. And about 25% of Canadians currently choose to take a pass on religion.

Apart from sheer identification, we have seen that about 30% of people across the country say that they are embracing religion, about 25% are rejecting it, and the remaining 45% are acknowledging that they are somewhere in the middle.

These kinds of data hardly document the growing disappearance of religion in Canada. On the contrary, the readings provided by Statistics Canada and our own surveys show that religion continues to vibrantly coexist with non-religion, with lots of people in between the two inclinations.

Let me be pointed and emphatic: it's time that we stopped navel gazing and pontificating about how growing secularity is going to virtually eliminate religion in Canada. It hasn't happened, and it's never going to happen. Likewise, let's be perfectly clear about the nature of religious polarization. Religion is also never going to eradicate secular inclinations. My central point is that pro-religious and no-religious inclinations – along with the choice of the religious middle – have always been with us, even if they haven't received the publicity they deserve. And the three inclinations will always be with us.

The Pew Report
Some near-definitive additional documentation is available. As discussed earlier, the Pew Research Center has made a major contribution to those of us who want to understand global religious trends with an April 2015 release of a report I think is of historical significance. With considerable

sophistication and rigour, Pew has offered current data and projections through 2050 for the world's major religions in a large number of national settings, including Canada.

We have already given a lot of attention to current patterns of identification. What's fascinating are the Pew projections as to what the Canadian religious situation will look like in 2050.

▶ By that point in time, we will see a drop of about 10 percentage points in those who identify themselves as Christians.
▶ The decline in the Christian religious "market share" will be primarily the result of a slight increase in Muslims (from 2% to 6%) and those who indicate that they have no religion (from 24% to 26%).
▶ But otherwise things will not change very much.
▶ Particularly newsworthy for Christian groups is the fact that 60% of the Canadian population will be in the market for Christianity. Unknown to us at this point is which Christian groups will step up and respond.

What is important about these projections is that the data point to anything but the disappearance of religion by the middle of the 21st century. Yes, one-quarter of Canadians will reject religion, but three-quarters will not – similar to our current situation, measured by both religious identification and religious inclinations.

Canada is currently experiencing polarization – as is every other society in the world. The balance among those embracing faith, rejecting faith, and opting for the religious middle – the pro-faith, low faith, and no faith – will not change all that much in Canada by 2050, according to the Pew Research Center (Table C.2).

The Last Word: Resilient Gods

So there we have it. In the end, it's a pretty simple reality that can be explained in pretty simple terms. In Canada and everywhere else in the world, people variously embrace religion, reject religion, or take something of a middle position.

TABLE C.2 Identification with major religious groups in Canada, 2010 and 2050

	2010		2050, projected	
	Membership (in thousands)	% of population	Membership (in thousands)	% of population
Christians	23,470	69	24,640	60
Unaffiliated	8,050	24	10,470	26
Muslims	710	2	2,260	6
Hindus	470	1	1,070	3
Buddhists	280	1	600	1
Jews	350	1	560	1
Other	690	2	1,350	3

Source: Pew Research Center (2015a).

Secularization describes the inclination for individuals and societies to move away from being religious; revival or desecularization describes the inclination for them to move toward being religious. A significant part of populations everywhere will find themselves between the two polar extremes. The polarization continuum on which people are located is dynamic, ever changing in keeping with organizational, cultural, and demographic factors.

But in the process, the gods remain resilient. They are embraced, ignored, abandoned, and scorned – only to be frequently rediscovered. In some cases, but far from always, the posture toward them is permanent.

As Canada enters a time of accelerated immigration, the configurations are going to be in motion. Things, as always, will be changing. In the foreseeable future, Christians will be numerically dominant, but their lead is going to decrease. Those who reject religion will continue to be significant in number, as will people in the religious middle.

Such changes will bring with them two central questions.

First, in Canada and around the world, can the growing number of Christians, Muslims, and people with no religion coexist? Can they live out their different expressions of religious faith – or no faith at all – in ways that make for positive individual and collective life? Tangibly, in a country like Canada, can they find commonality on policy issues that relate to areas of life – such as sexuality – where their values and views are very different?

Second, an ongoing question is one that has been central to this book: what are the implications and consequences for personal and collective life of individuals variously embracing, rejecting, and taking a middle position on religion?

The gods are resilient; they aren't going away. In the words of Harvey Cox, "All the signs suggest we are poised to enter a new Age of the Spirit and that the future will be a future of faith."[5]

The esteemed anthropologist Clifford Geertz has written that it appears "in all probability most [people] are unable ... to look at the stranger features of the world's landscape in dumb astonishment or bland apathy without trying to develop ... some notions as to how such features might be reconciled with the more ordinary deliverances of experience."[6] Sociologist Max Weber once put things this way: religion is the product of an "inner compulsion to understand the world as a meaningful cosmos and take up a position toward it."[7] Canadian philosopher Charles Taylor has argued that people continue to have a need for a sense of fullness that reflects transcendent reality. In his words, "Our age is very far from settling in to a comfortable unbelief."[8]

The problem with living without the gods is that there are times when we are forced to deal with the mysteries of life and death. There are experiences of ecstasy and euphoria, perplexion and despair, suffering and tragedy that sometimes seem to call out for something beyond us.

All that said, those who choose to ignore the gods aren't going away. As journalist Konrad Yakabuski reminds us, many young people, for example, "find the church steps to be little more than a good place to skateboard."[9] And then, of course, there are even more people who have opted for that middle position who likewise are not going away.

Therefore, the big challenge of this century and in centuries to come is to figure out how all these different postures toward faith can be made to work in ways that contribute to optimum living – and dying.

In one line, the great question is this: how can the presence and absence of faith coexist for the betterment of us all – now that it is clear that both inclinations will always be with us?

Notes

Preface

1 Thiessen (2011). Thiessen conducted 90 detailed interviews with people in Calgary, evenly divided among those who actively embrace religion, those who marginally embrace it, and those who reject it. These categories reflect in part my earlier "concentric" thinking, going back to 1995 and drawing on the work of Hadaway (1990).

Introduction

1 One of the most prominent recent distillations of global data is offered in Stark (2015).

Chapter 1: The Early Days of God's Dominion

1 Grant (1998, 1).
2 Ibid., 8.
3 Bramadat and Seljak (2008, 2009).
4 Grant (1998, 65).
5 Beyer (1997, 276–77).
6 Canadian Institute of Public Opinion (1945).
7 Bibby (1987, 16–17).
8 CBC (1973).
9 Grant (1998, 161).
10 Canadian census (1941, 1961).
11 Beaucage and LaRoque (1983, 31).
12 CBC (1973).
13 Noll (2007, 18).
14 Kristofferson (1969).

Chapter 2: Declining Religious Participation among Boomers

1 See, for example, Altizer (1966) about the US and D. Hall (1980) about Canada.
2 Noll (2007, 36–37). For a valuable set of responses to Noll, see *Church and Faith Trends* (2008).
3 Foote (1996, 1).
4 Yakabuski (2009).
5 Bibby (2006).
6 See, for example, Bigge (2008); Burson (2009); and Murray (2009).
7 Bibby (1990, 9).
8 Hordern (1966, 46).
9 Bibby (2006, 71).
10 Ibid., 67.
11 Leger Marketing (2007).
12 Vaisey and Smith (2008). Also discussed by M. Harris (2008).
13 Bibby (2002, 221).
14 Taylor (2007, 580).
15 Ibid., 588.
16 Putnam (2000, 195).
17 Some of these ideas, accompanied by data, are described in more detail in Bibby (2006).
18 Statistics Canada Catalogue 96F0030XIE2001015, 6.
19 Archdiocese of Toronto website, October 2016, http://www.archtoronto.org.
20 For a summary of the key findings regarding Aboriginals, see Bibby, Fox, and Penner (2010).
21 Valpy (2010).
22 Dueck (2010). A take on the debate is offered by Scrivener (2010).

Chapter 3: Pro-Religion, Low Religion, and No Religion

1 Valpy and Friesen (2010).
2 For a very readable overview of secularization, see Horton (2013).
3 Dobbelaere (1981, 2002).
4 Berger (1961).
5 Ibid.; Luckmann (1967).
6 Berger (1961, 41).
7 Cox (1965).
8 Stark and Glock (1968).
9 See Beyer (1997); Bowen (2004); Dawson and Thiessen (2014); Eagle (2011); Noll (2007); and Rouleau (1977).
10 See, for example, Berger (1999, 2; 2014) and Cox (1995, xv–xvi).
11 Specifically, the 1990 General Social Survey and the 2000 Survey of Giving, Volunteering, and Participating; for details, see Bibby (2002, 75–76).
12 Ibid., 73.
13 Ibid., 90.

14   See, for example, his work with Bainbridge (1985); Finke (Finke and Starke 1992; Stark and Finke 2000); and Iannaccone (1994).
15   Stark and Bainbridge (1985, 7).
16   Ibid., 2.
17   Ibid., 529–30.
18   Finke and Stark (1992, 238, 250).
19   Ibid., 252–55.
20   Stark and Bainbridge (1985).
21   Bibby (2002, 62 ff.).
22   The "no-religion" figure was 4% in 1971, 7% in 1981, and 12% in 1991.
23   This argument is developed in detail in Bibby (2002, 66 ff.).
24   Stark and Finke (2000, 259–74).
25   Bibby (2002, 68).
26   Bibby (1993, 282).
27   Chaves (1994).
28   Beyer (1997).
29   Casanova (1994, 2006).
30   Berger (1999, 2–3).
31   Taylor (2007, 21).
32   Demerath (2007, 66).
33   Gregg (2005, 21–22).
34   Dawson and Thiessen (2014, 171); Thiessen (2011).
35   Vernon (1968).
36   Zuckerman (2014, 60 ff).
37   Putnam and Campbell (2010, 135–36).
38   Davie (1994).
39   Zuckerman (2014, 63).
40   Ibid., 64–65.
41   Hunsberger and Altemeyer (2006).
42   Cited in Zuckerman (2014, 66).
43   Thiessen (2015, especially Chapter 3).
44   Chaves (2011).
45   Putnam and Campbell (2010, 3).
46   Email, August 7, 2012, used with permission; Brym and Lie (2005, 459); in Canada, Brym, Lie, and Rytina (2007, 508–9).
47   Brym and Lie (2013, 269).
48   Email, August 7, 2012, used with permission.
49   See, for example, Wilkins-Laflamme (2014, forthcoming).
50   Email, October 15, 2015, used with permission.
51   Reimer (forthcoming).
52   Gallup (2013, 2015); Pew Research Center (2012, 2015b); for detailed data and analyses, see Barna and Kinnaman (2014).
53   Bibby (2014).
54   For an example of the responses of some evangelicals to the increase in those with no religion, see White (2014); for a Catholic take, see Oakes (2015).

55 Burke (2013); Newport (2013).
56 See the WVS website at http://www.worldvaluessurvey.org.
57 See http://www.gallup.com and the backgrounder document http://www.
gallup.com/services/170945/world-poll.aspx.
58 See http://pewglobal.org. I again have to express my deepest appreciation to
the Gallup organization, the WVS researchers, the Pew Research Center, and
the International Social Survey Programme for providing the priceless data
that make many of the summaries and analyses that follow possible.
59 For a background sketch, see http://www.norc.org/Experts/Pages/tom-smith.
aspx.
60 T. Smith (2009, 2).
61 Ibid., 15. For common measures, see, for example, Winseman (2002), who
describes Gallup's measures of "spiritual commitment." The indicators are
very conventional.
62 T. Smith (2009, 15–16).

Chapter 4: The Polarized Mosaic

1 Bibby (2011).
2 Glock and Stark (1965).
3 Becker (1972).
4 Except where otherwise indicated, all data in this chapter, including figures
and tables, are based on the ARI Religion Survey (2015).
5 Putnam and Campbell (2010).
6 Bibby (1987).
7 Reid (2016).
8 I wrote some of this material for the initial findings report of the ARI Religion
Survey (2015), released on the ARI website on March 26, 2015.
9 Bibby, Project Canada national survey (1985).
10 Thiessen and Wilkins-Laflamme (forthcoming).

Chapter 5: Religious Inclinations and Personal Well-Being

1 Dawkins (2006, 281, 308).
2 Hitchens (2007, 13).
3 S. Harris (2004, 236, 79).
4 Gruending (1996).
5 Collins (2010).
6 Pew Research Center (2016b).
7 Fraser (2016).
8 Sluyter (2001).
9 Wallace (2010).
10 See Gilbert (2006); Bok (2010); and Graham (2009).
11 Furstenberg (2013).
12 Samuel (2009).

13 Vandore (2008).
14 See Castle (2010); also see Watson and Coates (2010).
15 Helliwell, Layard, and Sachs (2015).
16 Lim and Putnam (2010). For a brief synopsis, see the Harvard University press release (Brockmeyer 2010). A good journalistic take on the study is offered by the *Globe and Mail*'s Sarah Hampson (2010). General information on social capital material is available at https://socialcapital.wordpress.com.
17 C. Smith (2005, 218 ff.).
18 Zuckerman (2008, 2014).
19 Zuckerman (2014, 3).
20 Manning (2015, 8). A journalist's take on the importance of raising children without religion is offered by Arel (2015).
21 Drawn from Southard (1961).
22 Manning (2015, 173).
23 Hampson (2010).
24 For gender breakdowns, see Bibby (2009, 70).
25 See Bibby (2006, 115).
26 Bibby (2009, 66).
27 Newport, Agrawal, and Witters (2010).
28 G. Miller (2000).
29 Ibid.
30 Stokes (2007).
31 Pelham and Nyiri (2008).
32 Ibid.
33 See, for example, Crabtree (2010, 2).
34 See, for example, Stratton (2010).
35 Social Capital Blog (2010).

Chapter 6: Religious Inclinations and Social Well-Being

1   Zuckerman (2014, 11).
2   Ibid., 13–14.
3   Pew Research Center (2014).
4   Stark (2012, 4).
5   C. Smith and Emerson (2008, L61).
6   See the Science of Generosity, University of Notre Dame, http://generosity research.nd.edu/more-about-the-initiative.
7   Cited in Edge Foundation (2010).
8   Ibid.
9   S. Harris (2010). For two informative reviews, see Appiah (2010) and Horgan (2010).
10 Edge Foundation (2010).
11 Cited in ibid.
12 Ibid.
13 Ibid.

14 An excellent video of his views on science and morality is available via YouTube: "Sam Harris: Science Can Answer Moral Questions," posted by TED Talks, http://www.ted.com.
15 See S. Harris (2010).
16 Adler (2006).
17 For expositions of the emerging field, see, for example, Cacioppo et al. (2002) and Todorov, Fiske, and Prentice (2011).
18 Quoted in Stolberg (2010).
19 Quoted in Ferguson (2010).
20 Wood (2010).
21 See, for example, http://www.hockeyalberta.ca/members/respect-sport/ and https://www.hockeycanada.ca/en-ca/Corporate/About/History/Partners/Respect-Group.
22 ARI Religion Survey (2015).
23 Bibby (2011, 145–46).
24 Project Canada/ARI 2015 Survey.
25 A number of the same items were included in the 2000 national adult and youth surveys. For items and findings, see Bibby (2001, 17, 233).
26 This item appeared in both the teen and the adult surveys in 2000; it did not appear in the adult survey in 2005. That's why we do not have recent comparable adult data.
27 Bibby (2001, 148).
28 Bibby (1990, 9).
29 Ibid.
30 See, for example, de Souza (2010).
31 Martinuk (2011).
32 Murphy (2009).
33 Peters (2010).
34 Allemang (2010).
35 Bibby (2011, 76–77).
36 Cited by Putnam and Campbell (2010, 521) and attributed to "legal scholar Peter Schuck."
37 Environics (2016, 35).
38 Ibid.
39 Very similar findings for views of Islam by religion are reported by ibid.
40 S. Harris (2008, 7).
41 See, for example, Pew Research Center (2016c) for recent Muslim data by country that document this observation.
42 Kazemipur (2014, 181).
43 Ibid., 194.
44 Environics (2016, 7–27).
45 Valpy and Friesen (2010).
46 Persichilli (2010).
47 Valpy and Friesen (2010).
48 B. Smith and Stark (2009, 4).
49 Pelham and Crabtree (2008, 3).

50 B. Smith and Stark (2009, 2).
51 Lipka (2016).
52 Pew Research Center (2014b).
53 Lipka (2016).
54 For further documentation of that pattern, see Bibby (2011, 89).
55 Putnam and Campbell (2010, 4–5).
56 See http://www.charterforcompassion.org.
57 Moyers (2009).
58 Mead (2010, 3).
59 Noll (2007, 56).
60 Goar (2006).
61 Pennings and Van Pelt (2009).
62 Latest analysis of the GSS 2013 data set. Earlier analyses include M. Hall et al. (2009, 6, 41). Frank Jones (2002), using the 1997 and 2000 data sets, examines these correlations in considerable detail, including looking at differences among religious groups.
63 "Do atheists care less?" *Maclean's,* May 6, 2010, http://www2.macleans.ca/2010/05/06/do-atheists-care-less.

Chapter 7: Religion versus Spirituality

1 See, for example, Chandler (2011); Fuller (2001); Grossman (2008); Marler and Hadaway (2002); and Mercadante (2014).
2 Rolheiser (1999, 11).
3 Ibid., 6–7.
4 Ibid., 7–11.
5. http://www.sbnr.org, including "Welcome!"
6 Taylor (2007, 506).
7 Roof (1999).
8 Google search for "spirituality online Canada," January 22, 2016.
9 Nouwen (2011); Tickle (2008); Young (2008); McLaren (2011); and Rohr (2015). Titles for the other religions mentioned can readily be found with a simple scan of sites such as Amazon or Chapters.
10 See, respectively, Byrne (2006); Friesen (2000); Owen (2015); Davies (1987); and Saunders (2002). The books on the spirituality of wine, sex, grandparenting, and pets are among a series released by Wood Lake Books (Kelowna) between 2005 and 2009.
11 See, respectively, Hampson (2008); Arel (2015); Comte-Sponville (2007); de la Rouvière (2005); Blake (2003); and Brogaard (2010).
12 Todd (2008a, 4).
13 http://bodysoulspiritexpo.com/about.html.
14 See, for example, http://www.articlesfactory.com/articles/self-help/how-to-be-a-spiritual-atheist.html.
15 http://www.innerbonding.com/show-article/1021/accessing-your-spiritual-guidance.html.
16 Rigler (2008).

17 Allemang (2010).
18 L. Miller (2010).
19 S. Harris (2014).
20 Elliott (2009).
21 See Bibby (2011, 122–23).
22 *The Big Bang Theory*, season 3, episode 23, May 24, 2010.
23 See, for example, Mercadante's US research (2014).
24 Chandler (2011, 2013). Her website is http://spiritualbutnotreligious.ca/author/vidbloym.
25 See, for example, a Centre for Studies in Religion and Society (University of Victoria) presentation in 2013 at https://vimeo.com/81442374.
26 Paterson (2015).
27 Roof (1999, 91).
28 Ibid., 9.
29 Wuthnow (2007, 134).
30 T. Smith (2009, 14).
31 Chaves (2011, 460; emphasis in original).
32 T. Smith (2009, 15). See, for example, Davie (2006) and Gill (2008).
33 Luckmann (1967).
34 See, for example, Bailey (2006).
35 The Pearson correlation coefficient (r) is .418.
36 Todd (2009a, 2010a). The quotations that follow are from Todd (2010a).
37 Cox (2009, 2).
38 Ibid., 11–12.
39 Ibid., 13–14.
40 Ibid., 14.
41 See, for example, Todd (2008b, 2009b, 2010b); an academic take on hockey is Sinclair-Faulkner (1977), on American football French (2001).
42 McCaig (2010).
43 Cited in Cogley (1968, 171).
44 Crabtree and Pelham (2008).
45 Zuckerman (2014, 211).

Chapter 8: Dealing with Death

1 Harpur (1991, 16). See also his updated volume (2011).
2 For an evaluation of the Boomers' legacy, see, for example, Bibby (2006, 209–23).
3 Coren (2005).
4 Cited in Reinberg (2011).
5 Newman (1977).
6 Wente (2009).
7 Freud (1957).
8 Richler (2010, 18).
9 Zuckerman (2014, 168, 199).

10 For expositions of the positions that various religions take on life after death, see, for example, Harpur (1991, 2011).
11 A conference presentation in San Antonio, June 2017.
12 For trend data on teens raising questions, see Bibby (2009, 173).
13 Bibby (2002, 133–36).
14 For details, see Bibby (2011, 169).
15 Rigler (2008).
16 Pausch (2008, 191–92).
17 Philippians 1.23–25.
18 In our Project Canada 2000 survey, we gave people the opportunity to offer any other primary responses; no single response was cited by more than 3% of the sample.
19 *Lethbridge Herald,* September 25, 2010.
20 Bibby (2016); Bibby and Grenville (2015).
21 See, for example, Freud (1957).
22 See Bibby (2011, 226); the Pearson *r*'s for essentially the same data: attendance and God .270, life after death .232, heaven .303; God and life after death .411, heaven .531; life after death and heaven .639.
23 World Values Survey (1981).
24 World Values Survey, Wave 4 (2000–4).
25 Freud (1957, 89).
26 Wente (2009).
27 Stiller (2001).
28 Kreeft (1990).

Chapter 9: The Resilience of Religion

1 Durkheim (1965, 477–79).
2 An earlier version of some of the following material appeared in my chapter in Hewitt (1993).
3 See, for example, Sorokin (1957); Davis (1949); and Bell (1977).
4 Davis (1949, 542–44).
5 Bell (1977).
6 Rifkin (1979).
7 See, for example, Brady (1991); Koop (1991); and Roozen, McKinney, and Thompson (1990).
8 Naisbitt and Aburdene (1990).
9 Parsons (1964, 295).
10 Ibid., 296.
11 Ibid.
12 Greeley (1972).
13 Durkheim (1965, 477–79).
14 Davis (1949).
15 See, for example, Finke and Stark (1992) and Stark and Bainbridge (1985).
16 Stark (2015, K4162; original emphasis).

17 Bibby and Reid (2016).
18 See, for example, de Souza (2010) on the government's apparent commitment to secularism.
19 For details, see Bibby and Reid (2016, especially Chapters 3 and 4).
20 Durkheim (1965, 475).
21 For an example of Anglican financial issues, see Williams (2010).
22 Harpur (1991, 15).
23 For some forthright thoughts about life after death from an Anglican priest, see Nicolosi (2010).
24 Airhart (2014); Flatt (2013).
25 Noll (2015, 26, 28).
26 Bagnell (2011) offers a brief but excellent overview of the numerical decline of the United Church, its current problems with resources, and its hopes for the future.
27 Butler Bass (2006, 45); this is her central thesis.
28 D. Harris (2009).
29 For an exposition of 40 evangelical churches currently seen as vibrant, see Paddey and Stiller (2015). For a less enthusiastic research report on evangelicals, see Reimer and Wilkinson (2015).
30 Kelley (1972).
31 See, for example, Bibby (2002) and Bibby and Brinkerhoff (1973).
32 See ibid.
33 For a helpful analysis of "Christian," see Clarke and Macdonald (2007).
34 For a provocative recent work by a prominent evangelical, see Posterski (2013).
35 Cox (2009, 1).
36 Stark (2015, K28 and K44).
37 Yancey (2010, 4).
38 Reynolds (2011).
39 See Mead (2010) and Reynolds (2011).
40 Pew Research Center (2015a).
41 Mead (2010, 2).
42 Ibid.
43 Pew Research Center (2015a).
44 Allen (2009, 20).
45 Thomas (2010, 96).
46 Mead (2010, 2–3).
47 Thomas (2010, 94).
48 Pew Research Center (2015a).
49 Thomas (2010, 95); Stark and Wang (2015, KL 1416).
50 Thomas (2010, 93).
51 Ibid., 94–95.
52 Ibid., 94.
53 Allen (2009, 3).
54 Thomas (2010, 95).
55 Ibid., 101.
56 Allen (2009, 2).

57 Ibid.
58 Mead (2010, 3).
59 For research that includes examples of hybrid and non-hybrid possibilities and remains relevant, see Brinkerhoff and Bibby (1985).
60 Thomas (2010, 95).
61 Ibid.
62 Ibid.
63 Ibid.
64 Allen (2009, 98).
65 Thomas (2010, 97).
66 Pew Research Center (2015a).
67 See, for example, Stark and Bainbridge (1985).
68 Thomas (2010, 101).

Conclusion

1 Cited in Bonifacio (2013, 119). The organization is the evangelical Lausanne Committee for World Evangelization.
2 Researchers like Manning (2015) attest to the pressure on parents with no religion when it comes to raising their children.
3 Palmer (2011).
4 Bibby (2011).
5 Cox (2009, 224).
6 Geertz (1968).
7 Weber (1963).
8 Taylor (2007, 727).
9 Yakabuski (2009).

References

Adler, Jerry. 2006. "The new naysayers." *Newsweek*, September 11. http://www.newsweek.com/new-naysayers-109697.

Airhart, Phyllis D. 2014. *A church with the soul of a nation: Making and remaking the United Church of Canada*. Montreal: McGill-Queen's University Press.

Allemang, John. 2010. "A tournament of atheists, then and now." *Globe and Mail*, November 6.

Allen, John L. Jr. 2009. *The future church*. New York: Doubleday.

Altizer, Thomas. 1966. *The gospel of Christian atheism*. Philadelphia: Westminster Press.

Appiah, Kwame Anthony. 2010. "Science knows best." Review of Sam Harris's *The moral landscape. New York Times*, October 1.

Arel, Dan. 2015. *Parenting without God: How to raise moral, ethical, and intelligent children, free from religious dogma*. Charlottesville, VA: Pitchstone Publishing.

Association for Canadian Studies. 2010. "Survey on beliefs about life after death." With the Carleton University Survey Centre. February. Cited in PostMedia News, September 3. http://news.nationalpost.com/holy-post/heaven-tops-hell-in-canadian-belief-poll.

Bagnell, Kenneth. 2011. "Secular shift." *United Church Observer*, January. http://www.ucobserver.org/faith/2011/01/secular_shift.

Bailey, Edward I. 2006. *Implicit religion in contemporary society*. Leuven: Peeters.

Barna, George, and David Kinnaman. 2014. *Churchless: Understanding today's un-churched and how to connect with them*. Carol Stream, IL: Tyndale House.

BBC. 2004. "Death is not the end." Poll conducted by ICM Research Limited for BBC Two program *What the world thinks of God*. February 9. http://news.bbc.co.uk/2/shared/spl/hi/programmes/wtwtgod/pdf/wtwtogod.pdf.

BBC News. 2009. "Most Britons 'believe in heaven.'" April 12. http://news.bbc.co.uk/2/hi/uk/7996187.stm.

Beaucage, Marjorie, and Emma LaRoque. 1983. "Two faces of the New Jerusalem: Indian-Metis Reaction to the Missionary." In *Visions of the New Jerusalem*, edited by Benjamin G. Smillie, 27–38. Edmonton: NeWest Press,

Becker, Howard S. 1972. Conference call with a Washington State University graduate sociology class, October 17. Confirmed by email, October 3, 2016.

Bell, Daniel. 1977. "The return of the sacred? The argument on the future of religion." *British Journal of Sociology* 28: 419–49.

Berger, Peter L. 1961. *The noise of solemn assemblies.* Garden City, NY: Doubleday.

–, ed. 1999. *The desecularization of the world: Resurgent religion and world politics.* Washington, DC: Ethics and Public Policy Center; Grand Rapids, MI: Eerdmans.

–. 2014. "A conversation with Peter L. Berger: 'How my views have changed.'" With Gregor Thuswaldner. *Cresset* 77, 3: 16–21. http://thecresset.org/2014/Lent/Thuswaldner_L14.html.

Beyer, Peter. 1997. "Religious vitality in Canada." *Journal for the Scientific Study of Religion* 36: 272–88.

–. 2006. *Religions in global society.* New York: Routledge.

Bibby, Reginald W. 1987. *Fragmented gods: The poverty and potential of religion in Canada.* Toronto: Irwin.

–. 1990. *Mosaic madness: Pluralism without a cause.* Toronto: Stoddart.

–. 1993. *Unknown gods: The ongoing story of religion in Canada.* Toronto: Stoddart.

–. 2001. *Canada's teens: Today, yesterday, and tomorrow.* Toronto: Stoddart.

–. 2002. *Restless gods: The renaissance of religion in Canada.* Toronto: Stoddart.

–. 2006. *The Boomer factor: What Canada's most famous generation is leaving behind.* Toronto: Bastian Books.

–. 2009. *The emerging Millennials: How Canada's newest generation is responding to change and choice.* Lethbridge: Project Canada Books.

–. 2011. *Beyond the gods and back: The demise and rise of religion in Canada.* Lethbridge: Project Canada Books.

–. 2014. "Beyond the 'no religion' panic in the United States." Paper presented at the annual meeting of the Pacific Sociological Association, Portland, OR, March.

–. 2016a. "The future of an allusion: Using social and personal forecasts to uncover explicit and implicit religion." *Implicit Religion* 19, 3: 439–54.

_. 2016b. "Life after death: Data and reflections on the last information gap." *Studies in Religion* 45, 4.

Bibby, Reginald W., and Merlin B. Brinkerhoff. 1973. "The circulation of the saints: A study of people who join conservative churches." *Journal for the Scientific Study of Religion* 12: 273–83.

Bibby, Reginald W., Terri-Lynn Fox, and James Penner. 2010. *The emerging Aboriginal Millennials.* Lethbridge: Project Canada Books.

Bibby, Reginald W., and Andrew Grenville. 2016. "What the polls do show: Toward enhanced survey readings of religion in Canada." *Canadian Review of Sociology* 53: 123–36.

Bibby, Reginald W., and Angus Reid. 2016. *Canada's Catholics: Vitality and hope in a new era.* Toronto: Novalis.

Bigge, Ryan. 2008. "Death of the monoculture." *Toronto Star,* July 20. https://www.thestar.com/news/2008/07/20/death_of_the_monoculture.html.

Blake, Robert R. 2003. *The Christian atheist.* Bloomington, IN: AuthorHouse.

Bok, Derek. 2010. *The politics of happiness: What government can learn from the new research on well-being*. Princeton, NJ: Princeton University Press.

Bonifacio, Glenda Tibe. 2013. *Pinay on the prairies: Filipino women and transnational identities*. Vancouver: UBC Press.

Bowen, Kurt. 2004. *Christians in a secular world: The Canadian experience*. Montreal: McGill-Queen's University Press.

Brady, Diane. 1991. "Saving the Boomers." *Maclean's*, June 3, 50–51.

Bramadat, Paul, and David Seljak, eds. 2008. *Christianity and ethnicity in Canada*. Toronto: University of Toronto Press.

–. 2009. *Religion and ethnicity in Canada*. Toronto: University of Toronto Press.

Brinkerhoff, Merlin B., and Reginald W. Bibby. 1985. "Circulation of the saints in South America." *Journal for the Scientific Study of Religion* 24: 253–62.

Brockmeyer, Meghan M. 2010. "Religious networks promote happiness." *Harvard Crimson*, December 15. http://www.thecrimson.com/article/2010/12/15/religious-happiness-putnam-friends.

Brogaard, Betty. 2010. *The homemade atheist: A former evangelical woman's freethought journey to happiness*. Berkeley: Ulysses Press.

Brym, Robert, and John Lie. 2005. *Sociology: Your compass for a new world*. 2nd ed. Belmont, CA: Thompson/Wadsworth.

–. 2013. *Sociology: Pop culture to social structure*. Belmont, CA: Cengage.

Brym, Robert, John Lie, and Steven Rytina. 2007. *Sociology: Your compass for a new world*. 2nd Canadian ed. Toronto: Nelson.

Burke, Daniel. 2013. "Q & A with Frank Newport: Don't rule out a renaissance of religion in North America." *United Methodist Reporter*, January 29. http://unitedmethodistreporter.com/2013/01/29/qa-dont-rule-out-a-renaissance-of-religion-in-north-america.

Burson, Harry. 2009. "Michael Jackson and the death of monoculture." *Popmatters*, July 7. http://www.popmatters.com/feature/107582-michael-jackson-and-the-death-of-monoculture.

Butler Bass, Diana. 2006. *Christianity for the rest of us*. New York: HarperOne.

Byrne, Rhonda. 2006. *The secret*. New York: Atria Books.

Cacioppo, John T., et al., eds. 2002. *Foundations in social neuroscience*. Cambridge, MA: MIT Press.

CBC. 1973. "The quieter revolution." Documentary film. Toronto: Canadian Broadcasting Corporation.

Casanova, José. 1994. *Public religions in the modern world*. Chicago: University of Chicago Press.

–. 2006. "Rethinking secularization: A global comparative perspective." *Hedgehog Review*, Spring–Summer, 8–22.

Castle, Tim. 2010. "U.K. to measure happiness alongside GDP." *Globe and Mail*, November 25.

Chandler, Siobhan. 2011. "The social ethic of religiously unaffiliated spirituality." PhD diss., Wilfrid Laurier University.

–. 2013. "The way of the spiritual seeker: As above so below." In *Ways of the spirit*, edited by D. Bryant, 1–7. Kitchener, ON: Pandora.

Chaves, Mark. 1994. "Secularization as declining religious authority." *Social Forces* 72, 3: 749–74.

–. 2011. *American religion: Contemporary trends.* Princeton, NJ: Princeton University Press. Kindle edition.

Church and Faith Trends. 2008. "What happened to Christian Canada?" A panel response to Mark Noll with a reply by Noll. *Church and Faith Trends* 2, 1. http://www.evangelicalfellowship.ca/page.aspx?pid=6208.

CIA. 2016. *The world factbook.* Washington, DC: Office of Public Affairs, CIA. https://www.cia.gov/library/publications/resources/the-world-factbook.

Clarke, Brian, and Stuart Macdonald. 2007. "Simply Christian: Canada's newest major religious denomination." *Toronto Journal of Theology* 23: 109–26.

Cogley, John. 1968. *Religion in a secular age.* New York: New American Library.

Collins, Thomas. 2010. Easter Sunday homily. Podcast. Toronto: Roman Catholic Archdiocese.

Comte-Sponville, André. 2007. *The little book of atheist spirituality.* New York: Viking.

Coren, Michael. 2005. "Dignity in death comes with confidence in God." *Presbyterian Record,* April 1. http://presbyterianrecord.ca/2005/04/01/dignity-in-death-comes-with-confidence-in-god.

Cox, Harvey. 1965. *The secular city.* New York: Macmillan.

–. 1995. *Fire from heaven: The rise of Pentecostal spirituality and the reshaping of religion in the twenty-first century.* Reading, MA: Perseus Books.

–. 2009. *The future of faith.* New York: HarperOne.

Crabtree, Steve. 2010. "Religiosity highest in world's poorest nations." August 31. Washington, DC: Gallup.

Crabtree, Steve, and Brett Pelham. 2008. "The complex relationship between religion and purpose." December 24. Washington, DC: Gallup.

Davie, Grace. 1994. *Religion in Britain since 1945: Believing without belonging.* Oxford: Blackwell.

–. 2006. "Religion in Europe in the 20th century." *European Journal of Sociology* 47: 271–96.

Davies, Douglas James. 1987. *Mormon spirituality: Latter Day Saints in Wales and Zion.* Logan, UT: Utah State University Press.

Davis, Kingsley. 1949. *Human society.* New York: Macmillan.

Dawkins, Richard. 2006. *The God delusion.* New York: Houghton Mifflin.

Dawson, Lorne, and Joel Thiessen. 2014. *The sociology of religion: A Canadian perspective.* Toronto: Oxford University Press.

de la Rouvière, Möller. 2005. *Spirituality without God.* Tamarac, FL: Llumina Press.

de Souza, Raymond J. 2010. "Quebec worships the idol of secularism." *National Post,* December 30.

Demerath, N. Jay, III. 2007. "Secularization and sacralization deconstructed and reconstructed." In *SAGE handbook of the sociology of religion,* edited by James A. Beckford and N. Jay Demerath III, 57–80. London: Sage Publishers.

Dobbelaere, Karel. 1981 "Secularization: A multi-dimensional concept." *Current Sociology* 19: 201–16.

–. 2002. *Secularization: An analysis at three levels*. Oxford: Oxford University Press.

Dueck, Lorna. 2010. "Blair v. Hitchens: What you believe to be true matters." *Globe and Mail*, November 25.

Durkheim, Emile. 1965. *The elementary forms of the religious life*. 1912; reprinted, New York: Free Press.

Eagle, David E. 2011. "Changing patterns of attendance at religious services in Canada, 1986–2008." *Journal for the Scientific Study of Religion* 50: 187–200.

Edge Foundation. 2010. "The new science of morality." Transcript of seminar held July 20. https://www.edge.org/events/the-new-science-of-morality.

Elliott, Trisha. 2009. "'I'm not religious. I'm spiritual.'" *United Church Observer*, June. http://www.ucobserver.org/faith/2009/06/not_religious.

Environics. 2016. *Survey of Muslims in Canada 2016*. Toronto: Environics Institute for Survey Research. http://www.environicsinstitute.org/uploads/institute -projects/survey%20of%20muslims%20in%20canada%202016%20-%20 final%20report.pdf.

Ferguson, Eva. 2010. "Online program pushed to bring respect to the rink." *Calgary Herald*, January 24.

Finke, Roger L., and Rodney Stark. 1992. *The churching of America, 1776–1990*. New Brunswick, NJ: Rutgers University Press.

Flatt, Kevin N. 2013. *After evangelicalism: The sixties and the United Church of Canada*. Montreal: McGill-Queen's University Press.

Foote, David. 1996. *Boom, bust, and echo*. Toronto: Macfarlane, Walter, and Ross.

Fraser, Brian. 2016. "The vibe in your head." *Jazzthink Ezine* 1, 4. http://www. jazzthink.com/ezine/1604_ezine.html.

French, Hal W. 2001. "Religion and football." In *The secular quest for meaning in life: Denton papers in implicit religion*, edited by Edward I. Bailey, Chapter 19. Lampeter, UK: Edwin Mellen Press.

Freud, Sigmund. 1957. *The future of an illusion*. 1927; reprinted, Garden City, NY: Doubleday.

Friesen, John W. 2000. *Aboriginal spirituality and biblical theology: Closer than you think*. Calgary: Detselig Enterprises.

Fuller, Robert C. 2001. *Spiritual, but not religious: Understanding unchurched America*. New York: Oxford University Press.

Furstenberg, Frank F. 2013. *Behind the academic curtain: How to find success and happiness with a PhD*. Chicago: University of Chicago Press.

Gallup. 2010. *Gallup global wellbeing: The behavioral economics of GDP growth*. Washington, DC: Gallup.

–. 2013. "In U.S., rise in religious 'nones' slows in 2012." January 10. http://www. gallup.com/poll/159785/rise-religious-nones-slows-2012.aspx.

–. 2013. "In U.S., four in 10 report attending church in last week." December 24. http://www.gallup.com/poll/166613/four-report-attending-church-last-week. aspx.

–. 2015. "Percentage of Christians in U.S. drifting down, but still high." December 24. http://www.gallup.com/poll/187955/percentage-christians-drifting-down -high.aspx.

Geertz, Clifford. 1968. "Religion as a cultural system." In *The religious situation*, edited by Donald Cutler, 639–88. Boston: Beacon Press.

Gilbert, Daniel. 2006. *Stumbling on happiness*. New York: Alfred A. Knopf.

Gill, Robin. 2008. "The cultural paradigm: Declines in belonging and believing." In *The role of religion in modern societies*, edited by Detlef Pollack and Daniel V.A. Olson, 115–40. New York: Routledge.

Glock, Charles Y., and Rodney Stark. 1965. *Religion and society in tension*. Chicago: Rand McNally.

Goar, Carol. 2006. "Loss of faith imperils charities." *Toronto Star*, May 5.

Graham, Carol. 2009. *Happiness around the world: The paradox of happy peasants and miserable millionaires*. New York: Oxford University Press.

Grant, George Webster. 1998. *The church in the Canadian era*. Expanded ed. Vancouver: Regent College Publishing.

Greeley, Andrew. 1972. *The denominational society*. Glenview, IL: Scott Foresman.

Gregg, Allan. 2005. "The Christian comeback." *Saturday Night*, November 6, 21–22. http://allangregg.com/category/source/magazines/saturday-night.

Grossman, Cathy Lynn. 2008. "Survey: Non-attendees find faith outside church." *USA Today*, January 9.

Gruending, Dennis. 1996. *Revival: Canada's Christian churches*. Video. Ottawa: Carleton University.

Hadaway, C. Kirk. 1990. *What can we do about church dropouts?* Nashville: Abingdon Press.

Hall, Douglas John. 1980. *Has the church a future?* Philadelphia: Westminster Press.

Hall, Michael, David Lasby, Steven Ayer, and William David Gibbons. 2009. *Caring Canadians, involved Canadians: Highlights from the 2007 Canada survey of giving, volunteering, and participating*. Catalogue 71-542-XPE. Ottawa: Statistics Canada.

Hampson, Michael. 2008. *God without God: Western spirituality without the wrathful king*. Berkeley: O Books/Small Press Distribution.

Hampson, Sarah. 2010. "Happiness and the God spot." *Globe and Mail*, December 13.

Harpur, Tom. 1991. *Life after death*. Toronto: McClelland and Stewart.

–. 2011. *There is life after death*. Toronto: Thomas Allen.

Harris, David. 2009. "Start something unthinkable: The church needs to be flexible." *Presbyterian Record*, October 1. http://presbyterianrecord.ca/2009/10/01/start-something-%E2%80%A8unthinkable.

Harris, Misty. 2008. "Catholic teens don't harbor more guilt than others." *Ottawa Citizen*, June 14.

Harris, Sam. 2004. *The end of faith: Religion, terror, and the future of reason*. New York: Norton.

–. 2008. *Letter to a Christian nation*. 2006; reprinted, New York: Knopf.

–. 2010. *The moral landscape: How science can determine human values*. New York: Free Press.

–. 2014. *Waking up: A guide to spirituality without religion*. New York: Simon and Schuster.

Helliwell, John F., Richard Layard, and Jeffrey Sachs, eds. 2015. *World happiness report 2015.* New York: Earth Institute, Columbia University.

Hewitt, W.E., ed. 1993. *The sociology of religion: A Canadian focus.* Toronto: Butterworths.

Hiller, Harry H. 1976. "Alberta and the Bible Belt stereotype." In *Religion in Canadian society,* edited by Stewart Crysdale and Les Wheatcroft, 372–83. Toronto: Macmillan.

Hitchens, Christopher. 2007. *God is not great.* New York: Hachette.

Hordern, William. 1966. *New directions in theology today. Volume 1: Introduction.* Philadelphia: Westminster Press.

Horgan, John. 2010. "The acid test for doing the right thing." Review of Sam Harris's *The moral landscape. Globe and Mail,* October 9.

Horton, Michael S. 2013. "Secularization." *Modern Reformation* 22, 5: 26–41.

Hunsberger, Bruce, and Bob Altemeyer. 2006. *Atheists: A groundbreaking study of America's nonbelievers.* Amherst, NY: Prometheus Books.

Hunter, James Davison. 1991. *Culture wars: The struggle to define America.* New York: Basic Books.

Jones, Frank. 2002. "How is volunteering associated with religious commitment?" Religious Commitment Report 02-09. Ottawa: Christian Commitment Research Institute.

Kalbach, W.E., and W.W. McVey. 1976. "Religious composition of the Canadian population." In *Religion in Canadian society,* edited by Stewart Crysdale and Les Wheatcroft, 220–40. Toronto: Macmillan.

Kazemipur, Abdolmohammad. 2014. *The Muslim question in Canada.* Vancouver: UBC Press.

Kelley, Dean. 1972. *Why conservative churches are growing.* New York: Harper and Row.

Koop, Doug. 1991. "Are Canadians really going back to church?" *Christian Week,* September 10, 1, 4.

Kreeft, Peter. 1990. *Everything you ever wanted to know about heaven.* San Francisco: Ignatius Press.

Kristofferson, Kris. 1969. "Sunday morning coming down." London: EMI Blackwood Music.

Leger Marketing. 2007. "Profession barometer." *OmniCan Report,* May 15.

Lim, Chaeyoon, and Robert D. Putnam. 2010. "Religion, social networks, and life satisfaction." *American Sociological Review* 75: 914–33.

Lipka, Michael. 2016. "Muslims and Islam: Key findings in the U.S. and around the world." July 22. http://www.pewresearch.org/fact-tank/2016/07/22/muslims-and-islam-key-findings-in-the-u-s-and-around-the-world.

Luckmann, Thomas. 1967. *The invisible religion.* New York: Macmillan.

Manning, Christel. 2015. *Losing our religion: How unaffiliated parents are raising their children.* New York: New York University Press.

Marler, Penny Long, and Kirk Hadaway. 2002. "'Being religious' or 'being spiritual' in America: A zero-sum proposition?" *Journal for the Scientific Study of Religion* 42: 289–300.

Martinuk, Susan. 2011. "Told you gay rights would trump religion." *Calgary Herald*, January 14.

McCaig, Sam. 2010. "Death of Brian Burke's son reinforces what's really important." *Hockey News*, February 6. McCaig's blog, THN.com.

McLaren, Brian D. 2011. *Naked spirituality: A life with God in 12 simple words.* New York: HarperOne.

McLeod, Henry. 1982. "A comparison of trends in Protestant church membership in Canada: 1946–1979." In *Yearbook of American and Canadian Churches.* New York: Abingdon.

Mead, Walter Russell. 2010. "Pentecostal power." Blog in *American Interest*, May 28.

Mercadante, Linda A. 2014. *Belief without borders: Inside the minds of the spiritual but not religious.* New York: Oxford University Press.

Miller, Geoffrey. 2000. "Social policy implications of the new happiness research." *Edge.* https://www.edge.org/response-detail/10791.

Miller, Lisa. 2010. "Sam Harris believes in God." *Newsweek*, October 18.

Moyers, Bill. 2009. "Interview with Karen Armstrong." *Bill Moyers Journal*, March 13. http://www.pbs.org/moyers/journal/03132009/transcript1.html.

Murphy, Rex. 2009. "Crucifix out, warming in." *Globe and Mail*, November 6.

Murray, Noel. 2009. "One nation, still more or less under a groove." *The A.V. Club blog*, August 26. http://www.avclub.com/article/one-nation-still-more-or-less-under-a-groove-32173.

Naisbitt, John, and Patricia Aburdene. 1990. *Megatrends 2000.* New York: Avon Books.

Newman, Randy. 1977. "Old man on the farm." *Little criminals.* Warner Brothers.

Newport, Frank. 2013. *God is alive and well: The future of religion in America.* Washington, DC: Gallup Press.

Newport, Frank, Sangeeta Agrawal, and Dan Witters. 2010. "Religious Americans enjoy higher wellbeing." October 28. Washington, DC: Gallup.

Nicolosi, Gary. 2010. "Guest reflection: What happens when we die?" *AnglicanJournal. Com*, November 1. http://www.anglicanjournal.com/articles/guest-reflection-what-happens-when-we-die-9432.

Nielsen. 2009. "Special Nielsen poll: Faith in Australia 2009." December 16. Sydney: Nielsen.

Noll, Mark A. 2007. *What happened to Christian Canada?* Vancouver: Regent College Publishing.

–. 2015. "O Canada. Liberal evangelicalism: A case study." *Books and Culture*, September–October. http://www.booksandculture.com/articles/2015/sepoct/o-canada.html.

Nouwen, Henri J.M. 2011. *A spirituality of living.* Nashville: Upper Room Books.

Oakes, Kaya. 2015. *The nones are alright.* Maryknoll, NY: Orbis Books.

OECD. 2016. "Official development assistance 2015." Organization for Economic Cooperation and Development. http://www.oecd.org/newsroom/aid-to-developing-countries-rebounds-in-2013-to-reach-an-all-time-high.htm.

Owen, Sarah. 2015. *Celtic spirituality: A beginner's guide.* CreateSpace/Kindle Direct Publishing. Kindle edition.

Paddey, Patricia, and Karen Stiller. 2015. *Shifting stats shaking the church: 50 Canadian churches respond.* Toronto: World Vision Canada.

Palmer, Jason. 2011. "Religion may become extinct in nine nations, study says." March 22. http://www.bbc.com/news/science-environment-12811197.

Parsons, Talcott. 1964. "Christianity and modern industrial society." In *Religion, culture, and society,* edited by Louis Schneider, 273–98. New York: John Wiley.

Paterson, Gary. 2015. "Reclaiming loaded words: Discipleship and evangelism." Personal blog, July 13. http://www.garypaterson.ca/2015/07/13/reclaiming -loaded-words-discipleship-and-evangelism.

Pausch, Randy. 2008. *The last lecture.* New York: Hyperion.

Pelham, Brett, and Steve Crabtree. 2008. "Worldwide, highly religious more likely to help others." Washington, DC: Gallup. http://www.gallup.com/poll/111013/ worldwide-highly-religious-more-likely-help-others.aspx.

Pelham, Brett, and Zsolt Nyiri. 2008. "In more religious countries, lower suicide rates." July 3. Washington, DC: Gallup.

Pennings, Ray, and Michael Van Pelt. 2009. "The Canadian culture of generosity." *Policy in Public,* November 20. http://www.cardus.ca/policy/article/2155.

Persichilli, Angelo. 2010. "Resilient church will overcome latest scandal." *Toronto Star,* April 4.

Peters, Ted. 2010. "Evangelical atheism today: A response to Richard Dawkins." http://www.counterbalance.org/bio/ted-frame.html.

Pew Research Center. 2005. "Islamic extremism: Common concern for Muslim and Western publics." http://www.pewglobal.org/files/pdf/248.pdf

–. 2007. "A rising tide lifts mood in the developing world." July 24. http://pewglobal. org/2007/07/24.

–. 2008. "Where trust is high, crime and corruption are low." April 15. http://www. pewglobal.org/2008/04/15/where-trust-is-high-crime-and-corruption-are-low.

–. 2009. "Many Americans mix multiple faiths." December 9. http://www.pewforum. org/2009/12/09/many-americans-mix-multiple-faiths/.

–. 2011. "Global Christianity: A report on the size and distribution of the world's Christian population." December. http://www.pewforum.org/files/2011/12/ Christianity-fullreport-web.pdf.

–. 2012. "'Nones' on the rise." October 9. http://www.pewforum.org/2012/10/09/ nones-on-the-rise-new-report-finds-one-in-five-adults-have-no-religious -affiliation.

–. 2014a. "Worldwide, many see belief in God as essential to morality." March 13. http://www.pewglobal.org/2014/03/13/worldwide-many-see-belief-in -god-as-essential-to-morality.

–. 2014b. "How Americans feel about religious groups." July 16. http://www. pewforum.org/2014/07/16/how-americans-feel-about-religious-groups.

–. 2014c. "People in emerging markets catch up to advanced economies in life satisfaction." October 30. http://www.pewglobal.org/2014/10/30/people -in-emerging-markets-catch-up-to-advanced-economies-in-life-satisfaction.

–. 2015a. "The future of world religions: Population growth projections, 2010–2050." April 2. http://www.pewforum.org/2015/04/02/religious-projections-2010-2050/ pf_15-04-02_projectionstables8.

–. 2015b. "America's changing religious landscape." May 12. http://www.pewforum. org/2015/05/12/americas-changing-religious-landscape.

–. 2016a. "The gender gap in religion around the world." March 22. http://www. pewforum.org/2016/03/22/the-gender-gap-in-religion-around-the-world.

–. 2016b. "Religion in everyday life." April 12. http://www.pewforum.org/2016/04/ 12/religion-in-everyday-life.

–. 2016c. "The divide over Islam and national laws in the Muslim world." April 27. http://www.pewglobal.org/2016/04/27/the-divide-over-islam-and -national-laws-in-the-muslim-world.

–. 2016d. "Muslims and Islam: Key findings in the U.S. and around the world." July 22. http://www.pewresearch.org/fact-tank/2016/07/22/muslims-and-islam -key-findings-in-the-u-s-and-around-the-world/.

Posterski, Don. 2013. *Jesus on justice*. Toronto: World Vision.

Putnam, Robert D. 2000. *Bowling alone: The collapse and revival of American community*. New York: Simon and Schuster.

Putnam, Robert, and David E. Campbell. 2010. *Amazing grace: How religion divides and unites us*. New York: Simon and Schuster.

Reid, Angus. 2016. "Keynote address at the BC leadership prayer breakfast." April 22. http://angusreid.org/angus-reid-keynote-address-bc-leadership-prayer -breakfast.

Reimer, Sam. Forthcoming. "Protestants and Religious Polarization in Canada."

Reimer, Sam, and Michael Wilkinson. 2015. *A culture of faith: Evangelical congregations in Canada*. Montreal: McGill-Queen's University Press.

Reinberg, Steven. 2011. "Steve Jobs faces uphill battle against cancer: Experts." http://news.health.com/2011/08/25/steve-jobs-faces-uphill-battle-against -cancer-experts.

Reynolds, Neil. 2011. "The globalization of God in the 21st century." *Globe and Mail*, January 10.

Richler, Noah. 2010. "Author Christopher Hitchens in conversation with Noah Richler." *Maclean's*, December 27, 16–18.

Rifkin, Jeremy. 1979. *The emerging order: God in the age of scarcity*. New York: Ballantine Books.

Rigler, Sara Yoheved. 2008. "Spirituality without God." November. http://www. aish.com/sp/ph/48962441.html.

Rohr, Richard. 2015. *What the mystics know: Seven pathways to your deeper self*. New York: Crossroad Publishing.

Rolheiser, Ron. 1999. *The holy longing: The search for a Christian spirituality*. New York: Doubleday.

Roof, Wade Clark. 1999. *Spiritual marketplace: Baby Boomers and the remaking of American religion*. Princeton, NJ: Princeton University Press.

Roozen, David, William McKinney, and Wayne Thompson. 1990. "The 'big chill' generation warms to worship." *Review of Religious Research* 31: 314–22.

Rouleau, Jean-Paul. 1977. "Religion in Quebec: Present and future." *Pro Mundi Vita: Dossiers*, November–December.

Samuel, Henry. 2009. "Nicolas Sarkozy wants to measure economic success in 'happiness.'" *Telegraph*, September 14.

Saunders, Kevin. 2002. *Wiccan spirituality.* Somerset, UK: Green Magic Publishing.

Scrivener, Leslie. 2010. "Feisty chat for Blair, Hitchens." *Toronto Star,* November 27.

Sinclair-Faulkner, Tom. 1977. "A puckish look at hockey in Canada." In *Religion and culture in Canada,* edited by Peter Slater, 383–405. Toronto: Canadian Corporation for Studies in Religion.

Sluyter, Dean. 2001. *The Zen commandments: Ten suggestions for a life of inner freedom.* New York: Tarcher/Penguin.

Smith, Buster G., and Rodney Stark. 2009. "Religious attendance relates to generosity worldwide." September 4. Washington, DC: Gallup.

Smith, Christian. 2005. *Soul searching: The religious and spiritual lives of American teenagers.* New York: Oxford University Press.

Smith, Christian, and Michael O. Emerson. 2008. *Passing the plate: Why American Christians don't give away more money.* New York: Oxford University Press.

Smith, Tom W. 2009. *Religious change around the world.* Report prepared for the Templeton Foundation. http://gss.norc.org/Documents/reports/cross-national-reports/CNR%2030%20Religious%20Change%20Around%20the%20World.pdf.

Social Capital Blog. 2010. "Summary of recent happiness research." October 27. http://socialcapital.wordpress.com.

Sorokin, Pitirim. 1957. *Social and cultural dynamics.* Revised and abridged. Boston: Porter Sargent.

Southard, Samuel. 1961. *Pastoral evangelism.* Nashville: Abingdon.

Stark, Rodney. 2012. *America's blessings: How religion benefits everyone, including atheists.* West Conshohocken, PA: Templeton Press.

–. 2015. *The triumph of faith: Why the world is more religious than ever.* Wilmington, DW: ISI Books. Kindle edition.

Stark, Rodney, and William Sims Bainbridge. 1985. *The future of religion.* Berkeley: University of California Press.

Stark, Rodney, and Roger Finke. 2000. *Acts of faith: Explaining the human side of religion.* Berkeley: University of California Press.

Stark, Rodney, and Charles Y. Glock. 1968. *American piety: The nature of religious commitment.* Berkeley: University of California Press.

Stark, Rodney, and Laurence R. Iannaccone. 1994. "A supply-side reinterpretation of the 'secularization' of Europe." *Journal for the Scientific Study of Religion* 33, 3: 230–52.

Stark, Rodney, and Xiuhua Wang. 2015. *A star in the east: The rise of Christianity in China.* West Conshohocken, PA: Templeton Press.

Stiller, Brian C. 2001. *What happens when I die?* Toronto: HarperCollins.

Stolberg, Sheryl Gay. 2010. "Obama talks about his faith." *New York Times,* September 28. http://thecaucus.blogs.nytimes.com/2010/09/28/obama-talks-about-his-faith-2/?_r=0.

Stokes, Bruce. 2007. "Happiness is increasing in many countries – but why?" July 24. Pew Global Attitudes Project. http://pewglobal.org/2007/07/24/happiness-is-increasing-in-many-countries-but-why.

Stratton, Allegra. 2010. "Happiness index to gauge Britain's national mood." *Guardian,* November 14.

Taylor, Charles. 2007. *A secular age.* Cambridge, MA: Harvard University Press.

Thiessen, Joel. 2011. "Book review of Reginald Bibby's *Beyond the Gods and Back.*" *Church and Faith Trends* 4, 1: 1–4.

–. 2015. *The meaning of Sunday: The practice of belief in a secular age.* Montreal: McGill-Queen's University Press.

Thiessen, Joel, and Sarah Wilkins-Laflamme. Forthcoming. "Becoming a religious none: Irreligious socialization and disaffiliation." *Journal for the Scientific Study of Religion.*

Thomas, Scott M. 2010. "A globalized god." *Foreign Affairs* 89: 93–101.

Tickle, Phyllis. 2008. *The great emergence: How Christianity is changing and why.* Ada, MI: Baker Books.

Todd, Douglas. 1996. *Brave souls: Writers and artists wrestle with God, love, death, and the things that matter.* Toronto: Stoddart.

–. 2008a. *Cascadia: The elusive utopia: Exploring the spirit of the Pacific Northwest.* Vancouver: Ronsdale Press.

–. 2008b. "Are Trevor Linden and Mats Sundin bigger than Jesus?" *Vancouver Sun,* December 22.

–. 2009a. "Five spiritual trends to watch for in 2009." *Vancouver Sun,* January 2.

–. 2009b. "Hallelujah! Canucks unite British Columbians with religious zeal." *Vancouver Sun,* April 14.

–. 2010a. "Five spiritual trends for '10s." *Vancouver Sun,* January 9.

–. 2010b. "The new US cliché: Hockey is Canada's 'religion.'" *Vancouver Sun,* March 1.

Todorov, Alexander, Susan T. Fiske, and Deborah Prentice, eds. 2011. *Social neuroscience: Toward understanding the underpinnings of the social mind.* New York: Oxford University Press.

United Nations. 2015. *UN human development report, 2015 – HDI rankings.* http:// hdr.undp.org/en/2015-report.

–. Office on Drugs and Crime. 2010. "Global homicide rates stable or decreasing, new UNODC report says." February 16. http://www.unodc.org/unodc/en/ frontpage/2010/February/global-homicide-rates-stable-or-decreasing-new -unodc-report-says.html.

Vaisey, Stephen, and Christian Smith. 2008. "Catholic guilt among U.S. teenagers." *Review of Religious Research* 49, 4: 415–26.

Valpy, Michael. 2010. "Young Canadians increasingly shunning religious institutions." *Globe and Mail,* December 15.

Valpy, Michael, and Joe Friesen. 2010. "Canada marching from religion to secularization." *Globe and Mail,* December 11.

Vandore, Emma. 2008. "French use happiness as economic measure." *USA Today,* April 2. http://usatoday30.usatoday.com/money/economy/2008-01-10 -145885540_x.htm.

Vernon, Glenn M. 1968. "'Nones': A neglected category." *Journal for the Scientific Study of Religion* 7: 219–29.

Wallace, Kenyon. 2010. "Q & A: Canada leads in happiness research. A discussion with Chris Barrington-Leigh." *National Post,* November 28.

Watson, Roland, and Sam Coates. 2010. "'Happiness' index to be compiled by Office for National Statistics." *Times*, November 25.

Weber, Max. 1963. *The sociology of religion*. 1922; reprinted, Boston: Beacon Press.

Wente, Margaret. 2009. "When in doubt: An atheist's Christmas." *Globe and Mail*, December 18.

White, James Emery. 2014. *The rise of the nones: Understanding and reaching the religiously unaffiliated*. Grand Rapids, MI: Baker Books.

Wilkins-Laflamme, Sarah. 2014. "Toward religious polarization? Time effects on religious commitment in U.S., UK, and Canadian regions." *Sociology of Religion* 75, 2: 284–308.

–. Forthcoming. "The remaining core: A fresh look at religiosity trends in Great Britain." *British Journal of Sociology*.

Williams, Leigh Anne. 2010. "Council of General Synod approves balanced budget for 2010 – but treasurer warns of difficult years ahead." *AnglicanJournal. Com*, November 21. http://www.anglicanjournal.com/articles/cogs-approves-balanced-budget-for-2011-9447.

Winseman, Albert L. 2002. "How to measure spiritual commitment." Washington, DC: Gallup. April 30. http://www.gallup.com/poll/5914/how-measure-spiritual-commitment.aspx.

Wood, Michael. 2010. "Hockey Calgary scores win over disrespect." *Calgary Sun*, October 24.

Wuthnow, Robert. 2007. *After the Baby Boomers: How twenty- and thirty-somethings are shaping the future of American religion*. Princeton, NJ: Princeton University Press.

Yakabuski, Konrad. 2009. "Neither practising nor believing, but Catholic even so." *Globe and Mail*, August 14.

Yancey, Philip. 2010. *What good is God?* 3rd ed. Nashville: FaithWords.

Young, William Paul. 2008. *The shack: Where tragedy confronts eternity*. Newbury Park, CA: Windblown Media.

Zuckerman, Phil. 2008. *Society without God: What the least religious nations can tell us about contentment*. New York: New York University Press.

–. 2014. *Living the secular life: New answers to old questions*. New York: Penguin.

Index

Notes: Entries refer to Canada unless otherwise indicated; "religious inclination" means pro-religion, religious middle, or "no religion"; RC stands for Roman Catholic; "SBNR" means spiritual but not religious; "(f)" after a page reference indicates a figure; "(t)," a table.

Aboriginal/Indigenous beliefs: attitudes toward, 129; central feature in lives in early Canada, 14; Indigenous spirituality and Christianity, 9; percentage identifying as (Canada, 2011), 206(t); residential schools, 104; teenagers' level of religious non-affiliation, 35, 36(t)

Adler, Jerry, 108

After the Baby Boomers (Wuthnow), 158

age: demographics of SBNR, 151–52; immigrants' religious inclinations by birthplace and age, 218–19. *See also* Baby Boomers; Gen-Xers; Millennials; post-Boomers; pre-Boomers; teenagers

Age of the Spirit (Cox), 163

Airhart, Phyllis, 202

Alberta: atheists, percentage in Canada (2015), 119(f); breakdown of those claiming to be SBNR, 152(t); entry into Canada (1905), 11; province's correlation with religious inclination, 70–71

Allemang, John, 119

Allen, John: on Christian-Islamic relations in 21st century, 213; on growth of Roman Catholicism, 210; on majority of Roman Catholics in global South, 212; on Pentecostal competition with Catholicism, 211

Altemeyer, Bob, 52

Amazing Grace (Putnam and Campbell), 53

American Piety (Stark and Glock), 40

American Religion (Chaves), 53

America's Blessings (Stark), 105

Anglican Church: Anglican immigrants (2001–11), 78; Anglican immigrants (pre-1946 to 2000), 16(t); attendance at services (1957, 1980, 2005), 33; attendance stabilizing (1990 to 2000), 41; decline and future prospects, 200–203; disestablishment, impact of, 19; dominant religion in early Ontario, 10; failure to persuade younger people to get involved, 219; homosexuality and gender as divisive issues, 201; immigration patterns shifting away from, 17, 34–35, 78, 201; influence in early Canada, 14–15; median age of members (2011), 207; membership (1871–1966), 13(t), 14; membership (early 1840s), 10(t); percentage of Canadian population (1901–2011), 206(t), 207; recuperative powers, 46, 198, 200–201; religious middle identifying as, 81, 82(t); teen identification with (1984 *vs.* 2008), 35–36, 201, 202(f)

Angus Reid Institute, 5, 64–65, 87; survey in 2015 with author, 64–65, 87

atheists: acceptance of faith groups, 122–23, 124(t); attitude toward religion by religious inclination, 68(t); beliefs related to life after death, 174(t); forgiveness, importance of, 112; "new atheists" increasingly vocal, 119; percentage in Canada (1975–2015), 79, 80(f), 119(f), 120; percentage of teens, 37; personal well-being and (*see* well-being [personal] and religious inclination); religious inclinations, 66(t); self-image of teens, 95(t); social well-being and (*see* well-being [social] and religious inclination); spirituality and, 146. See also "no religion"

Atlantic region: atheists, percentage in Canada (2015), 119(f); breakdown of those claiming to be SBNR, 152(t); church attendance, decline, 7–8; region's correlation with religious inclination, 70–71. *See also* New Brunswick; Newfoundland; Nova Scotia; Prince Edward Island

attendance at religious services: acknowledgement of spiritual needs, 148–49; adults' weekly service attendance up (1957–2000), 41–42, 41(f); in Atlantic region, 7–8; attendance (1945–2005), 7–8, 12, 13(t), 14, 32–33; attendance and interest in spirituality in Europe, 159, 160(t); attendance

(Canada, 1956), 19, 20(t), 21(f); Baby Boomers, 17, 19–21; belief in heaven, hell, angels, contact with dead and, 173, 174(t), 175; belief in life after death, 173, 174(t); breakdown of those claiming to be SBNR, 151–52; demographics of those claiming to SBNR, 151, 152(t); development assistance and, 130, 131(t); donating and volunteering, and, 141; helping behaviour and, 129, 130(t); immigrants' religious inclinations by birthplace and age, 218–19; interpersonal values by religious inclination and attendance, 111(t), 112; in the North, 7–8, 8(f); in Ontario, 7–8, 8(f); Protestants compared with RCs, 21(f); responses to death and, 177–78; SBNR practices, values, beliefs by service attendance, 153, 154(f); suicide and, 100; teens' weekly attendance up (1984–2000), 40–41, 48; thinking about death, prevalence globally, 183; US weekly service attendance (1939–99), 39(f); view of what happens after death and, 176

Avatar (Cameron), 162–63

Baby Boomers: attendance at church declining, 17, 19–21; attitudes toward authority, 26(t); belief in life after death without belief in God, 175–76; churchgoing as duty *vs.* personal gratification, 23–25, 32–33; cohort's size, 19; confidence in leaders down, 27–28; death, dealing with, 167–68, 172; demographics of those claiming to SBNR, 151, 152(t); factors making religious involvement more worthwhile, 28–29; females in workplace, social impact, 29–32; heightened expectations, 28–29; highly selective consumers (of religion as well), 24–25; input/interaction insisted on, 25–27; interpersonal values by age cohort, 111(t); religious groups' poor

measurements of, 59, 60(t); religious salience, affluence, and life satisfaction, 96, 98(t); research into sources of happiness, 89; social well-being in, and religion, 129, 130, 131(t), 132(t), 133; thinking about death, prevalence globally, 183

British Columbia: atheists, percentage in Canada (2015), 119(f); breakdown of those claiming to be SBNR, 151, 152(t); entry into Canada (1871), 11; province's correlation with religious inclination, 70–71

Brockman, John, 106

Brown, Collum, 38

Bruce, Steve, 38

Brym, Bob, 53–54

Buddhists: acceptance of other faith groups, 122–23, 124(t); "engaged Buddhism," 161; immigrants (2001–11), 78; immigrants to Canada (20th century), 16(t); percentage globally (2010 and 2050), 208(t); percentage of Canadians (1921–2011), 205(t), 206(t); percentage of Canadians (1991 vs. 2011), 8, 9(t); percentage of Canadians (2010 vs. 2050), 223(t); teenagers' level of religious non-affiliation, 36(t)

Burke, Brendan, 165

Burke, Brian, 165

Cameron, David, 89

Cameron, James, 162–63

Campbell, David, 53, 64–65

Canada: balance among religious inclination to remain same in 2050, 222; death and (see death); declining religious participation, by age group, 19–21; disparate religious patterns today, 8–9; helping behaviour, by level of religiosity, 129–30, 131(t); meaning and purpose of life, reflections on, 197(t); Muslim populations (2010, 2030, 2050), 134, 135(t), 222, 223; Pew Center projections for religion

in 2050, 222; polarization (see polarization, religious); population identifying as Christian (2011), 206(t); population identifying as Christian (2016 vs. 2050), 221–22, 223(t); prominence until the 1960s, 7–8; religion as one source of meaning, 165; religion's influence, 14–17; religiosity compared with other countries, 59, 60(t), 61(t); religiosity, gender differences, 59, 61(t); religiosity, measurements of, 59, 60(t); religious salience, affluence, and life satisfaction, 96, 98(t). See also religious identification; religious participation; spirituality

Canada's Catholics (Reid and Bibby), 198–99

Canadian Charter of Rights and Freedoms, 17

Cardus, 141

Casanova, José, 47

Cascadia: The Elusive Utopia: Exploring the Spirit of the Pacific Northwest (Todd), 161

Cavanaugh, Perry, 109–10

Chandler, Siobhan, 149

Chaves, Mark, 47, 53, 158–59

Chi Tzi movement, 161

China: attendance at services and levels of suicide, 100; Christian population (1980–2040), 209, 210, 211, 212(t); Christianity and neo-Confucianism tacitly allowed, 213; meaning and purpose of life, reflections on, 197(t); Muslim population (2010), 213; Muslim population (2010, 2030, 2050), 135(t); religiosity, 59, 60(t); religiosity, by gender, prayer, and salience, 61(t); religious salience and quality of life, 99(t); thinking about death, prevalence globally, 183; views of Christians, Jews, and Muslims about each other, 137

Christian Orthodox: immigrants of this faith (2001–11), 78; percentage of Canadian population (1901–2011),

206(t); revival in Russia, 210; teen-agers' level of religious non-affiliation, 36(t)

Christianity: Age of Faith *and* Age of Belief, 163; Age of the Spirit, 163; Canadian percentage identifying as, 221; Christians in China (1980–2040), 212(t); Christians' views of Jews and Muslims in select countries (2005), 136–37; countries with largest Christian populations (2010), 209; dramatic growth in recent years, 4, 209–14; global Christianity more conservative than in Europe, 212; growth in global South, 210–11; majority of members in global South, 212; percentage identifying as (Canada, 2011), 206(t); religious makeup of world population (2010 and 2050), 133, 134(f), 208, 222–23. *See also* Roman Catholics; Protestants, Conservative; Protestants, Mainline; *and individual church groups*

civility, 109–10, 113–14, 140

coexistence: atheists in Canada, percentage (2015), 119(f), 120; attitudes toward religion by religious inclinations, 120–21; Canadians' endorsement of diversity, 120; Christians,' Jews,' Muslims' views of each other in select countries (2005), 136–37; Muslim migration to non-Muslim parts of world, impact of, 134–39; Muslim populations in select countries (2010, 2030, 2050), 134, 135(t); negative attitudes toward Muslims, 134–36; polarization between pro-religion and no religion people, 119–20, 129; polarization within religious groups, 119–20; religious diversity in Canada growing, 118–19; religious groups' acceptance of other faith groups, 122–23, 124(t), 125–26, 129; violence/terrorism of militant Muslim groups, impact of, 134. *See also* polarization, religious

Collins, Thomas, 87

compassion: association with interpersonal civility, 109–10; association with religious belief, 109; of Canadians, by religious inclinations, 116–17; donating time and money help others, 116–17, 155, 156(t); on need for belief in God to be moral person, 104–5, 113; sources of, 108–9, 128–29

Comte, August, 38, 191

Congregationalist Church in early Ontario, 10

Coren, Michael, 168

Cox, Harvey, 40, 163, 209, 224

crime rate: relationship with service attendance and trust, 130–31, 132(t), 133; Stark on religion's deterrent effect on crime, 105

Davie, Grace, 52

Davis, Kingsley, 193, 196

Dawkins, Richard, 86, 107–8

Dawson, Lorne, 40

death: Baby Boomers' coming to grips with, 167–68, 172; belief in contact with deceased, 179–81; cultural, clinical, and empirical responses to what happens after death, 181–82; dealing with death by differing outlooks on religion, 6; death not addressed by many expressions of spirituality, 164; funeral preferences, by religious inclination, 178–79; responses to the reality of death, 177–78; science little help in understanding, 168–69; thinking about death, prevalence globally, 183

death and life after death, beliefs: about, 172–76; in contact with deceased, 179–81; global survey, 183, 184(t), 185; options re believing in life after death, 170–71; in our having souls, 187–88; in reincarnation, 185, 186(t), 187; that death is not the end, 188

Globe and Mail, 38, 119
Glock, Charles, 40, 63
Gnostics, 44(t)
Goar, Carol, 140–41
Graham, Billy, 87
Graham, Carol, 89
Grant, John Webster, 9, 12
Greeley, Andrew, 194–95
Gregg, Allan, 48
Grenville, Andrew, 179, 187

Haidt, Jonathan, 106
Hampson, Sarah, 92
happiness and religion inclination: community trumps materialism, 101–2; generosity trumps selfishness, 102; individual to each person, 92; measuring and improving, research into, 88–90; personal concerns (health, time, money, etc.) and religious inclination, 95–96; personal outlook by religious inclination, 92–93; positive trumps the negative, 101; religion and, 90–91, 101; of SBNRs, 155, 156(t); self-esteem's relationship with faith, 94–95, 101; "set point" for happiness, 100; synthesis of findings, 97–98, 100
Happiness around the World (Graham), 89
Harpur, Tom, 168, 190, 201–2
Harris, David, 203
Harris, Sam: failure of science as justification for religious faith, 106–7; inspired by Eastern religions, 148; on religion as source of conflict, 86–87, 107; on understanding right and wrong, 107; views on moral values, 106–8
Hauser, Marc, 106
Helliwell, John, 90, 101–2
Hindus: acceptance of other faith groups, 122–23, 124(t); belief in reincarnation, 185; Canadians identifying with faith, 8, 9(t); Hindu immigrants (2001–11), 78; immigrants

(20th century), 16(t); percentage of Canadians identifying as (1921–2011), 205(t), 206(t); population globally, religious makeup (2010 and 2050), 133, 134(f), 208–9, 223(t); teenagers' level of religious non-affiliation, 36(t)
Hitchens, Christopher, 37, 86, 170
Hockey Calgary and civility, 109–10
The Holy Longing (Rolheiser), 143–44
honesty's importance to Canadians, 110–12, 155, 156(t)
Hordern, William, 23
Humanists, 44(t)
Hunsberger, Bruce, 52
Hunter, James Davison, 52

Iannaccone, Laurence, 42
immigrants: birthplace's correlation with religious inclination, 70–71; Christian monopoly in early Canada, 11; conservative views of sexuality and family life, 138; crucial for growth in organized religion, 78; ensuring children remain religious, 219–20; identification with "no religion," 16(t), 70, 71(t); importance for Canadian population growth, 4, 217; major religions of (20th century), 16(t), 34, 35(f); major religions of (2001–11), 78–79; religious inclinations and service attendance, 218–19; shift in immigration patterns mid- to late 20th century, 17, 78; shift in religious identification (last 30 years), 206–7; transformation of religious scene, 4, 8
International Social Survey Programme, 5, 57
Islam. *See* Muslims and Islam

Jehovah's Witnesses: membership in faith group (1941–1960s), 14; percentage of Canadians (1921–2011), 205(t), 206–7; share of population (1951 *vs.* 2001), 44(t), 45

Jews and Judaism: acceptance of other faith groups, 122–23, 124(t), 129; article "Spirituality without God" on Jewish website, 147–48; in early Canada, 10(t); Jewish immigrants (20th century), 16(t), 205; membership (1941–1960s), 14; percentage identifying as (Canada, 2011), 206(t); percentage of Canadians (1921–2011), 78(t), 205–6; population globally, percentage (2010 and 2050), 208(t); teenagers' level of religious non-affiliation, 36(t); views of Muslims and Christians in select countries (2005), 136–37

Jobs, Steve, 168

John Templeton Foundation, 105

Kazemipur, Abdie, 125–26

Kelley, Dean, 203, 207

Kristofferson, Kris, 17

Last Lecture, The (Pausch), 177

Latter-Day Saints, Church of Jesus Christ of: acceptance of other faith groups, 122–23, 124(t); percentage of Canadians identifying as (1921–2011), 205(t), 206–7; share of population (1951 vs. 2001), 44(t), 45

Layard, Richard, 90

Léger, Paul-Émile, 7, 14

Lie, John, 54

Life after Death (Harpur), 190

Lim, Chaeyoon, 90

Lipka, Michael, 134

Living the Secular Life (Zuckerman), 90–91

"low religion." See religious middle

Luckmann, Thomas, 39–40, 48

Lutheran Church: attendance at service (1957, 1980, 2005), 33; attendance stabilizing (1990 to 2000), 41; decline and future prospects, 200–203; failure to persuade younger people to get involved, 219; immigration patterns shifting away from, 16(t)17, 34,

35(f), 78, 201; Lutheran immigrants (2001–11), 78; membership (1871–1966), 13(t); percentage of Canadian population (1901–2011), 206(t); recuperative powers, 46; religious middle identifying as, 81, 82(t); teen identification with (1984 vs. 2008), 35–36, 201, 202(f)

Macleans, 141

Manitoba, 11, 70–71, 119(f)

Manning, Christel, 91

Manning, E.C., 7

markets and religion: addressing the "big" questions, 106–7, 192, 196–98, 214–15, 220; life-after-death market underserved, 182, 188; "market" for religion continues to exist, 78–79, 196, 220–21; "market model," demand for religious responses, 24, 42, 56–57; market models, explanatory value, 46–47

Martinuk, Susan, 118

Marx, Karl, 86, 91, 182, 191

McCaig, Sam, 165

Mead, Walter Russell, 139–40, 210, 212–13

meaning of life: meaning among SBNRs, 165; reflections on, comparison of countries, 196, 197(t); religion as source, 42, 165; science unable to answer "big" questions, 106–7, 192, 196

The Meaning of Sunday (Thiessen), 53

Methodist Church: membership (1871–1966) (under United Church), 13(t); membership (early 18402), 10(t); percentage of Canadian population (1901–2011), 204(t); prominence in early Ontario, 10

Millennials: belief in life after death without belief in God, 175–76; declining attendance at church, 17; interpersonal values by age cohort, 111(t); those seeing themselves as SBNR, 151, 152(t)

Miller, Geoffrey, 97–98, 100

The Moral Lamdscape: How Science Can Determine Human Values (Harris), 106–8

morality: failure of science as justification for religious faith, 106–7; innate foundations of morality, 106; on need for belief in God to be moral person, 104–5, 113, 140; "new science of morality," 106–8

Mormons. *See* Latter-Day Saints, Church of Jesus Christ of

multiculturalism, 118–19

Murphy, Rex, 118

The Muslim Question in Canada (Kazemipur), 125

Muslims and Islam: acceptance of, by religious groups, 122–23, 124(t), 129; attendance at prayer services (2006 *vs.* 2016), 207–8, 207(f); attitudes toward of Muslims of Canada, 125–26, 134–36; conservative views of sexuality and family life, 138; countries with largest Muslim populations (2010), 213–14; growth/revival of Islam, 4, 207–9, 213–14; immigrants to Canada (20th century), 16(t), 17, 218; immigrants to Canada (2001–11), 78; impact of violence/terrorism of militant groups, 134; median age of members (2011), 207; migration to non-Muslim parts of world, impact, 134–39; percentage of Canadians (1921–2011), 205(t), 206(t), 207–8; percentage of Canadians (1991, 2011), 8, 9(f); population globally, religious makeup (2010 and 2050), 133, 134(f), 208–9, 214; population in select countries (2010, 2030, 2050), 134, 135(t); religion's importance in daily lives, 213; religious terrorism as trend (2009), 161–62; teenagers' level of religious non-affiliation, 36(t); viability, reasons for, 207–8; views of Jews and Christians in select countries (2005), 136–37

Naisbitt, John, 194

National Opinion Research Center, 158

New Age, 44(t), 45

New Brunswick, 10, 10(t), 11(t)

New Thought, 44(t)

Newfoundland, 11

Newman, Randy, 169

Newport, Frank, 57

Newsweek, 108

"no religion": attitudes toward religion, 67–69, 80, 83(t); belief in life after death, 173, 174(t); belief that church-going a duty, 23(t); beliefs and practices, 73–75; correlation with birthplace and region, 70–71, 119(f); correlation with gender, age, and education, 69–70; correlation with religious identification, 71–72; correlation with religious indicators, 65–66, 67(t); correlation with religious/spiritual self-image, 72–73; funeral ceremony preferences, 178–79; immigrants to Canada (20th century), 16(t); immigrants with "no religion" (2001–11), 78(t); immigrants with "no religion" (pre-1961 to 2001), 16(t), 35(t); implications for society's well-being, 85; interpersonal values by religious inclinations, 111(t); movement in the "no religion" direction, 56; not candidates for religious recruitment, 80; percentage claiming to be SBNR, 152(t); percentage identifying as (Canada, 2011), 206(t); percentage of population (1891–1991), 44(t), 45, 49–51; percentage of population (2015), 119(f); percentage world population (2010), 133, 134(f); personal concerns and religious inclination, 95–96; personal well-being and (*see* well-being [personal] and religious inclination); prayer, 74–75; salience of religious involvement, 75–76; self-esteem, relationship with faith, 94–95, 101;

social well-being and (*see* well-being [social] and religious inclination); teenagers' level of religious non-affiliation, 36(t), 37. *See also* atheists; "spiritual but not religious" (SBNR)

Noll, Mark: on Christianity in Canada *vs.* U.S., 16; on marginalization of Christian groups as organizations, 19; on reasons for decline of United Church, 202; on secularization in Canada, 40; on "shadow effect" of Christianity, 140

North, 7–8, 8(f)

Northwest Territories, 11

Nova Scotia, 10–11

Obama, Barack, 108

O'Brien, Pat, 90

Ontario: atheists, percentage in Canada (2015), 119(f); Baptist slaves fleeing to Canada via Underground Railroad, 10–11; breakdown of those claiming to be SBNR, 152(t); church attendance in 1950s *vs.* in 1960s, 7–8, 8(f); province's correlation with religious inclination, 70–71; religious identification in early Canada, 10–11

Pagans, 44(t)

Parsons, Talcott, 194–95

Pasquale, Frank, 52

Passing the Plate: Why American Christians Don't Give Away More Money (Smith and Emerson), 105

Paterson, Gary, 149

Pausch, Randy, 177

Peers, Michael, 87

Pennings, Ray, 141

Pentecostals: dramatic growth in last 100 years, 210; membership (1871–1966), 13(t); Pentecostal immigrants (2001–11), 78; percentage of Canadian population (1901–2011), 204(t), 206(t); percentage of Canadian population (1931–2001), 34(t); regional distribution globally (2010), 210–12; religious

middle identifying as, 82(t); teenagers' level of religious non-affiliation, 35–36, 36(t)

Persichilli, Angelo, 127–28

Peters, Ted, 119

Pew Global Attitudes Project, 100

Pew Research Center: data on growth of Christianity, 209–11; on need for belief in God to be moral person, 105; on negative attitudes toward Muslims, 134, 136(f); religious makeup of the world population (2010, 2050), 133, 134(f), 208(t), 209, 214(t), 221–23; research into religious developments, 5, 57; study on religion's influence of US lives, 87

Pinker, Steven, 106

Platt, Kevin, 202

polarization framework: continuum ever-changing and dynamic, 55–56; continuum in US, 51, 56–57; degree of religious inclinations, 5, 54–55; "no religion" group growing, 49–50; orientation toward religion (2015), 64–65; polarization continuum ever-changing and dynamic, 55–56; sacralization or desecularization, 47, 56; secularization and desecularization, 54–55

polarization, religious: among religious groups, 119–20; Christians', Jews', Muslims' views of each other in select countries (2005), 136–37; culture wars in US and, 53; increasing in Canada, 61–62; "low religious" or the "religious middle," 51; makeup of world population (2010 and 2050), 133, 134(f), 208, 222–23; Muslim migration to non-Muslim parts of world, impact of, 134–39; Muslim populations in select countries (2010, 2030, 2050), 134, 135(t); Muslims' conservative views of sexuality and family life, 138; negative attitudes toward Muslims, 134–36; between religious and "no religion" groups,

revitalization of religion: adults'
weekly service attendance up (1957–
2000), 41–42, 193; congregational
trends (2000–15), 77–78; polarization
pattern growing, 51; sacralization or
desecularization, 47, 56; stimulated
by secularization, 45–46, 195; teens'
weekly service attendance up (1984–
2000), 40–41, 48. *See also* resilience
of religion

Reynolds, Neil, 210

Rifkin, Jeremy, 193

Rigler, Sara Yoheved, 147–48, 176; video
games and shift in concept of reality,
176

Rolheiser, Ron, 143–44, 171

Roman Catholics: acceptance of other
faith groups, 122–23, 124(t), 129;
attendance at church (1957, 1980,
2005), 32–33; attendance at church
compared with Protestants, 21(f);
attendance declines slowing (1957–
2000), 40, 41(t), 42; bright future
in Canada, 198–200, 208, 210; in
Canada (1871–1961), 11(t); Canadians
identifying with RC faith (1931–
2001), 33, 34(t); churchgoing seen
as duty (2005), 23(t), 25; confidence
in religious leaders vis-à-vis sexual
abuse, 127–28; conservative views of
sexuality and family life, 138; deference *vs.* discernment in younger
members (in US), 27–28, 28(f); in
early Canada, 7, 9–10, 10(t), 11(t);
growth in global South, 210, 212;
immigrants to Canada (20th century), 16(t); immigration "pipeline,"
11, 17, 18, 33–35, 78, 218; influence in
early Canada and later, 15; median
age of members (2011), 207; membership (1871–1966), 13(t); membership in Quebec (1871–1966), 12, 13(t),
14; nationalism in Quebec, impact
of, 19; "Pentecostalization" through
Charismatic movement, 211; percentage claiming to be SBNR,

152(t); percentage identifying as
(Canada, 2011), 206(t); percentage
of population (1891–1991), 44(t),
45; Quebec Act (1774), 9–10; Quiet
Revolution in Quebec, 8, 8(f), 16;
RC immigrants (2001–11), 78; recuperative powers, 46, 198–200; religious inclinations, 71–72; religious
middle identifying as, 81, 82(t); religious participation (1945, 1950s and
1960s), 7–8, 12, 14; resilience of, 46;
resources to help families cut back,
31–32; teenagers' level of religious
non-affiliation, 35, 36(t); teens' feelings of guilt, 28

Roman Catholics (outside Quebec):
attendance declines slowing (1957–
2000), 40, 41(t), 42; church attendance compared with Protestants,
21(f); churchgoing seen as duty
(2005), 23(t), 25; percentage claiming to be SBNR, 152(t); religious
inclination with religious identification, 71–72; religious inclinations,
71–72; teenagers' level of religious
non-affiliation, 36(t); weekly attendance at services, 20(t)

Roof, Wade Clark, 146, 157–58

Rouleau, Jean-Paul, 40

Russell, Bertrand, 165

Russia: attendance at services, correlation with interest in spirituality,
160(t); attendance at services, correlation with trust and crime rate,
132(t); belief in God, afterlife, heaven,
and reincarnation, 184(t), 185, 186(t),
188(t); Christian Orthodox religion,
revival of, 210; Christian population
(1980–2040), 209, 210; meaning and
purpose of life, reflections on, 197(t);
Muslim population (2010, 2030,
2050), 135(t); Muslim population at
present, 213; religiosity, 59, 60(t),
61(t); religious salience and quality
of life, 99(t); religious salience and
satisfaction with life, 98(t); views of

Christians, Jews, and Muslims about each other, 137(t)

Sachs, Jeffrey, 90
sacralization, 47
salience of religion: comparison of countries, 59, 60(t), 61(t); correlation with affluence and life satisfaction, 96–97, 98(t); correlation with quality of life, 99(t); enhancement of life, by religious inclinations, 75–76; gender differences, 59, 61(t); SBNR and, 153
Sarkozy, Nicolas, 89
Saskatchewan: atheists in (2015), 119(f); breakdown of those claiming to be SBNR, 151, 152(t); correlation with religious inclination, 70–71; entry into Canada (1905), 11
Satanists, 44(t)
SBNR. *See* "spiritual but not religious" (SBNR)
Science of Generosity initiative, 105
Scientology, 44(t), 45
A Secular Age (Taylor), 47
secularization: arguments supporting, 38–40; attendance at services (1945–2005), 7–8, 12, 13(t), 14, 32–33; congregational trends (2000–15), 77–78; declines in service attendance not irreversible, 46; difficult for new groups to break monopoly, 43, 44(t), 45; established Christian groups dominant, 43, 44(t), 45; experts on secularization and market models, 46–47; females in workforce, social impact, 29–32; movement in the "no religion" direction, 56; public interest in religion, 37; religion valued according to its costs, 43; religious decline, patterns of, 58; shift away from religion, 50–51; Stark's market model argument, 42–43; as stimulant for innovation/rejuvenation, 43, 45–46. *See also* Baby Boomers; religious identification; religious participation; spirituality

self-esteem, relationship with faith, 94–95, 101
Seljak, David, 11
Sikhs: acceptance of other faith groups, 122–23, 124(t); Canadians identifying with faith, 8, 9(t); immigrants (20th century), 16(t); percentage of Canadians (1921–2011), 205(t), 206(t); population globally, percentage (2010 and 2050), 208(t); Sikh immigrants (2001–11), 78; teenagers' level of religious non-affiliation, 36(t)
Smith, Christian, 90, 105
Smith, Tom, 57–58, 158–59
social environment's importance, 3
Society without God (Zuckerman), 90–91
Sorokin, Pitirim, 193
"spiritual but not religious" (SBNR): belief in heaven, hell, angels, contact with dead, and, 173, 174(t); books, websites, and conferences on, 146–47; definition on SBNR website, 144–45; demographics of those claiming to be SBNR, 151–53; diverse understandings of, 145–46; funeral ceremony preferences, 178–79; marketing of spirituality products, 147; meaning or purpose in life, 165; practices, values, beliefs by service attendance, 153, 154(f); practices, values, beliefs by spiritual-religious matrix, 154, 155(t); prevalence in Canada, 150; shift toward SBNR outlook, 158–59; spiritual-religious matrix by inclinations (2005), 151–53; well-being [personal and social] of SBNR, 155, 156(t), 157
spirituality: books, websites, and conferences on, 146–48; Canadians' acknowledgement of spiritual needs, 148–49; Christianity now in "Age of the Spirit," 163; complexity of religion/spirituality issue, 144–48; continues after move away from organized religion, 159–60, 162;

critics of contemporary expressions of, 165–66; death not addressed by many expressions of spirituality, 164; different meanings of, 144–46, 163; Eastern spirituality, 161; failure to address "big questions of existence," 164–66; Indigenous spirituality and Christianity, 9; search for alternatives to conservative versions of Western religion, 162; secular spirituality, 162–63; separate from religion, 143–44; shift toward SBNR outlook, 158–59; "spiritual tinkerers," mixing and matching beliefs, 162; spiritual trends (in 2009), 161–63; summary of, 163. *See also* "spiritual but not religious" (SBNR)

Stark, Rodney: on answers only "gods can provide," 42, 196; on crime and religion's deterrent effect, 105; estimates of Christians in China (by 2050), 211; on growth of Islam, 207; "market demand" for religious answers, 42–43; religion valued according to its costs, 43; on religiosity of world (2015), 209; research into religious developments, 5; secularization as stimulating innovation and rejuvenation, 43, 45–46, 195; secularization framework in *American Piety*, 40; viability of religious groups, 196, 198

Statistics Canada. *See* General Social Survey (GSS) by Statistics Canada

Stumbling on Happiness (Gilbert), 89

suicide, correlation with attendance at services, 100

Survey of Muslims in Canada 2016 (Environics), 125–26

Taylor, Charles, 29, 47, 146, 224

teenagers: atheist teens, proportion, 37; disapproval of anti-social behaviour, 113–14; feelings of guilt in RC teens, 28; identification with Mainline Protestant groups (1984 *vs.* 2008),

201, 202(f); interpersonal values by gender and region, 112; level of religious non-affiliation, 35–37; religiosity's link with good behaviour, 114–16; self-esteem, relationship with faith, 94–95; service attendance up (1984–2000), 40, 48; value of organized religion, 90

There Is Life after Death (Harpur), 190

Thiessen, Joel, 40, 51, 53, 80

Thomas, Scott: estimates of Christians in China (by 2050), 211; globalization's impact on religion, 213; growth in religion globally, 210; importance of religion for most people, 215; on increasing Pentecostal population in Muslim communities, 211; on Islamic renewal worldwide, 213; shrinking percentage of world population in global North, 212; on social consequences of spread of evangelical Christianity, 212–13

Todd, Douglas, 147, 161–63, 164

Trivers, Robert, 106

trust, service attendance, and crime rate, 130–31, 132(t), 133

Unitarians, 44(t)

United Church: attendance at services (1957, 1980, 2005), 33; attendance stabilizing (1990 to 2000), 41; decline and future prospects, 200–203; failure to persuade younger people to get involved, 219; focus on life, not on life after death, 202; governments' co-opting of welfare, impact, 19; immigrants' religious identification (pre-1946 to 2000), 16(t); immigration patterns shifting away from, 17, 34–35, 78, 201; influence in early Canada, 15; median age of members (2011), 207; membership (1871–1966), 13(t), 14; percentage of Canadian population (1901–2011), 206(t); recuperative powers, 46; religious middle identifying as, 81, 82(t); teen

of God, 104; honesty, importance to Canadians, 110–12, 155, 156(t); implication of religious inclination and, 6, 84–85, 128; interpersonal values by age cohort and gender, 110, 111(t), 112–13; interpersonal values by religious inclination and service attendance, 111(t), 112; morality and need for belief in God, 104–8, 113, 140; religion's contribution to social well-being, 103–5, 140–41; religion's deterrent effect on crime, 105; religious groups' acceptance of other faith groups, 122–23, 124(t), 125–26, 129; teen behaviour, link with religiosity, 114–16; trust in most people, relationship with service attendance, 130–31, 132(t), 133; well-being of SBNR, 155, 156(t), 157

Wente, Margaret, 169, 189

western Canada, church attendance (1950s *vs.* 1960s), 7–8, 8(f)

Wilkins-Laflamme, Sarah, 54, 80

Wilson, Bryan, 38

Wilson, Edward O., 106

women: employed outside home, Canada and US, 30(f); employment outside home, social impact, 29–32; time pressures, 31–32. *See also* gender

"World Happiness" reports, 90

World Values Survey: belief in life after death, 183, 184(t), 185; on belief that we have souls, 187–88; description, 57; on prevalence of thinking about death, 183; of religious developments, 5

Wuthnow, Robert, 158

Yakabuski, Konrad, 20, 224

Yancey, Philip, 209–10

Yukon's entry into Canada (1898), 11

Zuckerman, Phil: on absence of God in "Golden Rule," 104–5; awe rather than spirituality, 165; on nothingness after death, 170; on positive aspects of secular life, 90–91; on the religious middle, 51–52

About the Author

REGINALD W. BIBBY has held the Board of Governors Research Chair in the Department of Sociology at the University of Lethbridge since 2001. Born and raised in Edmonton, he received his PhD in sociology from Washington State University. He also has degrees in sociology from the University of Alberta (BA) and the University of Calgary (MA) and a degree in theology (BD) from Southern Seminary in Louisville. For more than four decades, he has been monitoring social trends in Canada through a series of well-known Project Canada national surveys of adults and teenagers. These surveys have produced unparalleled trend data and have been described by colleagues and the media as "a national treasure." His current surveys include a number carried out in partnership with Angus Reid.

Widely recognized as one of Canada's leading experts on religious and social trends, Professor Bibby has presented his findings in North America, Europe, Australia, and Japan. He has spoken at Canadian universities that include British Columbia and Victoria, Alberta and Calgary, Regina and Saskatchewan, Manitoba, Lakehead, Ottawa, Queen's, McMaster, Waterloo, Wilfrid Laurier, Toronto, Acadia, Prince Edward Island, and St. Francis Xavier. He has also made numerous presentations in Montreal and Quebec City. Outside Canada, he has presented his work at universities that include Oxford, Notre Dame, and Harvard.

His commitment to taking his work beyond the academic community has resulted in a large number of public appearances and a high media profile. *Maclean's* alone has featured his research with four cover stories. Professor Bibby has written fifteen books that to date have sold more than 160,000 copies. In recognition of his outstanding contribution to the nation, he was appointed an Officer of the Order of Canada in 2006.

Also by Reginald W. Bibby

Canada's Catholics (with Angus Reid), 2016

A New Day, 2012

Beyond the Gods and Back, 2011

The Emerging Millennials, 2009

The Boomer Factor, 2006

Restless Churches, 2004

Restless Gods, 2002

Canada's Teens, 2001

The Bibby Report, 1995

There's Got to Be More!, 1995

Unknown Gods, 1993

Teen Trends (with Donald Posterski), 1992

Mosaic Madness, 1990

Fragmented Gods, 1987

The Emerging Generation (with Donald Posterski), 1985

Printed and bound in Canada by Friesens

Text design: Irma Rodriguez

Set in Calibri, Helvetica Compressed, and Sabon
by Artegraphica Design Co. Ltd.

Copy editor: Dallas Harrison

Index: Patricia Buchanan